DICK, NO JANE

DICK, NO JANE

It's about me, Richard
I have some good life stories

Richard Groth

Library of Congress Control Number:		2021914818
ISBN:	Hardcover	978-1-6641-8616-3
	Softcover	978-1-6641-8615-6
	eBook	978-1-6641-8617-0

Print information available on the last page.

Rev. date: 04/13/2023

To order additional copies of this book, contact:
Xlibris
844-714-8691
www.Xlibris.com
Orders@Xlibris.com
820236

CONTENTS

BOOK BLURB

Sitting around with friends, I would usually have an opportunity to bring up one of my stories: Hey, that reminds me of this vacation, that sports road trip, or one of the movies I worked on. Finally, after years of listening, my good friend Brenda blurted out, "Would you just write a ——ing book?"

I've been to twenty-seven countries and have a lot of stories, starting in the spring of 1970.

Most of them good.

Most of them fun and interesting.

Some of them informative (a little bit of tour guide).

And alcohol has a part in a "few" of them.

My journey begins in June 1970, after graduating from Marist Catholic High School on the far southwest side of Chicago. A month earlier, thirteen college kids were shot at Kent State University while protesting the Vietnam War. Four died.

On July 1, I took Sue, my girlfriend, to the Indiana Dunes on the shores of Lake Michigan. That same day, the US government had a lottery for young men eligible to be drafted into the army. If you were born in 1951, you got a number based on the order the birthdays were picked. Most of my friends were born in '52, but I came along in November '51, so I qualified.

When we got home, her mom was waiting at the front door. The look on her face said it all. "November 24th, right?" She wanted to be sure. "Your number is eighty-one." Not good news, because it was low enough for me to be drafted.

I didn't want to go into the army and definitely didn't want to go to Vietnam. To this day, I've never fired a gun and never been remotely interested in doing so.

I had been accepted at Lewis College in Lockport, Illinois, about fifty miles southwest of downtown Chicago. As a full-time student, I qualified for a deferment that would exempt me from the draft. Sounds good, right? Except I was a screwup and almost flunked out my freshman year. Had that happened, my name would have been put back in.

What saved me was pledging TKE (Tau Kappa Epsilon), a fraternity at Lewis known for its partying. Luckily, the fraternities at Lewis had an agreement with the administration that every student pledging a frat had mandatory study hours at the library, Monday through Thursday. That agreement saved my ass, kept me in school and out of the draft.

My dad was a Purple Heart veteran from World War II. I can remember telling him if drafted, I would consider going to Canada to avoid going into the army and avoid going to Vietnam. I knew it wasn't exactly what he wanted to hear, but he told me to do what I needed to do. I've never forgotten what he said, especially coming from a dad in that era and especially coming from a Purple Heart veteran.

Let me backtrack to my first day at college. My mom and dad drove me there and waited, hoping to meet my roommate, but had to leave before he arrived. Pat got there a short time later with his mom, his dad, and (how could I forget?) his sister, a Chicago Playboy Bunny.

Now, the rest of my life.

70's

'71 Lewis Spring
_____

It's April of my freshman year, and I hadn't flunked out. During an intramural softball game involving an all-white fraternity and the BSU (Black Student Union), a fight broke out. Things escalated over the course of the evening, with a bunch of black students taking over the student lounge located on the first floor of Fitzpatrick Hall, a three-story dormitory that would remind you of a U-shaped Motel 6. It also included the switchboard and the school radio station. When word started to spread, the small campus started to heat up.

White students began to fill up the snack bar in the school's Student Union building, but quickly ran out of room, so everyone moved to the gym, where it turned into a full-fledged rally. Soon after that, a large group began the short walk across campus. Local police had been notified and showed up in full riot gear. They dispersed the white students first, then cleared out the lounge.

I was pledging TKE at the time, and most of us were at a fraternity party in Joliet the next day when we got a call, learning Smitty, one of our pledge brothers, had been jumped by a couple of guys from the BSU. Hearing that, a bunch of us hopped into three cars and headed back to the campus.

Somewhere on Route 53, the police pulled over the first car, so the other two cars pulled up behind them.

We had been drinking, but after explaining we were heading to Lewis to help one of our brothers, the officer let us go. When we got there, Smitty was OK, and things had calmed down. From that point on, everyone seemed to get along.

My room was also in Fitz, on the first floor, in the middle of the U, with a large window just above the desk. It conveniently opened at ground level, so it was easy to sneak girls in.

One evening, we welcomed in a few prospects who told us they attended St. Francis, a college in Joliet, about six miles from Lewis. You could actually take some classes at either school, so we had an immediate connection, but only until they clarified which school they attended. It was St. Francis, but it wasn't the college; it was a local high school. That meant it was time for them to get back on the desk and out the window. Looking back, I'm amazed we did the mature thing.

Our fraternity had a tradition that each pledge class could grab a few active members and escape for a weekend to a TKE chapter at another school. We picked the University of Wisconsin, Whitewater, warned them we were coming, and got the OK. The crazy stuff started on the drive up. It was me, my roommate, Ryno and a cooler of beer, nicely nestled into his Volkswagen. When it was time for a bathroom break, we were stuck in a long stretch of construction. Finally finding an exit, we made a beeline to a gas station, not paying attention to what was going on there.

At the last second, we noticed a couple of workers smoothing some freshly poured cement. When Ryno hit the brakes, it was too late, and his front tires dropped into it. So what did he do? He calmly put his car in reverse, found a parking spot, and we went in to use the bathroom. The workers were just noticing what happened as we pulled away. Sorry.

We made it to Whitewater, found the TKE fraternity house, and found a shortage of beds. It was obvious not everybody was going to get one, so a few of us pledges walked down the street, found a sorority house, knocked on the door, and introduced ourselves. Pretty sure we all ended up on a couch or the floor, but at least we were in a sorority house. After the fact, we heard some of our active members ended up sleeping on the floor. Yes, us pledges were a little smarter.

More crazy stuff: this time, it was Eddie Larry's car being driven around campus, not on its roads, but on its walkways, and not by Eddie. He had passed out, so a few of us decided to borrow it. Nobody was hurt, and nobody was arrested.

Shooting the moon seemed to be the thing to do that weekend, with

Gnat (Tim S.) being named the MVP after mooning some girls up close while they sat in the basement party room Saturday night. Easily, the highlight of the weekend was "HJ" Sally, who took care of a small portion of our pledge class. That's all I'll say.

Home safe Sunday night.

'72 Spain

On August 26, I left home to begin my junior year at Lewis College. What was different this semester was the location of my classes. They were in Spain. A group of about thirty-five students flew Air France to Paris, spending two days there. Then it was three weeks in Sevilla followed by two and a half months in Madrid.

I started feeling sick on the flight, but it wasn't airsickness; it was some kind of stomach virus. My first day was spent in bed or in the bathroom. On day two, I ran around the city, making it to Notre Dame, the Arc de Triomphe, Champs-Elysees, Eiffel Tower, and the Louvre Museum, where I saw the Mona Lisa. Not bad for a clueless twenty-year-old, but the most memorable stop was a bathroom break.

My stomach still wasn't 100 percent, so I went into a café to use their facilities. Oh no, a pay toilet? It was my first real day in France, so I wasn't too familiar with its currency, especially the coins. The stall door was floor-to-ceiling, so sneaking in wasn't an option. It gets worse. When I finally found the right change and opened the door, there wasn't a toilet. Actually, there was, but it was basically a large porcelain bowl at floor level with two footprints to show you where to stand. To this day, I thank God for blessing me with good aim.

The next morning, it was a train south to Spain, with a stop in San Sebastian, a city on its northwest coast, full of beautiful parks, gardens, and fountains. After a few hours, we boarded the overnight train to Sevilla.

Our hostel was a short walk from the train station, but we weren't impressed walking up to it. Slum was the word that came to mind. There are pictures of a handful of students, including me, leaving a few minutes later. Not positive, but I don't think anybody stayed there.

It was time to find a new place, so Smitty, two other friends, and I took a walk around the neighborhood. A few minutes later, we found another hostel and tipped off a few girls about it. On short notice, Brother Martin, our teacher/tour guide was able to work out a deal where the college would reimburse us so we could pay our rent at the new hostels. What a difference. Our new dorm had a nice deck with an orange tree.

Settled in, it was time to start our semester. We would earn sixteen credit hours as if we were home on campus. The first eight hours consisted of one Spanish language class in Sevilla that lasted three weeks, and another in Madrid during our 2 1/2-month stay. The other eight hours came from two philosophy classes taught by Brother Martin.

Looking back, I give him credit. He realized we weren't on the trip to take philosophy, so he made attendance optional. Read a book and do a paper? That was four hours credit. One more book and one more paper? That's right, the other four hours. I never did go to a philosophy class.

On September 10, Smitty and I hopped on a train and spent the weekend in Cadiz, a city on the Atlantic Ocean, in the far southwest corner of Spain. During the ride down, we met two girls, twin sisters from Pittsburgh. We hung out for two days, then it was time for us to return to school. The girls went on their way too, but will show up again. And I know it wasn't too exciting for the average American in 1972, but we did see a soccer game. Cadiz lost to Santander 1-0.

During our last weekend, Smitty and I met Anne and Michele, a couple of Canadians traveling through Spain. Instead of going to Lisbon with a few other classmates, we decided to stay in Sevilla. I would work on my paper in the park during the day, then we would hang out with the girls at night. That was my first four credit hours.

I took an incomplete for the other philosophy class, eventually doing a paper at home during Christmas break to finally complete my semester. Our three weeks in Sevilla were over, so it was time to go to Madrid.

After checking in to our new hostel, Smitty, Margie, Mo, and I hopped on a train. With a week before school started, we headed to Barcelona. We didn't see much of the city, spending a good portion of time looking for a place to stay, but did take a long walk down Las Ramblas, Barcelona's main boulevard, and wandered along its waterfront.

I remember seeing a statue of Christopher Columbus pointing out toward the water. It seemed a little strange for the average American because he was pointing east. After talking to a couple of locals, we learned he was pointing home to Genoa, Italy. We eventually found a room with one king-sized bed and the toilet/shower down the hall. Yeah, the girls got the bed and the guys got the floor. By then it didn't matter, just give me a pillow.

The next morning was another train ride, this time to Munich, Germany. We got there in the early evening, not really knowing what we were doing. When you travel in Europe, there is always a hotel-finding office in the city's main train station, but there was a line from the office in Munich's station that went out the door and down the street.

Now in line, it didn't take long before the girls struck up a conversation with the cute guy in front of us. He was an Aussie traveling through Europe solo and was the one who told us why the line was so long. We were lucky enough to arrive the night before the opening day parade of the 1972 Oktoberfest.

After standing in the same spot for a while, we noticed a woman making her way down the line. She was chatting away, with a little bit of English thrown in, but since everyone else seemed to have trouble understanding her, we didn't pay much attention. An hour later, still in about the same spot, the woman was working her way back up the line. This time we paid more attention. It was tough, but we finally figured out she was trying to rent a loft she owned about a mile from the Oktoberfest fairgrounds. After the hundreds of people who took a pass, including us the first time down the line, the four of us and our new Aussie friend stayed in one very large room for next to nothing.

The next morning, the woman woke us up early so we could make it to the parade, fed us, and even gave Mo an extra sweater. Being the smallest of the group, she got special attention from our landlady. She even got an extra blanket. Later that day, we took a break from the biergartens. Munich had hosted the Summer Olympics from August 26 to September 11, so we took a tour of Olympic Park. They were the games where eleven Israeli athletes were killed by terrorists. We saw the building where they died and the fences enclosing the site that had been covered with flowers, photos, and notes. It had only been two weeks, so it was emotional.

The next day, Smitty and I were back at the Oktoberfest, sitting at an outdoor table, talking with a middle-aged German man who was a World War II veteran. We learned how he had been drafted into the German army at the age of fifteen, luckily near the end of the war, so he never saw any action.

Our talk was interesting, but a little unsettling. It was only twenty-seven years since the end of World War II, my dad was a Purple Heart veteran who fought in the Battle of the Bulge, and I was talking to someone who could have been shooting at him. I'm glad we met.

On a lighter note, Smitty and I left a beer hall late that night, still in possession of our liter beer mugs. It was only a mile to our room, but we took the U-Bahn (subway). C'mon, we were carrying heavy beer steins. We got a few stares, but figured the locals were used to seeing things like that, especially during Oktoberfest.

Back at the loft, it was time to wake up the girls and show them our trophies. They weren't too thrilled, especially when I spilled what was left in my mug all over Mo. I still can't believe there was any beer left.

The next day was spent on a long, overnight train back to Madrid, and it wasn't pretty. None of us had showered in a while, so the couple we shared our compartment with kept opening the window. We would wake up shivering, close the window, and go back to sleep. Magically, the window would open again. I don't think they liked us because there were no hugs or nice goodbyes when we arrived at Madrid's Atocha Station.

Now it was time for school. Each day started with a two-block walk to the Anton Martin subway stop. After a quick ride to the Moncloa station, a few minutes on a city bus got us to the university. In 1972, a ride on the subway cost four pesetas (about six cents). A twenty-ride bus pass cost about fifty cents.

There was one thing our parents didn't learn until we were already in Spain. During the two years before our trip, foreign students had to be sent home because of riots at the university. The country was a dictatorship under the rule of General Franco, but our timing was pretty good. Looking back, I've often wondered if the administration at Lewis was aware of what had been going on leading up to our semester.

Our hostel was located in a great spot. A ten-minute walk in one direction was the Reina Sofia Museum, which is known for "Guernica," Picasso's famous work. Ten minutes in the other direction is the Prado, one of the top two or three art museums in all of Europe. Two minutes from there gets you to Retiro Park, Madrid's answer to Chicago's Grant Park or New York's Central Park.

When the culture's over, it's time for your tapas crawl. Walk through the old town around the Plaza Mayor, stop in a bar for a couple of small drinks and a tapa (appetizer), then move on to another place. You don't have to walk very far. Dinner starts after 9:00 p.m.

In October, Smitty and I took a trip out to Torrejon, a US air base about twenty miles outside the city. We had no problem entering the base, but we found out we needed an ID card and/or a ration card to do anything else.

Ready to head back, we learned of two places that didn't require identification. One was the cafeteria; the other was the bar. That meant we were able to scarf down some real hamburgers and some real pizza (sort of real, I'm from Chicago), and bring back some American beer. It was Schlitz and Budweiser, so back then, we came back heroes. We would return a month later.

Very late on November 7, the first Tuesday of the month, a few of us went to the Madrid Hilton to see the results come in from the US presidential election. As we watched Nixon get reelected, it quickly became Wednesday morning. There were still a handful of Americans there, so the hotel put out a free breakfast for us. Yes, Wednesday was a free day.

A few days later, while walking through old town Madrid, I heard a female voice: "Oh no, not again." It was the twin sisters from Pittsburgh, who happened to be in Madrid for a couple of days. We sat and talked for a while and traded stories on what we had been doing, then it was time to go our separate ways. Don't worry; they'll be back.

During my tapas crawl the next night, I met Marybeth, a girl from upstate New York who had made a short stop in Madrid while traveling through Spain. We hung out for two days, then it was time for her to move on. And like the sisters from Pittsburgh, she'll make another appearance.

Most of our group ate most of their dinners at the same restaurant. One night in early November, while explaining the holiday of Thanksgiving to Antonio, the owner, somebody mentioned that one of the guys on the trip had some cooking school experience. After hearing everything, Antonio gave him some space in the kitchen and gave us half of the restaurant so we could celebrate the holiday.

With a plan for Thanksgiving, it was another trip to Torrejon. Yes, we came back with Schlitz and Budweiser, plus we surprised everyone with six pumpkin pies and whipped cream for dessert. Then it was Antonio's turn.

He bought everyone a shot of cognac for dessert. We all agreed it was the coolest Thanksgiving we ever had.

The night wasn't over, so some of us, including Antonio, moved down the street to a local bar to continue the festivities. During our stay, the conversation turned to politics. Our semester had been quiet, but Spain was still a dictatorship, so talking politics in a public place wasn't a good idea. A couple of plainclothes cops had been listening to us, so they called in some uniformed police to check us out.

We had been living in Madrid for two months, and started to feel like Madrileños (citizens of Madrid). Some of us even stopped carrying our passports. We were young and really didn't think anything of it.

Anyway, the police came in, asking for identification. I was the one who asked, "Porque?" (why), came across as a smart-ass, and was told to step outside. At first, I refused, but Antonio said it was OK. Once outside, they pointed to one of their vehicles and told me to get in. Again, I refused, not knowing where they planned to take me. Again, Antonio stepped up.

After a short conversation with the police, he said not to worry; they were just taking me to a local precinct to check me out. While this was going on, a friend had run up the street to get my passport. I remember him running back down the street as we drove away.

At the police station, I was asked my address but wasn't sure what they meant, so my question to them was "Madrid or the US?" Again, I was the smart-ass. It didn't help when the name of the hostel wasn't familiar to either officer behind the counter.

That meant they had to drag out Madrid's version of the Yellow Pages, but their frustration continued. While standing at the counter, looking at a Spanish phone book upside down, I spotted the Hostel Galan and pointed it out to my new buddies. They were happy they found it, but not too thrilled a young, drunk American had to point it out.

A few minutes later, Antonio, Smitty, and a few other friends showed up, and so did my passport, but there was a little more drama before I was released.

An officer grabbed Smitty by the shirt and pushed him up against a wall. We just assumed he was paying the price because he was a friend of mine, but smoking a cigarette next to a sign that read "No Smoking" in Spanish didn't help. After that, we were allowed to leave, and since it was after midnight, I had officially turned twenty-one in a Madrid police station.

Some of the guys on our trip started getting into Spanish soccer. At the time, Lewis had a pretty good soccer program, great for a small Midwestern college in the early '70s. I think we got interested because a couple of fraternity brothers were on the team and because we watched *Wide World of Sports*.

Madrid has two professional soccer teams: Real Madrid and Atlético Madrid. It was like being in Chicago during the baseball season; it's the Cubs or the Sox. I don't remember why, but we went with Real Madrid. On November 26, we found a few tickets and saw them beat Burgos 2-0 at historic Estadio Bernabeu. Seeing a game there was like seeing your first game at Wrigley Field or Fenway Park.

Now, more interested in Spanish soccer, we learned about the lottery where you could put a bet down on the results of all fourteen games that took place in La Liga every Sunday. It was simple. For each game, you picked a team to win, lose, or draw. It paid off for fourteen, thirteen, or twelve correct picks.

We tried our luck for a few weeks, not really knowing too much about the teams and it showed. At school one day, we were talking to a couple of guys from New York. They had been in Madrid for the whole school year, so we were hoping they might have some insights about the teams we weren't familiar with, which meant all of them. They took a quick look at our picks and had us change two "obvious" bad choices.

As it turned out, we got twelve right. That was the good news. The bad news? Had we stayed with our original selections, we would have gotten all fourteen right and won somewhere around twenty thousand dollars. Twenty thousand dollars in 1972? I might never have come home. Instead, we split about twenty dollars.

After class one day, somebody was talking about a new restaurant that had recently opened in our neighborhood. A few of us went to see what the big deal was, but didn't eat in; we got our food to go. It was twenty pieces of fried chicken from KFC! Not positive, but I think it was the first one to open in Spain.

As the semester came to a close, a group of students decided it wasn't time to go home yet. The plan was to travel separately for about a week, then meet in Rome for Christmas—sounded good to me.

Yes, there's more.

'72 Spain—After School

School was over, so Smitty and I headed east to Milan, Italy, but not before two quick stops.

Monaco was first where we spent a couple of hours walking the area—no gambling. Next was the small Italian town of Ventimiglia also on the Mediterranean Sea. I took two pictures there. One has a few palm trees in it; the other has the snow-covered Alps in the distance. Similar pictures will show up again, years later, while traveling in Switzerland. This time, the snow and the palm trees are in the same photo, and yes, it was in Switzerland.

Arriving in Milan, Smitty had a change of heart and headed to Rome for an early flight home. I stayed, played tourist for a few hours, then took a train to Venice, getting there late that night, but not before a little drama.

Seeing a sign for Venice's Mestre Station, I grabbed my bag, jumped up, and headed for the nearest exit. An old man stopped me and, in his limited English, kept me on the train because he had a feeling I was getting off at the wrong stop. He was right. The Mestre Station is on the mainland. There was one more stop to go. Grazie, signore.

A few minutes later at the Santa Lucia Station, I walked out the door, and I was welcomed by a young guy playing a guitar and singing "Guantanamera," a popular Cuban song at the time.

Stopping for a second to get my bearings, I looked up to see the Grand Canal staring me in the face. "Wow, I'm in fucking Venice!" My stop there was short, just one day, but I'll be back. It was time for a train to Florence, another quick stop that included a trip to Pisa to see the Leaning Tower.

Naples was next. What made this stop noteworthy was what I did on my only night in town. I went to the movies and saw *The Godfather*, which

11

had just been released in Italy. It was in Italian, of course, but it wasn't too hard to figure out what was going on.

The next morning, I took a train that would get me to the bottom of the country. This is where it gets serious. I was heading to Sicily and the small village of Nicosia, hoping to meet relatives from my mom's side of the family. It would be the first meeting ever since my grandmother boarded a boat to the United States at the age of sixteen, eventually ending up in Chicago.

From the mainland, I took the ferry to the port city of Messina, never leaving my seat because the train actually boards the boat. I think it was wide enough for three tracks. Anyway, after backing a few cars onto each one, the boat is ready to sail.

On the ride across the bay, I went up on deck to check out the view and grab something to eat. The train wasn't crowded and the compartment I was traveling in was empty except for me, but somebody was paying attention. Returning to my seat, I immediately noticed my bag had been messed with. My cash was gone, but on the positive side, I still had one traveler's check, which left me with a little bit of money to live on.

Arriving in Messina, I decided to keep going and took the train down the east coast of the island to the city of Catania. The sixty-mile ride took about ninety minutes. Nicosia was next, also about sixty miles, this time on a much cheaper bus. The drive inland down a winding two-lane road would have taken over two hours, but my bad luck continued.

A couple of days before I arrived, the area had been hit by some torrential rainstorms, and the road to the town had been shut down because of mudslides. Almost out of money, I had to give up my quest and grab a train to Rome for an early flight home. It left me about eight hours to see what I could of this amazing city, reminding me of the one day in Paris at the beginning of the trip.

Now two days ahead of schedule, in a city with so much to see, I ran into some friends from our group. First, it was Ray H., who spotted me on the Spanish Steps. Then, maybe an hour later, while lining up a picture in St. Peter's Square, I backed up into somebody. Turning around to say "mi scusi," I discovered Pam and Margie, two girls from our trip.

At the airport, I learned about something called a departure tax. You had to pay an extra fee when flying out of Rome. After four months in Europe, I was going home with a little over three thousand Italian lira in my pocket. It might sound impressive, but it translated to about two dollars.

On the flight home, there were some weather problems along the east coast of the United States, so TWA thought it would be a good idea to play it safe and stopped in Shannon, Ireland, to refuel.

Arriving in New York, I went through Customs and walked up to the TWA counter, knowing what was coming. Yes, my flight to Chicago was long gone, but there was a small window of opportunity. An employee at the desk said, if I ran, it might be possible to make the final boarding call of a flight to San Francisco. It stopped in Chicago and Pittsburgh, so she gave me the gate number and I took off. And yes, she said Pittsburgh.

Not positive, but I think I was the last one to board the flight. Walking down the aisle, still catching my breath, I heard, "Oh no, not again?" It was the twin sisters from Pittsburgh. Yes, again.

Remember, I was flying home two days early, plus I missed my connecting flight, so the chances of me ever being on that plane were astronomical. After hearing the story about our coincidences, more than a few people, usually women, have said I should have married at least one of the girls. Fate? I'll never know. They got off the plane in Pittsburgh; I didn't.

OK, I finally arrived in Chicago, but I was two days ahead of schedule, so I had to call home to see if somebody could come and pick me up. The problem was the only money I had was in Italian lira, and this was back when you needed coins to make a collect call from a public payphone. I actually had to ask someone (beg) for some change to make the call.

During the semester, I made a collect call home because of a problem with a personal check my parents sent me. After getting the phone bill that included it, they wrote a letter, telling me not to call collect again because it was so expensive.

This is what was going through my mom's head when she answered the phone and heard the operator say it was a collect call from me. She freaked, then told the woman to hold on. While the operator and I waited, she yelled to my dad, asking him if they should accept the call. He told me later after giving her a funny look, he said, "Yes, take it."

Not looking forward to begging again, I asked the operator to explain to her I was calling from Chicago. After hearing that, my mom let out a little scream then, thankfully, accepted the call.

Home broke.

'73 Lewis Thursdays

I'm back from Spain and halfway through the second semester of my junior year, so six of us in the three-room section of our dorm decided it would be a good idea to host Thursday night parties. We weren't that far from the Chicago metropolitan area, so a lot of the students living on campus would head home for the weekend. Because of that, Thursday night kind of became Friday night.

It was a five-minute drive to Gabel's, a bar in Lockport, where we would buy a half barrel of beer. For some reason, $22 rings a bell, so that's probably why we charged our classmates one whole dollar for all they could drink. If it wasn't Thursday, we would get our six-packs of Buckhorn or Hi-Brau for $0.87, or our case of bottles for $2.49. Remember, it was 1973.

Anyway, after four or five Thursday nights, we received a letter from the director of residence because a couple of things disturbed him. He had gotten calls from a few students complaining about the noise and figured the parties had gotten too big and probably bothered more than just a few students. But the noise wasn't the main issue; it was the age of the drinkers. Students were allowed to drink in their rooms, but only if they were twenty-one, so the real problem was we were allowing minors to drink as long as they paid the $1 fee.

He was disgusted by our lack of maturity, looking at it as not only a party, but also a profit-making scheme. Yes, we also looked at it both ways. And here's a quote from the letter, which I still have: "If you want to open a bar, go into Lockport, get a license, and set up shop." We didn't, we shut down.

Here are a few other things that happened that year, although not necessarily on Thursday:

Based on the statute of limitations, I can tell you this one. The university had a place called the Catacombs, which was kind of a snack bar/hangout in the basement of the Student Union. Its windows matched up with ground level, so once in a while, we would leave one unlocked, then return with a shopping list after it closed. Forty years later, we still talk about how I sent one of our pledges back because he returned to our dorm with the wrong buns. "I told you poppy-seed."

On other nights, when we needed some beer and snacks, somebody would drive a few miles either north or south of the school to do some "shopping" in a local late-night grocery store. This was before cameras were everywhere, and we had perfected our technique. Take a six-pack of beer, fold it out, then place it under your arm and under your coat. Stuff a couple of things down your pants and it was time to go.

We would actually buy a few things, go through the checkout line, then sometimes send one of the pledges back into the store to borrow what we forgot.

'73 Spring Break

Five of us (Big Don, Ted, Chuf, Jonzy, and I) drove down to Fort Lauderdale for spring break. Ted's green Dodge Demon was our mode of transportation. Not one small person in the group, so you can imagine how enjoyable the ride was. It gets worse.

In Daytona, we picked up Slink (John), another old friend, who had gone down a few days ahead of us with two female friends. That makes six. We gave him the wheel for the last leg into Lauderdale, figuring he was the soberest and least tired of the group. We were wrong. Maybe thirty minutes into his shift, he decided to take a nap, so for a few seconds, we took a tour of Interstate 95's grassy median. Five minutes later, he was sound asleep in the back seat. The rest of the drive was uneventful.

We checked into the Sierra Motel on Route A-I-A, about a mile from the beach. It was an efficiency room with a kitchenette, two double beds, and plenty of floor space to accommodate the six of us.

In the early afternoon of our first hangover, we found a great cure right across the street from our motel. It was a fast-food place called Neba's, where we inhaled tater tots by the pound. It worked like a charm.

Then there was the day clerk at our place. We got to know him when a couple of the guys had trouble getting their cigarettes out of the lobby's moody vending machine. He would get down on his knees, give the machine a big hug, then deposit $0.60. Magically, the cigarettes would pop right out, but only for him.

And speaking of cigarettes, Big Don, when at home, would walk into the local convenience store and always ask the young clerk for "two packs of Camel filters, no matches." One day, in the elevator of a hotel where some fraternity brothers of mine were staying, he heard a young voice behind him ordering two packs of Camel filters, of course, without matches. By coincidence, the girl from the store was in Florida on her high school's senior class trip.

Let me continue with coincidences. One afternoon, Big Don and I were walking down a street along the beach. Don't worry; it was just a short stroll between bars. As we crossed a side street, a girl walking toward us made eye contact with me. After reaching our respective curbs, we both stopped and turned around. It was Marybeth, the girl from upstate New York I met in Madrid the previous November. We caught up and moved on. Sorry, that's all.

Not done yet. Chuf met a couple of girls from Chicago. When he told them his name, their response was "We know you!" They had actually been at a party in his basement when he was passed out on the floor. Not every coincidence is good.

That same night, I met a girl and found a secluded spot by the motel. As soon as I got lucky, it was time to disappear. A few minutes later, Chuf found her sitting alone and tried to "console" her. It didn't work. "Get away from me. You're one of his friends."

The guys in the room next to us were from Cleveland and had come down to Fort Lauderdale in one car, just like we did. They also had an accident, but it was a little more serious than our trip through the grassy median. Once a portion of the car's front end was cut away, they continued south on their spring break quest.

Once we met, a few of us got together and hit an all-you-can-eat restaurant, which I think was called Steak and Brew. If I remember right, it was also all-you-can-drink. An hour or so into our dinner, Don, the one from Cleveland, decided to take a spot under our table. After getting comfy, he proudly announced to anyone in earshot that he successfully drank himself under the table. Minutes later, we were asked to leave. Can you believe that?

Later that night, back at the motel, we heard the same Don pleading for someone to come and help him. We found him standing under an outdoor cement stairway, claiming his head was stuck under one of the steps. We guessed it was more than alcohol, because marijuana was a close second when it came to partying on this trip.

Let's continue for a minute with the marijuana theme. Whenever we would get tired of listening to Ted, I would write a prescription, then somebody would magically appear with a pipe or a joint. Twenty minutes later, he was ready for bed. Good night, buddy. By the way, my nickname on the trip was Dr. Bong, which would get a reaction from my daughter years later.

A couple of days into our stay, we hooked up with some college friends of mine who also came down for the break. They had rented a motor home for the trip and christened it the Magic Bus. Their drive was different from ours, because they made a stop in Georgia to see Lewis play a baseball game against Valdosta State University during the school's southern tour.

Not surprisingly, they were asked to leave about halfway through the game. Yes, it had something to do with alcohol. They quickly got over it, continued south to Fort Lauderdale, and found an open spot next to the Biltmore Hotel, which was across the street from the beach.

It was perfect. We would walk off the beach into a nice, cool motor home, have a quick drink and maybe a "cigarette," then head to the hotel bar. We never found out if their parking spot was legal, but our guess was it didn't matter once the hotel bar checked the ring on its register. They loved us, even after we sent a bunch of chairs off the balcony into the hotel pool one night.

There was one more incident at the Biltmore, and it involved the hotel sign. It was low enough so somebody sitting on somebody's shoulders could scramble the letters. I'm not positive, but for a couple of days, we think it read something like "We're open for c——ts during happy hour."

Next was Salvation Army Day. We decided to use our kitchenette and our cooking skills to take care of any hungry person, whether it was a homeless guy or just a college kid who spent all his money on booze. After cooking up a couple of pounds of pasta and some Italian sausage, we opened the door to our room and were amazed at the amount of people who came by that afternoon—definitely our good deed for the trip. I'd love to know the final totals of people and pasta, because we actually went out to get more food.

I was passed out on the floor one night, snoring away, when my friends thought it would be a good idea to put a not-so-clean bucket over my head. It wasn't. I was told it actually amplified the noise. Anyway, it didn't have any effect on me. Neither did the maid vacuuming around me the next morning.

Finally, we decided to throw an outdoor party at poolside, financing it by knocking on doors and asking for a couple of dollars to help us out. It worked! We even got some donations from people at the motel next to us.

The funniest one came from a middle-aged guy who slipped us a few dollars while looking over his shoulder at his wife and baby. I don't remember seeing him at the party, but he did give us a wave when we noticed him sitting alone on his balcony.

The beer choices that night were Genesee, Shell City, and Old Milwaukee. Our best guess was somewhere around sixty cases, with the cost somewhere around $4/case. Since Old Milwaukee was the only one we were familiar with, a lot of it discreetly ended up in our fridge.

The highlight of the party was provided by the three magi, who danced the night away, in costume, after arriving from New Orleans where they had just performed at Mardi Gras.

The final blur was the ride home. Pretty sure only four of the six were in the car. Anyway, we all made it home safe.

STREAKING '73

The streaking fad had peaked in California in the summer of '73, so by the time it got to northern Illinois, it was starting to get cold. Not good if you're trying to impress the women.

I was out on a Friday night with three friends at a bar called the Pepper Mill, on the far southwest side of Chicago. Tequila Sunrise was the drink of choice that night, but if you're not used to drinking it, tequila can be dangerous.

It was dangerous enough that we thought it would be a good idea to go into the bathroom, get undressed, then streak through a crowded bar. It was me, Ted, and Mike, friends from grammar school. Steve, who was two years older and a little more mature, kept his clothes on and left first with ours.

Walking out the front door, he freaked when he saw a Chicago Police car parked in front of the building. So what did the mature one do? He threw the clothes up in the air and took off. Seconds later, we came out and knew we were in trouble. Ted was the unlucky one.

After grabbing what he thought were his clothes, he ran around the corner and tried to climb a fence. And here's the quote from a Chicago cop: "Come on down, Cheeks." This is back when the police had a sense of humor.

With all the commotion, people started filtering out the front door, then quickly started chanting, "Let him go, let him go" when they saw Ted in the backseat. They even rocked the squad car a little bit. Sense of humor or not, it was time for the cops to drive him to the local precinct.

When he got there, the sergeant at the desk asked Ted to empty his pockets, and he wasn't amused with what landed in front of him. It was Mike's underwear. We never figured out how they got there.

Ted eventually went to court, charged with disorderly conduct, and ended up in a room full of real criminals. The judge read his ticket, then asked him, "Will you promise to never do this again?"

"Yes, your honor."

That's when the judge leaned forward and quietly told Ted, "Then get the hell out of here."

Friday night was the Pepper Mill, so Saturday was Parkwood, a tavern about a mile down the street. I got there late after bartending a wedding at the Golden Age Restaurant in Oak Lawn, so I had some catching up to do. I was up to the task.

We were reminiscing about the night before and thought it would be a good time and place for an encore, but it was gonna be different. We weren't interested in running around, so we got undressed, stayed at the bar, and continued drinking, naked.

While laughing, the bartender, whom we knew before we turned twenty-one, put down a round of drinks and told us what we owed. We all kept trying to put our hands in our pockets but had to apologize because nobody seemed to have any money on them. It's the only time I have ever seen a bartender down on one knee, laughing and crying at the same time. Needless to say, the drinks were on him.

It got more bizarre. Parkwood was a long building with a long bar and doors at either end. We were at the back near the pool table and the bathrooms, with the front occupied by some off-duty Chicago police officers and their wives. They never said a word, but when the women needed a bathroom break, they would walk out the front door and reenter the bar through the back door so they wouldn't have to walk by us.

Bizarre continued. My brother and his best friend happened to be sitting in the middle of the bar that night but hadn't picked up on what was going on; that is, until I walked over to say hello. I was standing between them for a couple of seconds before they realized my lack of clothing.

Remember the old bar-bowling game with the puck? The bar had one, so I tried to get the two of them to play a game with me. Luckily, they talked me out of it, then told me to go away.

Final bizarre: one of the guys (no, not me) got up on the bar and started to do a little dance as he made his way from the back of the place to the front. That was the breaking point. It was time to get dressed.

Anyway, we were naked for about twenty minutes. Not a bad effort, but the best would come a few months later at Lewis University during the spring semester. At the time, there was a bar on campus located in the Student Union Building, so one night a few of us went into its bathroom and got undressed. Then it was a sprint through the place, out the door, and safely back to our dorm.

Back in one of the rooms, we made an earth-shaking decision. Streaking was dead! Strolling was the new fad! We called the school radio station to tell them about the new craze and that we would be strolling over to do an interview in about ten minutes. How bad could it be? We didn't know anybody that listened to the school radio station, but boy, were we wrong. It was located on the first floor of Fitzpatrick Hall, a dorm with outdoor balconies, which amazingly had some students waiting for us and cheering us on.

On the walk over, one frat brother bailed out, but the rest of us kept our cool and walked in. As stunned as they were, the staff still tried to present a professional face and ushered us into a room, where we sat around a conference table and did a live interview. The DJ did his job but had a hard time keeping a straight face. And to his audience, he proclaimed, "Yes, they really are naked."

After a few minutes, the students at the station thought it would be good idea to get us the hell out of there. They were right, but nobody expected what was next. As we left, the balconies had a lot more people and the cheering was a lot louder.

Later that week, there was a rumor going around that the AP/UPI Wire Service ran a story about "strolling," a new fad that had started on a college campus somewhere in the Midwest. Nobody was ever able to verify it.

I think the most amazing thing about the story is we did a live interview, naked, on a Catholic university radio station and didn't get thrown out of school. Our theory was when the story made its way around campus, nobody in the administration believed it really happened.

'74 KITZBUHEL

It's January, and I'm between semesters during my senior year at Lewis. The interim is usually around six weeks, so the university sponsored a ski trip to Kitzbuhel, Austria, run by Brother John M., a teacher who also doubled as a moderator for one of the fraternities.

Don't remember what it cost, but I do remember it being cheap because we were able to apply some of our Illinois State Scholarship money to help pay for it. Thanks, Brother John.

The first day in the Austrian Alps was unseasonably warm. It actually rained for a while. When the temperature dropped back to normal, everything iced up. These would be the conditions for my first attempt at skiing. All I knew was what I saw watching *Wide World of Sports* on television as a kid. It didn't take long for me to twist a knee hoping to avoid killing myself, so I went on the DL for a couple of days.

I could still walk, so it was time for a couple of day trips with a few friends. The first one was to Munich, Germany. No Oktoberfest this time, but I did get two great pictures of Mike T., one of my oldest friends. The first one takes place in a bier hall, where he is being fed a large beer by a not-so-pretty fraulein. The other is in an empty cathedral, where he decided to climb up into the pulpit and make an emotional speech. I'm pretty sure it was after we left the bier hall, not before we got there.

The second one consisted of two short stops about an hour bus ride apart. Innsbruck was first followed by St. Anton. It was a short walk around each town, followed by a tour of the ski museum in each town, where we saw exhibits from the '64 Winter Olympics that took place in Innsbruck.

Our stay in Kitzbuhel coincided with the Hahnenkamm-Rennen,

Europe's most famous downhill ski race. We weren't there for the actual race but did spend a couple of days on the slopes, watching the time trials. Seeing those skiers fly by us was incredible. They go a lot faster up close than they do on TV.

Now off the DL, I hit the slopes. It was a memorable day, probably because it took place on a slope commonly known in English as the bunny hill. There were a few pictures taken of me in the horizontal position in the snow, but only one of them shows me drinking wine from my bota bag.

The icing on the cake was when I finally stood up and tried to make it down the hill. Things were going OK until it was time to stop. Remember, I'm a rookie.

Nearing the bottom, two things stood out. One was the ticket booth. The other was a wooden fence that led to the ski lift. All I could envision was me going through the booth with my arms out, like in a cartoon, so it was time to throw myself down. I slid to a stop just short of the fence and somehow popped right up, giving everyone the impression I knew what I was doing. There was actually a smattering of applause.

Thank God this was back in the day when there were no camera phones to record me running back to my room to change my underwear. As of this writing, it's the only time I've ever skied, so when people ask, I tell them, "I only ski the Austrian Alps."

The trip took place during the oil embargo/gas crisis, so we found out there was a chance our flight home on Icelandic Air might be delayed or even canceled. At the time, Icelandic also flew to the Bahamas (no, I didn't believe it either), so Brother John told the airline they needed to get us on a flight out, even if it meant going there first. Not surprisingly, our flight left on time. Looking back, I would have loved to see us land in the Bahamas dressed for snow skiing instead of waterskiing.

Home without a sunburn.

'74 NAIA Baseball

On a Thursday morning in early June, I hit the road with Pete, Ryno, and Byrd, three fraternity brothers. Our destination was St. Joseph, Missouri, for the NAIA College Baseball World Series.

Lewis had qualified, but we hadn't done our homework. What we thought was a long weekend was actually a double elimination tournament. That meant the four- or five-day trip quickly turned into a nine- or ten-day trip. It also turned out to be one of my cheapest vacations ever—more on that later.

During the drive through Missouri, the weather took a turn for the worse. While channel surfing on the car radio, we heard about a tornado warning. A funnel cloud had been sighted in "Smith" county (don't remember the actual name), and people were being warned to take shelter. It didn't make much of an impact on us until we saw a sign welcoming us to "Smith" County a couple of minutes later.

Later we learned as we were heading west, the storm was heading east, separated by just a few miles. We made it to St. Joe's in one piece, and very sober.

We knew what hotel the team was staying at, so after knocking on a few doors, the four of us ended up sleeping on the floor in a couple of their rooms. This was the beginning of our cheap vacation.

The next day, two fraternity brothers who were on the team set us up with transportation to the games. We would travel on the team bus, and when we got to the park, they would give us some equipment to carry in so it looked like we were part of the squad. Free rides to the games and free entry into the games—not bad, but it gets better.

Every school in the tournament was sponsored by a local business.

Our sponsor was McDonald's, so we also ate for free after each game. On our first off day, we found a buffet that offered all-you-can-eat waffles for $0.99. That meant, for our time in St. Joe's, most of our meals consisted of McD's burgers, waffles, and ice water. We didn't have a choice because the money we brought was only supposed to last a few days.

After our third night sleeping on the floor, it was time to leave because their head coach felt we were a bad influence on his players. His reason was we had been keeping them up way too late. We thought it would be in our and the players' best interest not to tell him how the guys on the team kept tripping over us when they were coming back in.

Leaving the hotel that morning, we were back at our favorite buffet, trying to figure out a plan for the rest of the tournament. Going home early seemed to be the only option, but our good luck returned.

While scarfing down our waffles extraordinaire, guys wearing TKE shirts (that's our frat) were spotted across the room. Pete jumped up, went over, and introduced himself, and about a minute later, we had a place to stay. School was out, so there was plenty of room at their frat house, plus we got to sleep in real beds. They even apologized for not putting together a party that night. That meant we had to wait twenty-four grueling hours.

The next night, we witnessed something we had never seen before, or thankfully, since. When Byrd would tell the story years later, he would start with "I left my jeans in the bathroom." So what happened? The frat house had a piano, and Byrd decided to play it with his organ. He was a "big" hit but, surprisingly, was not called back for an encore.

Returning to the bathroom, he realized his wallet was missing. Somebody pointed to a girl who just left there, so he walked up behind her, cracked her on the ass, and asked for it back. She denied taking it, so he turned around and went back for his pants. When he came back out, he apologized to the girl after finding it in another pocket. Oops!

The next evening, we took a quick trip across the Missouri River to the town of Wathena, Kansas. Our Missouri brothers told us about a bar with an awesome special. It was pitchers of beer for $2—a great price, plus it was Coors. Back then, it wasn't available east of the Mississippi River. I'm not sure, but at the time, I don't think it was even sold in Missouri.

We proceeded to put a major dent in the barrel but couldn't understand why we were all still sober. The bartender overheard us and started laughing. Then she broke the news to us. It was 3.2 beer. Not a lot of alcohol, so thank God it was cheap.

Now it's time for your Lewis U update: Tom B., one of the best college pitchers in the country, hit a sacrifice fly as the DH, driving in the winning run as Lewis beat Sam Houston St. 3-2 to win the national championship. A month later, the Cleveland Indians selected him fourth in the draft—not bad, coming from an NAIA school in northern Illinois. He toughed it out in the minor leagues, eventually pitching for the Indians, the Dodgers, and finally, his hometown White Sox.

And here's a little known fact. Tom and I worked on the movie *Rookie of the Year*. He was the home plate umpire with a speaking part, and I was an extra holding a camera during the press conference. I made fifty dollars a day. Yeah, he made a little bit more.

There's one more thing. It was our drive home. There were five of us now because we added Jim B. Turned out we really needed him.

I remember checking my rearview mirror and seeing a car flying up behind us. It was an Iowa state trooper, because I was speeding. The way it worked then was, pay the fine on the spot or return to somewhere in Iowa for a court hearing. Since I was guilty, it was time to pay up.

We pooled our money and handed it to the officer. He put it in an envelope, sealed it, then drove me to the nearest mailbox so I could personally drop it in. Remember how we were almost out of money halfway through the trip. Having Jim and his cash with us really helped. If we didn't have the money to pay on the spot, it would have been a long drive back to a local courthouse.

We made it home Saturday morning. Money spent for nine days was around sixty dollars.

'75 Larry and Chickie

In the spring of '75, five old friends (Big Don, Slink, Chuf, Jack M., and I) drove out east because our old friend Larry was getting married to Jenny. She was a Jersey girl he met at Quincy College in Illinois. Not too many people knew her real name. Everyone knew her as Chickie.

We stayed at a hotel called the Golden Dolphin, in Brigantine, an island town just north of Atlantic City. No gambling took place; this was before the casinos moved in. It was five guys in one efficiency room with three beds. Jack, the smallest of the group, got the single bed. It's where we passed out for three nights.

On day two, somebody discovered a second fridge. We never would have looked for one, except Larry's dad came to our room and donated a couple of cases of Schaefer's, or maybe Schmidt's, beer. Holy shit! There's a fridge behind this cabinet door.

That night, we left the island and drove across a bridge, looking for somewhere else to drink. We saw a bar with a sign telling us Peter Noone and Herman's Hermits were playing that night, so we stopped. After a long night of drinking and a little bit of singing along with the Hermits, we drove back to the hotel on State Road 87. Everything was kind of blurry, but a couple of us remember driving across the divided bridge on the wrong side of the road—not positive.

Late that night, safely back at the hotel, we got a visit from Larry's older brother, who ordered us to quit with the disgusting language. Evidently, we were pretty loud. After telling him to get fucked, we quickly passed out.

Chuf and Big Don were sharing one of the double beds. Chuf was a relatively normal-sized guy, if you didn't count his beer belly. Big Don wasn't. At some point, Chuf started complaining and told Don to roll over because he was hogging the bed. He did, but rolled the wrong way, so Chuf quickly disappeared. The only thing visible was one arm and one leg. The only thing audible was a muffled cry for help, with quite a few X-rated words thrown in. Luckily, they were muffled, or Larry's brother would have been forced to make another appearance.

The next day was spent at poolside for Larry's makeshift bachelor party. After some sun and some alcohol, we thought it would be funny to wrap him in a bedspread and throw him in the water. It took a few seconds before we realized he was in the process of drowning. Fortunately, for all of us, the bedspread was pretty old and pretty thin, so he was able to shred it and fly up out of the water. The language was a lot worse than what his brother heard the previous night.

Now the wedding. The church and the reception hall were across the street from each other in a neighborhood close to the hotel. We were parked down the block, so we finished our beers in the car and went into the church. After the ceremony, we immediately returned to the car. We had a few beers in reserve and a few minutes before the banquet bar opened, so we sat down at curbside to empty our cooler. The reception was a blast, but kind of tame compared to the two previous nights. Now, the icing on the cake: Slink (John) paid two hookers $20 to go up to Larry/Chickie's room. It wasn't real; we were just messing with them. Everybody, including the women, had a good laugh.

Home the next day.

WESTGATE '75—GROTH INVITATIONAL

In June, a group of guys who knew each other from grammar school, high school, or college got together for a day of golfing, drinking, and reminiscing. We met at Westgate, a golf course in Palos Heights, a Chicago suburb on its far southwest side.

I was a little drunk, but somehow shot the best round of the day. Everyone else must have been worse than me, because everyone else shot worse than me. I even came close to a hole in one, missing by a few feet.

After eighteen holes and a stop at the nineteenth, we joined our women at a nearby forest preserve for a picnic, adults only. That's when I made a decision that would change the way we thought of golf outings. There would be another one. On May 30, 1976, we returned to Westgate, where the Groth Invitational came into existence. That's my last name.

In 1977, on the Saturday before Memorial Day, the second Groth Invitational took place, but at a different venue. It was at Hickory Hills Golf Course, which would be our home for another twenty years. Every year, there would be a different-colored T-shirt and some trophies, which ranged from "closest to the pin" to "worst twosome of the day." They were awarded at the picnic that followed each outing.

Over the years, only one golf cart was wrecked, and only one ended up in a lagoon. One other cart was hurt when Marto lost control of it on a slope and turned it over. He was OK, but Ben, the passenger, broke his arm. All things considered, that's not too bad for twenty-three years of drunken idiots.

Wait, there's one more golf cart story. My brother and Pops (his best friend) overturned one but didn't have a scratch on them. That's because the accident was staged. While Pete and I were making the rounds in the beer cart, we came over a rise to find the two of them lying on the ground, "unconscious." As we ran over to help, they jumped up, flipped the cart up, and drove away—very funny.

And here's a golf cart encore: I don't remember how it started, but for a few years, Pete and I would drive around the course with a half barrel of beer, but without clothes. Yes, it was weird, but the reactions were priceless. Guys would be in the fairway with their head down, lining up a shot, when we would pull up in front of them. One quick look up was all it took.

My favorite was when Chuf spotted the beer cart not too far from him. He was waving and yelling, "Hey, hey!" then as we got closer, it was *"Hey!"* accompanied by a large grimace.

Now it's 5/25/85, the tenth year of the Groth Invitational, and they said it wouldn't last. After eighteen holes of golf and eighteen holes of alcohol, we moved into a banquet room at the golf course for the anniversary party, women and parents allowed. I even hired a DJ.

Looking back, I'm really glad I put this party together. There are some great pictures. The best ones are of my mom and dad, and Vic's mom and stepdad, with a close second being my oldest friend Ted's mom and dad, and finally, my aunt Phyllis and her husband, Charlie.

There was one downside to the night. It's a photo I have of my sister on the dance floor with Big Don. We never learned why he was allowed out there.

At some point, the golf course stopped selling half barrels of beer. That meant we had to buy it by the case. It was expensive, so to cut costs, somebody would make a beer run, then pull up to a fence at one of the distant holes and proceed to throw the cheaper cases of beer over to us.

Then, in 1991, I decided women would be allowed to golf in the outing that year, actually, just one foursome. My good friend Carolyn and three of her friends got the OK, but only if they golfed in the outfits they wore the previous night. If the request sounds a little strange, it's because Jim, my old roommate, married Carolyn the previous night.

On Saturday morning, the female foursome showed up at the course in proper attire and golfed the full eighteen holes. After receiving my permission, they got to change clothes after the first nine.

In 2003, after a five-year hiatus, the Groth Senior Invitational took place. Yeah, I organized one more. Last outing and last T-shirts—that would be a wrap.

'75 New Orleans

It's mid-November, and Don Stu provided the van for our trip to New Orleans. It was me, Jesse and Danny D., and Stu. The trip was basically a blur. The parts I remember are the parts I would like to forget.

Pat O'Brien's was first, where we attacked their very long drink list. Every fourth drink was mine, and I was the one who got to drink an absinthe cocktail. It wasn't very good and, luckily, didn't have the high alcohol content it had in other parts of the world. It has a strange history. You'll have to look it up.

Later that night, Jesse and I went out on our own. It wasn't long before we spotted a really cool restaurant sign carved out of a big piece of dark wood and hung out over the sidewalk. For some reason, we thought it would be a good idea to "borrow" it.

A homeless guy volunteered to help us, thinking he might make a couple of dollars, so he got on my shoulders and unhooked it. We got it to the ground, then Jesse and I picked it up and took two steps. That's when I felt someone tapping me on the shoulder. We stopped and turned around, then were arrested by two cops who had been watching us the whole time.

We were taken to a local precinct, where the police were able to contact the restaurant owner and get an approximate value of the sign. I don't remember the amount, but it was enough to qualify as a felony. That meant we would be charged with one count of felony theft and one count of felony possession. All of a sudden, things got serious.

Because it was a felony, it wasn't possible to bail yourself out of jail; a bail bondsman had to do it for you. We asked for the Yellow Pages and basically closed our eyes, put a finger down on the page where they were listed, and called that number. We've wondered what the odds were of getting a legitimate lawyer at that time of night. We didn't know it at the time, but we had hired a crook.

Our bondsman, the busy little bee that he was, immediately made a couple of phone calls. One went to Jesse's parents, the other to mine. He explained to them how we had been arrested, and they needed to wire him money to bail us out. Luckily, our dads agreed to wait until they actually heard from their sons. His next move was a stop at our hotel, hoping to get money from Stu and Danny. The problem was he had to wake up two passed-out drunks. They promptly turned him down and went back to bed. I'm guessing they weren't as polite as our fathers.

Finally, it was time to be processed and sent to New Orleans' Parish (county) Prison, which is similar to Chicago's Cook County Jail. Once inside, we got to stand in a long hallway with a dozen or so other prisoners, get undressed, then get deloused. That means I was sprayed over every inch of my body. Not the most pleasant thing I've ever done. After that, with our clothes back on, we had our picture taken, then handed a towel, cup, toothbrush, and our prison ID card. That's when it sank in. We might be here for a while.

Next was a large holding cell, joining about twenty-five other prisoners. Looking around, a couple of things stood out. The first one was the lone toilet in the far corner, with no stall. And two, I was one of two white guys in the place. Jesse is Hispanic, so he didn't count. Seeing two guys spooning on the floor didn't help either.

Now it's mid-morning, and our roommates have gotten up and started to remember the visit from our bondsman a few hours earlier. They were moving slowly, but at least they were moving and found a law office near the hotel. The people there knew exactly whom Stu and Danny were talking about. The story of us getting screwed was already making the rounds. They said not to worry; they would get us out. They did.

During that time, Jesse and I got to go out to the yard for recreation. It was just like in the movies. Standing outside, I had my first positive thought since being arrested. If we ended up staying for a while, at least we could compete on the basketball court. They weren't that good.

I can still hear the sound of the cell door slamming shut behind us after returning from the yard. About an hour later, a guard called our names, then let us out of the cell. The guys still inside kept yelling for us to give them our cups, toothbrushes, hand towels, and any change we still had in our pockets. I remember hoping this wasn't a false alarm.

As an employee finished the process to release us, I politely asked if there was any chance of keeping my ID. His response: "Get your ass outta here, boy." You don't have to tell me twice.

That night, the four of us went to the Superdome to see the New Orleans Jazz play Golden State. White standing during the national anthem, Jesse and I started to nod off. We might have been done, but our ordeal wasn't quite over yet.

Before leaving for home, we had to hire a lawyer. With no plans to return for a hearing, we needed someone to get us out of the state legally. He did, then also sent us a couple more bills a few months later. My dad told me to throw them out.

I'll return to New Orleans in '91, assured the statute of limitations has run out.

CONDESA DEL MAR
'75 AND '76

In early '74, at the age of twenty-two, I went to a bartending school on the far southwest side of Chicago. Shortly after that, I got a job at the Golden Age Restaurant/Banquet Hall in Oak Lawn. Shortly after that, I went to school again. This time, I was tutored by a forty-year-old hostess. First, she took me home, then she took me to school.

Two brothers-in-law owned the Golden Age but split up just months after I started there because one of them was building Condesa del Mar, a huge restaurant complex in Alsip, a nearby suburb on the southwest side of Chicago.

I followed him there in November 1975, getting my first real job as an assistant to the general manager. Condesa was a huge complex with a restaurant, show lounge and a twenty-four-hour coffee shop. It also had four banquet rooms that could open up into one large room with a stage at one end. It sat around 1,200 people, which gave us the ability to bring in some big-name performers, and yes, we took advantage of it.

As an assistant manager, I was exposed to all aspects of the business, and here's one of the first things my boss told me: "Don't shit where you work." There were waitresses everywhere, but I had a position with some responsibilities, so messing around with them would only come back to haunt me. I only "shit" a few times.

In February 1976, Bob Hope became the first of a string of celebrities who would appear there, doing two nights in the big room. I met him the first night and was impressed. He was a real class act.

That same weekend, I met and got an autograph from baseball Hall of Famer, Lou Boudreau. He wrote, "Best wishes, Rich. The food was great."

In March, it was Bobby Vinton, followed by Vikki Carr a week later. After her encore, I gave her my hand to help her down the stairs from the stage. Still don't know why she didn't bring me directly to her dressing room.

The presidential primaries were also going on in March. Ronald Reagan was running for the nomination, and Condesa hosted a luncheon for him. He was fighting a sore throat at the time, so they sent me out to a drugstore for some throat spray. He actually made a point of meeting me so he could thank me in person. I thought that was pretty cool.

On July 10, I had the honor of escorting Muhammad Ali and his entourage around the complex. Another great guy, plus I got his autograph.

During my two and a half years there, I learned some interesting words in Greek when I heard my boss yelling at some of the employees. They would come into play years later in Stockholm, Sweden.

Montreal '76

In July, Montreal hosted the Summer Olympics, so it was time for a road trip. Six of us—JD, Stu, Slink (John M.), Jesse, Big Don, and I—drove there. Three were in Stu's van and three in my '70 Monte Carlo.

It was four years after the tragedy at the Summer Olympics in Munich, where eleven Israeli athletes were killed by terrorists, so crossing into Canada was tougher than normal. At the border, we had to explain the purpose of our trip to security, then show them the event tickets to prove our story.

There was a small problem because all the tickets were in my car. Luckily, Stu was only a few minutes ahead of me, because the border guards had them pull over, not sure if they should believe their story. When I got there, we produced tickets for all six of us, then got the OK to proceed to Montreal.

Actually, our destination was St. Hyacinthe, a town about thirty miles east of the city. Before the Games, people with rooms to rent could sign up with a government agency to have travelers stay in their homes. Our reservation was in a private home with three bedrooms for us and a home-cooked breakfast every morning, and it was cheap. It came out to about $10/day per person.

Remember, we were in Quebec and away from the big city, so French was the main language. The couple who owned the home were seniors who only spoke a few words of English. I'll come back to the language barrier later.

Our first day, the 18th, the six of us got in Stu's van and drove into the city to see the US men's basketball team beat Italy in the afternoon. That was followed by a MLB game, with the Montreal Expos playing the Houston Astros in the early evening. The Expos had to wait until the Olympics were over before they could move into Olympic Park, so we saw them play at Parc Jarry, the city's minor-league park. Tickets were $4.

It's our first night in Montreal and the beer was flowing. We were at a baseball game, so that's what you do. Sometime during the middle of the game, laughter, then applause broke out in our section when people spotted Big Don coming up the stairs with two rounds of beer. Yeah, that's right; he had a six-beer holder on top of another six-beer holder.

Just before that, he had been penalized by the commissioner (me) for spilling a beer the previous inning. His penalty was to buy a round, but since he was next in the rotation, he naturally came back with two. Our section loved us. They also loved Stu falling asleep an inning later.

That night, we quickly learned how far the house was from Montreal. Somehow, we made it home safe, but not before a couple of interruptions. The first one was a bathroom break on the side of the road, but the next one was a little more serious. We got a little lost in St. Hyacinthe because of the confusing numbering system of streets and home addresses. A van with Illinois plates driving around the neighborhood had to look suspicious, so it didn't take long before a police car appeared behind us, then pulled us over.

We were a little nervous as the officer approached the van because we were a little drunk. It got worse when a second officer appeared with a gun in his hand. We explained our problem in English, and luckily, they understood and directed us to our house. Merci.

For our week in Quebec, we had tickets to six events and decided to pay a scalper's price for one more. They included basketball, volleyball, soccer, boxing (2), and track and field (2), leaving us one free day. In between events, we would head to the Old Town section of Montreal, where they would close off some streets to make room for daily street parties. During the course of a few days, we saw O. J. Simpson and Frank Gifford, and Andre the Giant, who was easily the biggest person I have ever seen.

We also saw Quinn Buckner and Scott May from the US basketball team. Scott May had been selected by the Bulls in the second round of the college draft, so Slink, aka the Wanderer, ran up and told him to make sure he stuck it to Bill Wirtz, the Bulls' owner.

A couple of days later, we were back partying in the Old Town when I turned around to see what all the commotion was. Amazingly, I discovered

Mick Jagger standing next to me. He was as small as Andre was big. Seconds later, he was on the move along with two large bodyguards.

That same day, the Wanderer came back to our group after a little wandering, laughing his ass off. He wouldn't tell us what was so funny; he just ordered us to follow him, so we walked through the crowd until we reached the sidewalk.

As the crowd parted, we saw a group of young Canadian guys sitting on the front steps of an apartment building. As we got closer, he started pointing in their direction, then specifically at a guy in the front row. Seconds later, their group began laughing, pointing back specifically at me. That's when it sank in.

The story is that everyone has a doppelganger (twin) somewhere in the world. Based on the reactions from my friends and the guys on the steps, mine was in Montreal. What made it official was the reaction of the people standing between us. After some head-turning and some pointing, they wholeheartedly agreed. We acknowledged each other with a quick wave, then moved on.

Tuesday night, with the street parties still going on, a taxi pulled up next to us. Nobody thought anything of it until an oompah band crawled out, instruments in hand. We weren't hallucinating; other people saw them too. As the partying continued, another band started playing, and people started dancing. Standing there drinking, we noticed someone whom we thought was the Wanderer glide by. He wasn't walking; he was bodysurfing, being carried along by the crowd. It was never confirmed.

On Wednesday, the 22nd, after a women's volleyball game in the late morning, it was back to St. Hyacinthe. We needed to change clothes because we had a reservation that night at the Montreal Playboy Club. And since Thursday was our free day, we needed some help from our landlord.

We were hoping to find a local golf course, but remember the language barrier. That's when Big Don broke into his best high school French: "Club d' golf?" Still nothing. In desperation, Don showed him his best golf swing and said, "Johnny Carson," with an accent on the "son." That did it. Our landlord looked down at the map we had provided and immediately pointed to a golf course. Sacrebleu!

With that problem solved, it was time to drive to the Playboy Club. As we headed to Stu's van, the wife came running out, holding a pair of scissors. She was yelling, in French, for Big Don to stop. We all breathed a sigh of relief when she cut the price tag off his new sport coat, a coat he had bought from the Robert Hall department store in Chicago specifically for that night. Anybody remember Robert Hall's?

At dinner, we tried to show how cultured we were and ordered a couple bottles of wine. When the wine steward put the corks down in front of us, it was our turn to show how uncultured we were. Nobody ever did that with our beers.

That night, we were lucky enough to see Jason Steele perform. Don't remember him either? The highlight of the night, and of the trip, was a picture of me trapped by two beautiful Bunnies, Sage and Danielle. Yes, I remember their names.

We closed the place, then started the long trek back to St. Hyacinthe. Stu claimed he was sober enough to drive his van, but after failing to stop at three straight red lights, Big Don took over. Stu got the benefit of the doubt for the first one because he was driving in a torrential downpour, but after two more, it was time to make a call to the bullpen.

The monsoon continued after getting on the highway, so Don's plan was to follow the taillights of the vehicle in front of him. It seemed to be working just fine until we realized we were going through a rest area at around sixty-five miles per hour. After slowing down, we made it safely to the house.

Sleep was next, but there was a minor problem. It was almost sunrise by the time we made it home from the Playboy Club, so we found a little diner and scarfed down some hangover (still drunk) food. Golf was next. Sleep? Nah.

Evidently, we got there too early, because the course hadn't officially opened yet. It seemed a little strange since it was light out, but it didn't stop us. We found the first tee and started our round.

The way the course was laid out, the eighth green was right by the clubhouse. You then had to walk back to the ninth tee to play a short par three that would get you back to the clubhouse again. Jesse finally hit the wall after putting out on the eighth green, laid down in a sand trap, and went to sleep. While we finished the last hole, the foursome behind us got a little surprise as they approached the eighth green. That's when Jesse got up, stretched, and walked off toward the clubhouse. Huh?

After two days of track and field and no more naps on the golf course, we were allowed to reenter the country.

'76 Condesa del Mar, Wayne Newton

It's November, and I was still working as an assistant manager when Wayne Newton came to our place for four nights. All four banquet rooms were opened up, and about twelve hundred people showed up each night, no empty seats.

Once the lights went down and Wayne Newton hit the stage, most of my work was done. That meant I got to see quite a bit of each show. After his last performance, he surprised and impressed everyone on our staff. While setting up the four rooms for the next night's parties, he came out of the dressing room, sat his ass down on one of the banquet tables, and hung out for the next half hour. He signed autographs and talked to the help. He was the only one who ever did that.

I also got to meet his female backup singers, but it's not that good of a story. I had the honor of driving them to and from a mall in a nearby suburb so they could get their shopping fix. Remember, I was an assistant manager.

While talking with Wayne Newton's conductor, I mentioned my upcoming trip to Las Vegas in January with three friends. He told me to give him a call on the day we were interested in seeing the show, and he would try to help us out.

Two months later, the four of us landed in Las Vegas, spending three days in the city. The nights were spent seeing three different shows.

First up was Bob Newhart. Our strategy each night was to give the maître d' a $20 bill and see what it would get us. Bob was great and the seats were good.

Night two was Redd Foxx. The seats were off to the side, but not too bad, considering my arm was resting on the stage. Oh, and Redd was just as disgusting as advertised, and just as funny.

Wayne Newton was next, performing at the Sands Hotel at the time. I got a funny look from the maître d' when I walked up and asked how to get in touch with his conductor. After telling him how we met, he picked up the house phone, dialed a number, and handed it to me.

There were two lines of people waiting to get into the show. One line was for the VIPs. The other, much longer one was for us average folk. Standing there holding the phone, I could feel people's eyes on me, especially the ones in the VIP line.

Nobody answered, so I explained we hadn't planned on standing in line, then pulled out the magic $20 bill. Even though it was the hottest ticket in Las Vegas, we were immediately ushered in, walking past both lines. You could see people craning their necks, trying to get a glimpse of this famous foursome. If they only knew.

Seconds after sitting down, our waiter appeared. We still had an hour before the show started, so I asked if it was possible to go back out and do a little gambling. No problem, he walked us back to the entrance and told the same maître d' what we wanted to do, then assured us he would be waiting when we returned to our seats.

We got back with about ten minutes to spare and were able to strut past the VIP line again. And yes, our waiter was waiting at our table. It was nice to be a big shot for a little while, and Wayne Newton didn't disappoint. $5 well spent.

Home the next morning.

Condesa del Mar '77—Last Call

In March, Tom Jones came to Condesa for one night. I got to meet him before the show while checking on a problem with the thermostat in his dressing room. He impressed me because he didn't seem to be on some big ego trip. He was very polite and very patient.

At the end of the show, one of the other assistant managers told me about a beautiful woman who was interested in me. Our guess was I was going to be the stepping-stone to Tom Jones, but I never did see her. His name will come up again in October 2013 when I spent a few days in Cardiff, Wales.

In May, Al Martino did a couple of weeks in our show lounge, another great guy. He was a vegetarian and a wannabe chef, so he had permission to come in at lunchtime and make his own meals.

Walking through the restaurant one day, he called me over because he needed some help. A couple of newspaper reporters were going to be in the house that night to review him and he wanted to use the line "If I do really good here in Alsip [funny-sounding suburb where Condesa was located], next stop . . .?" He was hoping I could come up with another odd-sounding suburb.

Having gone to Lewis, the answer was easy. It was Romeoville, a town just up Route 53 from the campus. He laughed, but he had to ask if it was a real place or just something I made up. I assured him it was real, so he used the line that night. It got a big laugh and actually made it into one of the papers. My only regret was never getting a copy of it.

Finally, a couple of weeks later, Bob Hope returned for his second appearance and did two nights in the big room. It would be his last time at Condesa. Soon after that, it was my last time at Condesa—time to move on.

'77 West—RV

It's early July, so four of us (Pete, Jonzy, Big Don, and I) hit the road at the crack of dawn in a motor home we rented for a two-week vacation. Our goal was to make it to Mt. Rushmore before dark.

There were a couple of detours on the way. The first one was a drive through the Badlands National Monument, which became a national park a year later. The other was a stop at the infamous Wall Drug in South Dakota, but I don't remember ever going there. Don owns a Wall Drug hat and insists he bought it that day, so I tend to believe him. He does remember it being one of those quick "yeah, I've been there" stops, and he's pretty sure I never left the van.

After that, about seventy-five miles got us to Mount Rushmore. Somehow, we made it before the sun went down and were able to get some great pictures. The monument was impressive and so was our effort to get there, but it was time to crash.

Another twenty-five miles got us back to a KOA Campground near Rapid City, South Dakota. Well, it was almost time to crash. Some locals directed us to a bar just a few minutes away where we were lucky to rock out with a Peter Frampton cover band—sort of lucky.

With help from the long summer day, plus the hour gained going from Central time to Mountain time, we did almost 1,000 miles, averaging about 55 miles per hour, including stops—impressive.

Day 2. We got ambitious that morning and hiked around Devil's Tower in northeast Wyoming. Since we were a little hung over and did our walk before breakfast, we got real hungry, real fast.

The area around the Tower was infested with these tiny little prairie dogs, which started to look pretty appetizing. The RV's oven was ready, but we were way too slow to catch one. We even tried sticking our hands into some holes in the dirt, thinking that was where they lived, but struck out there too. It turned out to be a good thing after a park ranger lectured us about a big rabies problem that originated with them.

Since we took a pass on the prairie dogs, it was time to find a real restaurant. About thirty miles later, in the town of Moorcroft, we found a local diner for a late breakfast, with a young waitress who wasn't quite ready for us.

Pete, the smallest of the group, was the first to order. He ordered stuff, with sides of stuff and extra stuff and two large glasses of milk to wash down all the stuff. It continued around the table until she got to Big Don. That's when the teenage waitress blurted out, "Sir, I'm afraid to even ask what you want to eat!"

She returned a couple of minutes later to ask if it was OK to bring the drinks one at a time, explaining she was the one who had to wash the glasses. No problem, all five of us made it through the rest of the meal.

Now, we were at a crossroads. It was either time to take a nap, or time to play tourist. Since we were on vacation, we played tourist, heading about 200 miles into southeast Montana and Little Bighorn Battlefield.

We took a short drive around the area, then parked the RV and started walking up to the spot where Custer's Last Stand took place. A park ranger was leading a tour, so we slid in with them and got to listen to his explanation of what really happened.

There are markers showing where each soldier died, but what surprised us were the markers scattered in a nearby ravine. The story from the guide was they were trying to run, but weren't very fast.

There was still plenty of daylight, so an hour drive got us to Billings, Montana, where we stocked our fridge, then continued our driving and restarted our drinking. A few hours later, we made an emergency stop in the city of Great Falls because Big Don forgot to replenish his stock of Budweiser in Billings. Before we got there, two strange things happened on our ride north on US Hwy 87.

After a couple of hours, the Big One needed a bathroom break. Not a big deal, except he was driving the van. No problem, he calmly set the cruise control, got up, and made his way back to the bathroom. While sitting in the passenger seat, I calmly set my beer down, leaned over, and calmly steered the RV. Getting up and moving over never crossed my mind.

Traffic was light, but the few vehicles going the other way all seemed to notice the "ghost RV." At the time, nobody gave it a thought. Years later, our reaction was "What the hell were we thinking?"

Not long after that, everything in the van became airborne when Don swerved to avoid a collision with a purple Dodge Charger. We avoided the collision because there wasn't a car in sight, let alone a purple Charger. Don said he would go to his grave swearing he saw one. Don, don't swear.

Yes, it was time to find a campsite. We didn't have any luck in the immediate area, so about an hour later, we entered the small town of Choteau, where we ran out of gas. It wasn't the RV; it was us because of the long day. The first parking lot we saw became our bedroom.

It quickly got interesting when we realized the lot was adjacent to the town's police station. Don was the soberest of the group, so we sent him in to see if it was OK to park there. They said yes and congratulated us because an RV parked on a side street would have gotten a knock on the door, especially one with Illinois plates. That's right; we spent the night in a police station parking lot—different era.

Day 3. It was about a 100-mile drive to St. Mary, a town located at the eastern entrance to Glacier National Park. Don was elected to drive out of Choteau because he was the mature one who got us the parking spot.

We made it to St. Mary in mid-afternoon, but instead of finding a campsite, thought it was more important to find a bar. It's a very small town, so it didn't take long. Although most of the night was a blur, I do remember falling in love with the band's fiddle player. It was a girl.

Then there was the couple at the table next to us. Every time the guy left his seat, Jonzy would slide over and start hitting on the girl. The guy finally confronted him, but once Jonzy stood up, the drama was over. He was about 6'5" and the other guy wasn't, but nobody was surprised when Jonzy went home with us, not her.

A couple more things. There was a brook that ran behind the bar, which later became known as the babbling brook when I puked there at the end of the night. And finally, I may have "borrowed" a book from the gift shop just before babbling.

After that, we all hopped into the RV, thinking it would be a good idea to drive drunk into a national park and look for a campsite. Maybe four or five seconds later, lights started flashing, and we were pulled over. A park ranger walked up and asked Don where the hell he planned on going. This is the point where Pete, Jonzy, and I thought it would be a good idea to gather by the driver's window and tell him our strategy.

When we finished, he shook his head, then had us make a U-turn, exit the park, and take a left. An easy mile drive got us to a campground, no problem. Today, it would have been four arrests and an impounded vehicle—again, a different era.

The campsite was full, so we found a spot in a field and shut down for the night. Getting an electrical hookup wasn't important; we just needed somewhere to park. A hot shower the next day would've been a bonus, but it didn't happen.

Day 4. After a slow start, we realized the van hadn't been parked on a level surface. That's a no-no in an RV, so we lost the gas to power the fridge for a good part of the day. On our drive to the park entrance, which we assumed was the same route we took into the camp the night before, things sure seemed different. Where did all the potholes and overhanging trees come from? This must be the wrong road. It wasn't, we were sober.

Then it was time to officially and soberly enter Glacier National Park and the Going-to-the-Sun Road. It runs about fifty miles east/west through the park, and it's pretty narrow. When we left the campsite, pulling in the side mirrors was our main concern, but unfortunately, we forgot to pull in the stairs to the side door. The sound of them scraping along the mountainside quickly reminded us.

Soon after that, we came around a turn and found large motor home coming toward us. We both stopped, then the three nondrivers (Pete, Jonzy, and I) jumped out to guide the two RVs past each other. There's a size limit for motor homes, but we learned there wasn't one for animals, when we noticed a very large moose running along with us. Yes, Going-to-the-Sun was an interesting drive.

The plan was to spend two nights there. While looking for somewhere to park, a wrong turn got us on a one-lane road, which ended rather abruptly. Instead of backing out, we decided to stay and do some exploring. A few minutes later, we discovered Hidden Lake and its small waterfall. The small beach was strewn with a lot of big tree branches, making it a perfect place for a jousting tournament. It ended quickly when somebody noticed a sign telling us to beware of bears. Back on the Going-to-the-Sun Road, we got lucky and found a campsite a few minutes later.

I was the self-appointed chef/wine steward for the first night and was still employed at Condesa, so I borrowed a few things from my job, including silverware, a few bottles of wine, and real napkins. I cooked the dinner and served the wine, getting it all out of my system in one night.

The jealous people in the campsite next to us sat back, waiting for some service, but it didn't happen. It was time to return to vacation mode.

The next day, after crossing the Continental Divide at Logan's Pass, about thirty miles got us to the park's west exit. Two hours south got us to Bison National Range, where we drove the twenty-mile loop assuming we'd see herds of bison. There were a few, far off on a hill, but we did see plenty of antelope. At one point, we slowed down to check out a herd, and we were joined by a guy from Liverpool, England, who had been driving behind us in a Triumph convertible. Our guess is he thought we knew what we were doing. Sorry, chap.

We pulled over for this cool photo op but didn't realize the RV had cut off some of the young ones from the herd, which meant they were cut off from their parents. Anyway, we jumped out of the van with beers and cameras in hand and started a slow walk toward a small group of antelope. Jonzy was in the lead.

In hindsight, stopping wasn't a good idea, because we were in the way. What confirmed it was an adult pawing the ground and breaking into a trot in our direction. Even with an afternoon of drinking under our belts, we knew this wasn't a good thing.

It was a quick retreat to the safety of the motor home, where we got to watch the older antelope shuttle the young ones across the road and reunite them with the rest of their family. We also got to watch the guy from Liverpool have a good laugh at our expense.

After leaving Bison, we made a quick stop in Missoula so I could buy a sleeping bag. I kept putting it off because it was July, but the two nights in the mountains changed my mind. Then it was on to Livingston, Montana, about an hour north of Yellowstone National Park's north entrance, where we found a place for the night.

Entering Yellowstone the next morning, we just missed Old Faithful, which meant we had to wait somewhere around an hour for its next eruption. Not counting the geyser, the thing I remember most was the noise made from the clicks of all the cameras when it finally blew. When it was over, everyone got up and left, which meant one thing: a traffic jam.

We weren't in a hurry, so we grabbed some beers and our folding chairs, and plopped our asses down next to the RV. It was time to sit back and watch everyone else who was in a hurry. As one couple with two young kids walked by, the dad stopped for a few seconds so he could take a quick look in our van. He never said a word to us, but we heard him as they walked away: "Honey, that's the way to see a national park."

It was a quick stop, so after a fifty-mile drive from the south exit, we entered Grand Teton National Park near Jackson Hole, Wyoming, and found a place to park near Jenny Lake. It was uneventful, that is, until Jonzy got going. It's a night anyone near us will remember, as he staggered through just about every campsite, annoying everyone in his path. Luckily, nobody was harmed, and nobody (Jonzy) was arrested.

Craters of the Moon in southern Idaho was next because Don talked us into going about 200 miles out of the way to see this cool place with a lunar landscape. It wasn't that cool, so after a quick stop, we dumped the holding tank, then drove another 400 very windy miles south then east, ending up in the town of Vernal, Utah, where we found a campground.

We might have stopped, but the wind didn't. When sand/dirt started piling up inside the van, it was time to move on. After four quick showers, we were back on the road. Less than an hour later, we found another campground in a cool, lush forest area that ran on the honor system. Since we paid for the first one and didn't stay, we felt this one should be free.

A quick note about the RV: One of our favorite things was Pete's bed, which was basically a coffin above the doorway to the back of the van. He had no choice in the matter; he was the only one that fit. Whenever he woke up, he would automatically sit up and automatically hit his head. It never stopped being funny. "Hey Pete, get up!"

With a couple of days to go, we headed to the western entrance of Rocky Mountain National Park. There wasn't much daylight left, so we quickly drove through it and found a campground near Estes Park, Colorado, reentering the park the next morning.

Once inside, we took about a half-mile walk along the Continental Divide. At that elevation, it only took a few steps before we started gasping for air. It was a tough hike, but it was worth it. Don took a pass. For our last night, we got a motel in Boulder, about an hour drive south. It was time to get out of the van for a night before our drive home, and this is where it happened.

At some point, while chowing down on a non-Chicago pizza, Pete got what turned out to be a small piece of green pepper lodged in his nose. About an hour later, he sneezed and sent it flying across the room—true story. And no, Big Don didn't eat it.

Last call was Golden, Colorado. We stopped there because it was our last chance to buy Coors beer. This was before it was available east of the Mississippi River, so we took a tour of the brewery, then drove across the street to a liquor store to stock up. I'm not sure how many cases we bought that day, but around a dozen of them made it home.

While helping load our big order, the owner noticed the Illinois plates. And yes, he was from the southwest side of Chicago, just five or six miles from where we lived. Because of that connection, he threw in a few ashtrays and a bunch of Coors Styrofoam beer holders. Thanks?

Home safe and sober (?) after driving about 4,500 miles.

'77 Cubs

In late September, five of us (Big Don, Ab, Slink, Ted, and I) booked two rooms at a motel on Halsted Street, a short walk from Wrigley Field. The reason was a couple of afternoon games against the Philadelphia Phillies.

Don had called the place a couple of weeks earlier to make a reservation, so walking in, he gave the clerk his name. Remember, this was before computers. The guy opened up a small box and pulled out an index card with the right name on it. What caught our attention were all the other cards; oh wait, there weren't any. The only other customers were women who made a living after dark.

On Tuesday, the Phillies beat the Cubs 15-9 to clinch the Eastern Division title. After a little neighborhood bar crawl, we ended up at Ray's Bleachers, just across the street from Wrigley's right-centerfield wall.

At some point, we noticed Jack Brickhouse, the Cubs' television announcer, who had also ended up there. Big Don approached him and said something like "Mr. Brickhouse, it's really good to meet you." His reply: "Please call me Jack, and feel free to buy me a drink." He didn't.

After the bar closed, it was time to head into the neighborhood. We had planned for this little outing by bringing along a pair of tin snips, "donated" by a Sears department store. When we got a couple of blocks from the park, a small guy got on top of a big guy, then proceeded to cut down some Clark Street and some Addison Street signs. I still have mine.

The next afternoon, our tickets were in the first row next to the Phillies bullpen, and it didn't take long to see we weren't the only ones moving a bit slow.

Before the game, we watched Jay Johnstone, an outfielder who kept following Phillies manager Danny Ozark. With help from a couple of players in the bullpen, we learned he was trying to get the OK to take the lineup card out to the umpires before the game.

They told us Ozark was old school, and they were pretty sure it wasn't going happen. That's when Johnstone started a slow walk to the bullpen, we think because he spotted our beers sitting on the ledge. He walked over, saw the cup with the most beer in it, and asked permission. After getting the OK, he took a nice, long drink, set the empty cup down, thanked Big Don, and returned to the dugout.

Finally, when Ozark walked out to home plate to turn in the lineup card, Johnstone solemnly followed him at a discreet distance, pretending to look interested. Then as the two managers and four umpires converged at home plate to go over the ground rules, Johnstone ran up, grabbed the lineup card from Ozark's hand, and handed it to one of the umpires. When they were finished, he followed his manager back to the dugout without ever saying a word. His teammates loved it.

Anyway, five hungover guys watched a hungover Phillies team beat the Cubs 5-2.

'78 NCAA BASKETBALL

At the end of March, four of us (Big Don, JD, Slink, and I) headed to the Checkerdome for the NCAA men's basketball finals. That would be St. Louis. The four teams that headed there with us were Kentucky, Duke, Arkansas, and Notre Dame.

And here's how we got our tickets: One year before the tournament, we mailed in our ticket request. Nobody remembers where we sent it, but there was only a two-day window for it to be postmarked. Once at the location, the bags full of mail would be dumped on the floor, then a few employees would walk around, randomly grabbing some envelopes. When Don learned that, he made sure his was an airmail envelope with red and blue trim on it. The hope was it might draw a little more attention than a plain white one. I guess it worked.

It's an easy 300-mile drive there from Chicago's southwest suburbs, but we had a stop on the way down. Smitty, a college roommate, lived in Decatur, so the plan was to meet him and spend the evening at the local VFW Hall.

The three-hour drive to Decatur turned into a 6-7 hour trek when an ice storm hit Central Illinois. By the time we got there, Smitty was long gone, and the VFW Hall was closed.

We found a Holiday Inn for the night and got two rooms. Luckily, we weren't there very long, because there was no heat and no hot water at the inn. Looking back, we definitely overpaid.

The next morning, the roads going south had turned to slush. We made it to St. Louis without any problems and saw Kentucky beat Arkansas 64-59 and Duke beat Notre Dame 90-86 in the semifinals.

The next day, Kentucky beat Duke 94-86 for the national championship, with Jack Givens scoring 41 points.

Then home.

'78—ALCS in Kansas City

While sitting at dinner with the family on Tuesday, October 3, my brother and I decided to drive to Kansas City for an ALCS playoff game. The Royals were playing the Yankees, so after a couple of quick showers, we hit the road. Our first stop was Dupo, Illinois, about ten miles southeast of St. Louis.

Why Dupo? Because Danny, one of my brother's college roommates lived there. It was a little strange because my brother's nickname is Du, and Danny's dog was named Du. It got a lot stranger when it was time for Du to pee outside in the town of Dupo.

Early the next day, we made it to Royals Stadium for the game, and it didn't take long before we spotted a guy trying to sell a couple of tickets. They were cheap, so we grabbed them. Then we found somebody else selling a couple of cheap tickets, so we grabbed them too. We did this for a while, reselling the tickets for a profit, pretty much paying for our trip.

Kansas City won the game 10-4. When it was over, we started our drive home, but we had downed a "few" beers during the game, so after a couple of hours, we thought it would be a good idea to find a motel. It was only 9:00 p.m. The last thing we remember was watching Jerry Martin hitting a home run for the Phillies in their 9-to-5 loss to the Dodgers that night. Unfortunately for my brother, I passed out first—unfortunately because I'm a snorer. After a few hours of almost sleeping, he woke me up, and we started our drive home around three in the morning.

Amazingly, home safe.

'79 New Year's Day

In the fall of '77, my brother and I rented an apartment in Oak Lawn and hosted our first party on New Year's Eve. It was a success, so we did it again a year later, on 12/31/78.

That one drew a lot more people, with a handful of them never leaving. You either slept where you dropped or didn't sleep at all.

When some of us finally started moving and before the other ones passed out, I fired up the grill. Nobody realized it at the time, but a tradition had been born.

The grilling portion continued until the early '90s, including seven years of marriage. Yes, my wife had a sense of humor.

On 1/1/79, we had the first official party, making 1/1/15 the thirty-seventh and the last.

80's

'80 Lake Placid

In the summer of 1979, I sat down with my friend Jesse and went over the schedule for the Winter Olympics that would be taking place in Lake Placid, New York, in February 1980. With eight days to work with, our goal was to try and fit a little bit of everything into the time we had, purchasing tickets to twelve events. It came out to about $25 per ticket. Three of them were hockey games.

The lack of snow was a big concern leading up to the opening ceremonies. For the first time in Olympic history, snow cannons were used because without them, the first few days would have been in jeopardy. Can you guess when the biggest snowfall of the month occurred? It was the night of February 15, as we drove through upstate New York on the way to our hotel. We stayed at the Panther Mountain House in Chestertown, sixty miles south of Lake Placid.

On the 16th, we had tickets for the men's and women's luge. That's when we learned it wasn't possible to drive directly into the city, only to the parking lots that were set up on the outskirts of town, and they were a mess because of the previous night's snow. We also learned it was the area where everyone would stand in the snowdrifts, waiting for the shuttle buses.

On day two, we saw the women's downhill at Whiteface Mountain, about fifteen miles outside of town, where Austrian Anna Marie Moser-Proell won the gold medal. Then it was time to do some Olympic drinking. Safely back in our room that night, we started throwing together some sandwiches to cure the munchies. One of the things I remembered was spreading mustard on the food with my fingers.

The next day, the 18th, we were back on the mountain for ski jumping.

At one point, we took a break and went into one of the chalets to warm up and get something to eat. It was also time for my bathroom break.

Have you ever laughed out loud while alone in a stall in a public bathroom? Sitting down, I noticed some strange yellow stuff on my underwear. Apparently, I used them to wipe the mustard off my fingers the night before. Waking up late and hungover, I threw on some clothes and ran out the door. Never saw it. One more question. Have you ever laughed out loud while walking out of a public bathroom by yourself? I was still laughing at the table when I told Jesse. He cracked up and so did the people near us, who couldn't help but listen in.

On the 19th, we saw Eric Heiden win the 1,000-meter speed skating race. It was number three of the five gold medals he won that year. Later that evening, we saw the men's figure skating short program. Don't say it.

The next morning was women's speed skating. Yeah, we actually went to see something in the morning. We remembered it too, because Eric Heiden's sister, Beth, won the bronze medal. Then at five o'clock, we had back-to-back hockey games. In the first one, we saw Russia hold on to beat Canada 6-4. The late game was better, with the United States beating West Germany 4-2.

On the afternoon of the 21st, we had one official event, watching Linda Fratianne take second place in the women's short program. In the evening, we had one unofficial event. Again, it was Olympic drinking. On the recommendation of our hotel owner, we drove about twelve miles down a two-lane road for a late dinner at a small family-run restaurant in the town of Warrensburg.

We had a nice, quiet dinner, and with the night coming to a close, it was time for last call. The only people left in the place were Jesse and me and one other couple with a teenage daughter. We all said yes to one more, except for the girl, who just wanted to go home.

After quickly finishing our last drink, we got ready to leave, but were ordered to stay. That's when the husband (chef), his wife (hostess), and the two waitresses sat down and joined the five of us. After a bunch of last calls, we finally made it back to our room. Thank God it was a straight shot down that two-lane road to the hotel. At least I think it was.

The next morning, we got up to see the finals of the Men's slalom skiing. Phil Mahre took the silver medal. I have no idea how we made it to that event, but on a positive note, I didn't find any more mustard.

Don't know if you lost track of time, but today is the 22nd. It's time for The Game.

Like I mentioned earlier, our ticket order included three hockey games. We got lucky with the first two and even luckier when the third game turned out to be the United States vs. Russia. No sane person would have, or could have, predicted this matchup. One week before the games began, Russia beat the United States 10-3 in an exhibition game at New York's Madison Square Garden. Nobody ever thought the United States would be in the medal hunt. Now they were in the final four.

You also have to remember the era this game took place in. The Cold War was still an issue, there was the hostage crisis in Iran, and the USSR had just invaded Afghanistan. We were playing the Russians on US soil, so emotions were high. Everyone assumed Russia would kick our ass, so we considered selling our tickets, hoping to pay for a portion of our trip. Emotions might have been high, but demand wasn't, so we kept them. Thank God.

Jesse and I were two of about 8,500 people who saw what many consider the most amazing upset in the twentieth century. My seat number was 27, row C, section 59. To this day, I still get goose bumps talking about it. We won 4-3. "Do you believe in miracles?" Thank you, Al Michaels.

Besides the ticket stub, I have one other keepsake in my possession. It's a button I bought before the game that reads, "USSR SUKS." It's my all-time favorite.

After the game, the streets were filled with people waving flags, chanting "USA" and drinking heavily because guys were walking around, passing out beers to whoever needed one. And it wasn't only beer. The bottles of choice were blackberry brandy and peppermint schnapps. When you wanted a shot, you would walk up to a guy holding a bottle and help yourself.

The next day, the 23rd, we somehow made it to the four-man bobsledding event. Jesse got an autograph and a picture with Willie Davenport, who ran hurdles in four different Summer Olympics, winning a gold medal in Mexico City in 1968. In 1980, he was a runner on the US bobsled team and the first African American to compete in the Winter Olympics.

We left late that night, hoping to get home in time to watch the United States play Finland. A lot of people didn't realize the game against Russia wasn't for the gold, and back in 1980, the gold-medal game was not a primetime event. The game was at 5:00 p.m. but not televised until 8:00 p.m.

Home safe, but not before a little drama the next morning, when I got pulled over in Ohio for speeding. We explained to the officer it was important for us to make it home in time to see the gold-medal game. After showing him the tickets stubs from The Game he let us go with these departing words: "Be safe, hurry home."

We beat Finland 4-2.

Years later talking with Jesse, I learned he got autographs from speed skater Beth Heiden and figure skater Linda Fratianne on his tickets from each event. How come I never got one?

'80 STL Chuck's Band

On Friday morning, a group of friends, divided into a few cars, invaded St. Louis for a Cub/Cardinal weekend. No hotel, we would be staying in South County at the home of my future mother-in-law. Nobody's positive, but we think it was August 15–17, 1980.

The partying started early, with Big Don drinking around thirty-six beers beginning in the afternoon, then continuing as we watched the Cubs beat the Cardinals Friday night. It was an unofficial estimate, with a six-pack plus/minus.

Our slow start on Saturday wasn't a big deal because it was another night game. This is gonna sound a little weird, but since the Cubs were up big, we left early and headed to Mehlville High School. It was because Vicky's brother Chuck and his band were playing there. We had to check them out.

We also thought it would be a good idea to bring some beers up to the gym's balcony, but we weren't very discreet. So almost eleven years after graduating from high school, I was kicked out of a high school dance.

The Cubs swept the Cardinals that weekend.

'80 Kansas City

The Phillies were in Kansas City on Friday, October 17, to play game three of the 1980 World Series, so Larry B. and I decided to hop in my car and go to the game.

Not having a ticket wasn't important because you can usually find one. What you end up paying is the interesting part. We walked around for a couple of hours, asking everyone in earshot if they had any extras. The answer we got in the local language was "Sure don't."

Then I spotted a guy with his young son, walking toward us with an envelope in his hand. My gut feeling was he had tickets, so we walked up and asked him. Sure do. $15 was the price printed on each ticket, and that's what we paid; that's right, face value for a World Series game.

It might have been a World Series game, but what impressed us most was the politeness of the Kansas City fans. During the game, most of the people on the first base side were getting on Pete Rose. Those crazed fans were chanting, "Rose stinks, Rose stinks." Not *sucks*, *stinks*. Can't imagine that happening in Philadelphia. Anyway, KC won 4-3 in ten innings.

After a long day and maybe a beer or two, we got lucky and found a motel not too far out of town. It's where we decided to stay for game four. It was an afternoon game, and we found tickets for face value again, this time standing room for only ten dollars. The Royals won 5-3, so when it was over, we hit the road.

Home safe.

'80 Bears in Cleveland

On November 3, four of us went to Cleveland's old Municipal Stadium for a Bears/Browns football game; so did 84,000 other people. The Browns were good that year, winning their division with an 11-5 record. They also beat the Bears, 27-21.

When it was over, we took a short drive to a bar recommended by some of the locals. A couple of drinks later, we took a short drive to a bar recommended by some of the locals. One more recommendation and it was time to find our hotel.

Since we got back hungry, a new tradition was born. That night, I took a walk through the hotel kitchen in search of some snacks. I was successful, so it would happen again.

When my brother and Big Don passed out, Larry B. and I decided to rearrange some of the hotel's furniture. After a quick stroll through the lobby and down a few hallways, we put some of the stuff in our room. That meant potted plants, chairs, and anything else that wasn't bolted down.

We filled the room, even rolling a big flower cart on to the elevator and up to our floor. Unfortunately, or luckily, it didn't make it through our door, so we left it in the hallway.

We also hid a big sign that was supposed to tell people about the hotel restaurant's taco special, in the bathtub, behind the shower curtain. I'm pretty sure the turnout was light. We weren't malicious; we were just stupid.

The next morning, once our roommates stopped laughing, we checked out and started our hungover drive home. Our only concern—let me rephrase that: Big Don's only concern was he would get pulled over by the

Ohio State Police because his name and license plate number were used when we checked into the hotel. He breathed a big sigh of relief when we crossed the state line into Indiana.

Then home.

'81 Canada RV

At the end of June, four of us rented a motor home and hit the road. Western Canada was our destination. The roster consisted of me, Larry B., Pete L., and Big Don. Also accompanying us was Don's private stock of Budweiser beer. His concern was he wouldn't be able to find it north of the border.

Our drive took us through Fargo, North Dakota, then north on I-29 to the border, where we got to meet our first Canadian Mountie. While taking a quick look at the motor home, inside and out, he asked us what we planned on doing during our stay in Canada. The stash of Budweiser made him even more curious. "So you guys planning on doing some fishing?"

"Nope."

"Going hunting?"

"Nope."

"Oh, a little raping and pillaging, eh?"

We really didn't know how to answer that one.

Our first stop was Edmonton, about a 900-mile drive northwest after meeting our Mountie. On our way there, I made a major miscalculation regarding the amount of gas left in the tank and our ability to find a gas station to fill it. Today, you can always find a gas station open any time and on any day. In 1981, a twenty-four-hour gas station/convenience store was a rarity.

We got off the highway in Bethune, Saskatchewan, population 350, found a closed Shell gas station and parked there, knowing we wouldn't be going anywhere any time soon. And guess what was located directly across the street; that's right, a bar. It was around eleven o'clock on a Saturday night.

The plan was to gas up whenever we got up, so the four of us walked into a local bar in a town of 350 people at eleven o'clock at night. Needless to say, the place came to a dead stop. It didn't take long to find out how nice everyone was, but the first couple of minutes were a little unsettling.

The bartender served us our drinks and immediately struck up a conversation. Everybody was dying to know who we were and how we ended up in their town.

After we told him our story, he updated his customers, then picked up the phone. It was a quick call, with a great result. He called the couple who owned the gas station and told the wife our problem.

She apologized for not being able to open it right away because her husband was taking a bath.

Remember, it was a Saturday night.

A little while later, clean and refreshed, the owner arrived and opened the station. We gave him fifty dollars, which in 1981, filled the tank and left enough for a good tip. He was happy and we were lucky—actually, very lucky, because the station was closed on Sundays.

On to Edmonton. We didn't see much of the city, but did see the Edmonton Trappers play the Tacoma Tigers in a minor-league baseball game. Edmonton got a little press in Chicago in late May when one of the Trappers was arrested after breaking into a Hudson Bay department store. He was drunk and thought it would be a good idea to try stealing some watches. It made our local news because the Trappers were an affiliate of the White Sox.

The next morning, July 1, we drove about four hours to Jasper, Alberta and crept down Main Street, looking for a place to grab a late breakfast or early lunch. We found a restaurant with an open parking spot right in front, so we went in and chowed down. It was time to get a good base because it wouldn't be long before we started drinking again.

After accomplishing our goal, we walked out and discovered the street had been closed down because it was Canada's Independence Day. Not able to leave, we were forced to sit up on the roof of the motor home and watch the parade that was coming down the street. With no time constraints, plus the best seats on the route, we sat back and enjoyed the moment. One thing stood out. It was the four of us constantly being pelted, in fun, with candy from the people marching by.

I think it was later that day when we discovered Red Deer, a local beer brewed in the city of . . . wait . . . Red Deer, located about halfway between Edmonton and Calgary.

It didn't take long before we renamed it Deer Piss. You know what it's like after drinking for a while and somebody screws up and gives you the wrong beer. Usually, it's not until you put down the empty bottle and read the label that you notice it.

Red Deer was different. It didn't matter if you had a couple of beers or a twelve pack, you couldn't sneak one past any of us. It was nasty. Oh, and the word *nasty* will show up again soon.

Leaving Jasper, we drove about thirty-five kilometers, which would be about twenty miles in the US, to Robson Provincial Park. It's adjacent to Jasper National Park, but located in the province of British Columbia. The only reason to go there was to add BC to our list of Canadian provinces. The plan was to drive about a mile, get out and touch park soil, then turn around and exit the place. We paid dearly.

I was relaxing in the bed over the driver's seat, checking out the scenery as we pulled up to a booth at the park's entrance. Looking down, I let out a gasp. The park ranger was a large woman with her hair plastered across one side of her face, similar to actress Veronica Lake (look it up), but not nearly as beautiful.

She stood there holding a cup of tea with her little pinky sticking out, but you could barely see the cup because of the size of her hand. We instantly dubbed her Nasty Samples, because she reminded us of Junior Samples from the TV show *Hee Haw*. You might have to look that one up too.

One of the highlights of the trip through Western Canada was the drive on the Icefields Parkway through Jasper and Banff National Parks. Four years earlier, we did the drive through Glacier National Park in Montana, and we were blown away by the scenery. I think the Parkway might have been better, and there was a bonus. It was a lot wider than the road through Glacier.

For most of the drive, we had the RV's side door tied open with somebody's belt. Not sure, but I'm guessing it was Big Don's. It allowed us to hang out the door and take pictures. We would snap a couple of shots of some awesome mountain vista, drive ten to fifteen minutes around a bend in the road, then discover another great photo op staring us in the face. This went on for a couple of hours.

We dropped anchor in Banff National Park and spent two days there. I have three pictures in my possession that were taken during that time and need to be mentioned here.

One is cute. It's a picture of a deer that had walked into our campsite and was eating beer nuts out of Pete's hand. The other two aren't as cute, and they both involve Big Don. At the time, Banff was known for its glaciers, but they have continued to shrink over the years. We're not positive, but the picture of Big Don lying spread-eagled in the snow may have been the start of the problem.

The other picture was taken in the woods. This time, we are 100 percent sure it's him and not Bigfoot. We had our doubts when we looked at some other photos, but the footprints absolved him.

With one day left, we went to the Calgary Stampede, the biggest and most famous rodeo in the world. Because of the crowds, we ended up parking the van in a field about a mile away. No problem, shuttle buses were there to get everyone to and from the fairgrounds.

While waiting for the next bus, we struck up a conversation with the people parked next to us. It went something like this:

"Where are you from?"

"Chicago."

"Where in Chicago?"

"Southside."

"Where on the south side?"

"Oak Lawn."

"Where in Oak Lawn?"

Amazingly, one of their relatives owned a jewelry store two blocks from my place.

At some point, we lost track of Big Don. We were a little concerned because he hadn't been feeling up to par, plus par for him is different from the average person. We took the shuttle back to see if he had returned to the van, but he wasn't there, so we turned around and went back to the Fair Grounds.

A few steps inside the main entrance, we spotted him at a corndog stand, with a half-eaten dog in his hand. Based on the wide smile across the vendor's face and the mustard smeared on Don's face, he had been there for a while. Later that day, we heard a story about the vendor retiring right after Don's visit—unconfirmed.

I was behind the wheel when we left Calgary to start our long drive home. Medicine Hat, about three hours south, was actually a scheduled stop because it had the nearest glass bottle return depot. It meant we could get ten cents for every empty beer bottle we turned in.

A guy on the dock waved us in, not knowing what he was getting into, so we started our own production line from the back of the van to where he was standing. I don't remember what we got back, but Don seems to think it was around $40. About fifteen cases? Yeah, that seems right.

Our last stop was Winnipeg to change our money, arriving two hours before the banks opened. After a little nap, we got some US dollars and headed home.

'81 Mich. City

Some friends rented a large beach house in Michigan City, Indiana, for the month of September. It was a bit of a gamble for that time of year, but we got lucky, with it turning out to be one of the warmest Septembers in some time. The drive to the house was a little over an hour. The walk down the back stairs and across a small sand dune to Lake Michigan was a little over a minute.

At the time, I was working twelve-hour days for Winchell's Donuts, in charge of opening a new store. It was located in Chicago's western suburbs, which boosted my drive time to almost two hours. Once there, the short walk to the beach sure helped, but after a few drinks, it was time for bed.

On September 6, I took a few hours off to see the Bears lose 16-9 to the Packers at Soldier Field. I should've stayed at work.

Then a week later, I was fired by the new division manager, who conveniently waited until my work at the new store was done. It would have been nice if he had taken the time to meet me, or fire me two weeks sooner. That way, I could have spent the whole month in Michigan City.

Our rental had a large balcony that faced southwest toward the water, which meant it faced downtown Chicago. At that time of year, from our location on the east side of the lake, the sun would set through the Loop—pretty cool.

For most of the weekdays during the last half of the month, it was usually just JD and me. Our dinner routine was to hit the balcony and fire up the grill. One night, I mentioned jokingly how romantic it was, sitting there as the sun went down. He quickly got up and ran inside so he could finish his dinner alone. Later that month, during the full moon, a few of us were on the beach after dark, throwing a Frisbee around. This was not any

Frisbee; it was the one Stu bought in Montreal when we were there for the '76 Olympics. An errant toss landed it in the lake. We never saw it again.

On September 20, it was back to Chicago for another Bears game. This time they won, beating Tampa Bay 28-17.

The way the schedule worked out, we had the house until Sunday morning, October 4. Since Saturday was last call, it became an all-day party. Everyone was hanging the next morning, so to try and jump-start the day, a few of us broke into a sprint and dove into Lake Michigan. Yes, it was early October, and yes, it was an instant hangover cure.

Almost twenty-five years later, while attending Loyola University in Chicago, my daughter and a few of her friends jumped into Lake Michigan on Halloween Night. You win, Steph.

In 2004, a few of the same group started renting a house in the same neighborhood. One of the first things we did, on the first day we were there, was walk down to the beach to see if the Frisbee had washed up. The year 2014 was our last in Michigan City. Still nothing.

'81 Bears in Detroit

The Bears were playing the Lions in Detroit on Monday night, October 19, so it was time to rent a motor home. Our roster was me, JD, Big Don, Larry B., and Snake. The rental came with a three-day minimum, so we looked around for something else to do.

After checking the college and pro schedules, we picked Cleveland because the Browns were home on Sunday afternoon against the New Orleans Saints. The Browns won the game 20-17, with Jeff Groth catching one pass for seventeen yards—nope, not related. When the game ended, it was time to hit a couple of bars. Not sure, but they might have been the same ones recommended by some of the locals the previous year.

After a slow start Monday, we drove about sixty miles south to Canton, spending a couple of hours at the NFL Hall of Fame. We could have stayed longer, but we had a Bears game to go to, so it was time to head to Detroit.

At a stop for gas, we noticed a semi with the Stroh's Beer sign across its side, so we showed the driver our half barrel of Stroh's, which happened to fit perfectly in the RV's shower. After a good laugh, he took a picture of us drinking Stroh's Beer in front of a Stroh's Beer truck.

We made it to the Silverdome in time to watch Eric Hipple, Detroit's quarterback, have his best game as a pro. He threw four touchdown passes and ran for two more, and we got our asses kicked 48-17.

When the game was over, we started our drive home. Maybe an hour later, near Ann Arbor, we had a munchies attack. A Burger King drive-through was about to become our solution (salvation).

Don was pretty sure the RV wouldn't fit, so he parked it and we walked up, still in the spots we were in when he drove up. There was a driver, a passenger in the front seat, and two guys sitting on the couch. Oh yeah, and one more guy just zipping up after coming out of the bathroom.

After Don placed our order, the girl calmly replied, "Please walk through." Guess we weren't as cool as we thought. We got our food, found I-94 and continued our ride home. Once dinner settled in with the alcohol, Don hit the wall. Since nobody else was in any shape to take the wheel, we found a rest area and called it quits.

Early Tuesday, we woke up and restarted the drive home, but there was a problem. The half barrel wasn't empty. Yes, that was the problem. Five minutes into Illinois, and about thirty minutes from home, we accomplished our goal. Timing was perfect.

'82 Phoenix

It's March, and I was engaged to be married. It was scheduled for late May and I had a big decision to make. Should I go to Hawaii with Vicky (my fiancée), her mother, sister, and little brother, or go to Mesa, Arizona, for Cubs' spring training with my brother and Big Don? Honey, I'll see you at the wedding.

We rented a small RV but got a late start because of my grandmother's death. It changed our plans by about thirty-six hours. Arriving in Phoenix late at night and not really knowing where we were going, we ended up on Van Buren Street. It didn't take long to figure out what part of town we were in.

While we were at a red light, a young prostitute casually walked up to the motor home, opened the passenger door, and invited herself in. Yeah, we were definitely at a red light. We took a pass on the local entertainment, eventually finding a campground/trailer park in Mesa, not far from Hohokam Park, where the Cubs played their spring training games.

It was too late to get an electrical hookup, so we grabbed a parking spot in front of the main office. Around noon, we met the owner and struck up a friendship. Yes, we'll be back.

Part of our first day was spent at poolside, where we met some of the people staying at the campground. Most of them were from Alberta, Canada, and most of them were seniors. We were about half their age, but I think we might have been a breath of fresh air. It was fun for all of us.

The next day, we drove to Hohokam to see our first game. I don't remember what it cost to enter the grounds, but I do remember the three of us commenting on how cheap it was. Then it was bonus time. While looking for somewhere to park, we discovered it was possible to pull our van up to the right field fence and leave it there for the day. That meant we paid for parking, but not for any tickets to the game.

It would become a tradition, returning three out of the next four years. Each time, we would find our spot and sit up on the roof before, during, and after the game. If we didn't drive to Phoenix, we would fly there, then rent a motor home. And yes, we had a spot.

I've lived my whole life in the Chicago area, so being in Phoenix in late March is about as good as it gets when we're talking weather. The low-seventies is perfect when you've come south out of a Chicago winter.

And if you're a college basketball fan, it's also time for the NCAA men's basketball tournament. We would run an extension cord up to the roof, keep the generator running, and plug in a small TV.

Baseball in front of us, mountains behind us, college basketball on TV, alcohol, BBQ and a sun tan. "We must be in heaven, man" (Wavy Gravy at Woodstock in '69).

We decided to take a short break from baseball and headed to Las Vegas. After some alcohol and a few boring hours driving up State Road 93, we did the smart thing and found a Holiday Inn in Kingman, Arizona.

It was a quiet night at the hotel, so we quickly made friends with the woman at the front desk. It was because she doubled as the bartender in the hotel's lounge. A couple of good tips and the bar stayed open a lot longer than it would have on a normal night. She loved us!

None of us were big gamblers and none of us had much money, so Las Vegas was a quick stop. It was mainly tourist stuff, including a tour of the Hoover Dam.

A couple more days of baseball and it was time to start the drive home. Our first stop was about 250 miles north from Phoenix, at the south rim of the Grand Canyon. It was windy and cold, with a little snow thrown in for good measure, but the sun did come out a few times. When it did, the view was amazing.

Leaving the canyon, Big Don, with nothing else to do, began his calculations, trying to predict when we would get home. His conclusion was if we averaged sixty miles per hour, including stops, we could make last call at our bar . . . the next night.

The drive home wasn't a whole lot of fun. The weather we experienced at the Canyon followed us through New Mexico, the Texas Panhandle, and Oklahoma. And to make matters worse, the heat in the RV stopped working. I was wearing a hat, gloves, and a blanket, and I was driving.

And just as Don predicted, we made last call at Bootlegger's in time to see my fiancée and her best friend staggering to their cars.

'82 Honeymoon

I made it home from Phoenix, so Vic and I were married on May 30, 1982. The next day, we flew to the Florida Keys because her boss gave us the use of his condo on Isla Morada for a week. It was a gated area where we had to use an ID card to enter the grounds. The card also doubled as a credit card for anything we purchased there.

The use of his car was also part of the gift, so on June 1, we left for Key West. As we headed south on Route 1, Hurricane Alberto was moving north. In case you didn't know, June 1 is the official start of the hurricane season. Our drive didn't last too long. There is nothing on Route 1 to break the waves, so when they started rolling up by the roadside, we thought it would be a good idea to turn around.

Back at the condo, we waited to see what would happen, then got lucky when Alberto took a slow turn east into the Atlantic Ocean. The only downside was having to spend a couple of days holed up in our place because of the torrential rains. I guess if I had to be stuck in an apartment for a couple of days, my first choice would be my honeymoon.

We were pretty selective when it came to spending money in our little community because everything was on the expensive side, but after two days of rain, I broke down and took off to the bar. We both drank Bacardi and Coke, so I went in and asked if it was possible to buy a bottle, not a drink. It was, so I did. They even threw in a few limes. I knew it was going to be expensive, but it didn't matter. They ran my ID card. I grabbed the rum and the limes, and ran back to the condo.

Walking in, I made a beeline to the kitchen and made two drinks. Vic stood there, waiting to hear what the damage was, so I handed her a Bacardi and Coke, and told her I had no idea. When they put the bill in front of me, I signed it and ran back. She shook her head for a second, then started drinking.

Later that month, when Vic was back at work, the bill came in for our stay in Florida. That's when we learned about the rest of his wedding present. Everything was free. Hindsight?

Two months later, we decided to treat ourselves to another honeymoon and flew to Cancun, Mexico. It was around the time the city was coming into its own as a tourist destination. In the mid-'70s, it got clean water, an international airport, and its first handful of hotels. After that, the population exploded, going from around 20,000 to about 250,000 by the early '90s. I looked it up.

We spent one day on Isla Mujeres, now a quick ferryboat ride from Cancun. Even then, the island was a draw because of some archeological sites and some great snorkeling spots, but the ferryboats didn't exist in 1982. What you did was pay a local to drive you there in his little motorboat.

This was also the site where I almost killed my wife. We rented a motor scooter to tour the five-mile-long island but, for some reason, rented only one. I drove and Vic sat on the back. Pulling away from the rental place, I let the clutch out a little too fast, and she flew off the back. She claimed, half-heartedly, that it was on purpose. It was an accident—really.

During our short stay, we scheduled a day trip to Chichén Itzá. As the ancient center of Mayan culture on the Yucatan Peninsula, it has some amazing ruins. It's about a three-hour ride from Cancun, but we got our time, or our time zones, mixed up and missed the bus.

Other than eating, drinking, and lying around our all-inclusive, that was pretty much it, but it's OK when you're on your (second) honeymoon.

Thirty-one years later, Vic, now my ex-wife, and I returned to Cancun for our daughter's wedding at the El Dorado resort on the Riviera Maya. Still never made it to Chichén Itzá.

'82 Cincy

It's July, and four of us (Big Don, Larry B., Bruce, and I) got a couple of rooms in Covington, Kentucky, a few miles south of Cincinnati. The Cubs were playing the Reds, so it was time for a little road trip. Two things would stand out on this trip. One took place during the game; the other came later.

I don't remember where our seats were for Saturday's game. What I do remember is standing behind home plate because it was close to one of the stadium bars.

After a couple of innings, we noticed the empty upper-deck suites in left field. Larry B. and I decided to investigate and discovered an unlocked door, so we walked in and took a seat in the front row. We wouldn't have stayed because it was so hot, but once Larry spotted the thermostat and turned on the A/C, we got comfy.

Looking up from the lower deck behind home plate, Big Don and Bruce couldn't believe it took three innings before we were noticed. When an usher finally came in and asked what we were doing, we quickly apologized and walked out, but not before turning off the A/C.

At a local bar after the game, two girls approached Bruce, thinking he was Chicago Cub Ryne Sandberg. With that, Larry immediately became the Cubs' trainer. With that, Don and I immediately gave the girls our seats so we could watch the show from a safe distance.

And here's the quote of the night, which has qualified as one of the best I've ever heard, given with a bit of a Southern drawl. "I hope you don't think I'm that kinda girl just 'cause I'm not wearin' any underwear." 'Nuff said.

Home safe the next day.

BOOTLEGGER'S

I worked at Bootlegger's Bar in Oak Lawn for about five years starting in the summer of 1978. Here are some stories in no particular order:

Christmas Eve was easily the most hysterical night of the year. We stayed open every year and had a blast every year.

Our next-door neighbor was the Oak Lawn Pet Store, and Bob, the owner, would keep his place open too. Why? Bwana Bob's punch. It was self-serve. Walk in, dip your glass into a fish tank, and come back into the bar. You just had to make sure you dipped it in the right tank.

We had a scare one year that sent all the women and a few of the men racing for the back door. Larry B. had been sampling the punch, so when he returned to the bar with a very large and very live boa constrictor draped over his shoulders, people freaked.

Yes, Larry had too much of Bob's punch in his system, but we didn't realize how much VO was in Bob's system. It had to be a lot for him to let someone walk out of his store with a large live snake around one's neck.

We had something called the guest tender. A customer would get picked, at random, then put behind the bar for a while—always worth a few laughs.

We also had something called the designated sitter. A bar stool would get picked at random, then drinks were free for the customer who happened to sit there.

One afternoon in '81, my boss dragged me to a White Sox game. It wasn't at gunpoint, but it was close; I'm a Cubs fan. This was during the time Harry Caray was their play-by-play announcer, and this is when I learned Jim and Harry actually knew each other.

Back then, during the middle of the game, Harry would leave the press box for a short break. The story was break time was beer time, and that day was no different. Jim and I were able to meet up with him at the last row of the lower grandstand even with third base.

We picked that spot because Nancy Faust, the Sox organist, was set up there, so for an inning or so, the three of us got to hang out with her. Harry might have been on a break but Nancy was still working, and even though I was at a Sox game, it was still a lot of fun. Harry and Nancy were great.

Oak Lawn turned 100 in 1982, so a big party was in order. Bootlegger's was located on Ninety-Fifth Street, a major artery on the southwest side that runs through the heart of the village. For the weekend celebration, the bar was lucky enough to have another spot directly across the street in a big beer tent.

Amazingly, Oak Lawn got the OK to close the street. That meant people hung around all night, a lot of them just sitting on the curb and drinking. And they stayed after the bars closed, which was 4:00 a.m. at the time, and they did it peacefully. Today?

Another noteworthy thing happened that weekend. After changing a barrel of Miller Lite, Big Don returned to the tap to start pouring the new one. He would stay there until the new one went dry. It never stopped.

And here are a couple more stories involving Bwana Bob:

One night, he enlisted our help at closing time because he needed some strong drunk guys to lift his SUV off the railroad tracks at the Ninety-Sixth Street/Cook Avenue crossing. I guess the construction and detour signs didn't make an impact. What was important was moving his vehicle before the early morning commuter trains started running into the city. Luckily, there was enough time and enough of us still in the bar.

The other story involves goldfish. Bob made a $100 bet with a customer to see if he could down twenty goldfish in thirty minutes. They were a little bigger than everyone expected, but he got them all down in the allotted time. A little while later, he calmly walked out the front door and threw up. Eighteen fish hit the pavement, two still flopping. Two are still unaccounted for.

With his stomach now empty, Bob tried to recoup his loss with a new bet. How about ten tiny little turtles in twenty minutes? It was a quick "no thanks" when the customer saw their tiny little claws.

John McC., my brother's best friend, worked for a small local radio station and was able to get some Chicago athletes out to the bar for some interviews. I remember Al Secord and Murray Bannerman from the Blackhawks, Dave Corzine (Bulls), Tom Filer (Cubs), and I'm pretty sure, some others. One more weird one: A girl who played on one of the softball teams we sponsored had grown up in St. Louis. Not long after graduating from high school, she got married, and not long after that, her husband was transferred to Chicago. After three years of marriage, they split up, and she decided to stay in the area. I married her.

OK, one more: My best friend Ted and I tried to buy the bar, but the owner wouldn't sell to us. A few months later, the place caught on fire. No comment.

'82 PLAYOFF BASEBALL

On a whim, my brother Jim and I drove up to Milwaukee County Stadium on October 8 to see the Brewers play the California Angels in an American League playoff game. We found two tickets and saw the Brewers win 5-3. After winning the next two games at home, it was time for them to face the St. Louis Cardinals in the World Series.

World Series games don't happen too often in Chicago, so we headed back to Milwaukee to see a game, this time with my wife, my brother's girlfriend, and our friend Larry B.

We weren't too worried about finding tickets. My brother and I were successful in '78, when we drove to Kansas City to see a Royals/Yankees playoff game, actually turning a profit, buying then reselling a handful of tickets.

And in 1980, Larry and I were in Kansas City for a World Series game against the Phillies. This time, it took a while, but we got into a World Series game for face value.

Now, back to Milwaukee. Again, it took a while, but I found five standing-room tickets for $20 each. Face value was eight dollars, so not too bad. We found a spot in the lower grandstand directly behind home plate. It even had a small ledge we could sit on. We didn't sit; we used it for our beers. Priorities.

It was a good game, with Willie McGee hitting two home runs and making two great catches in centerfield, one of them robbing Gorman Thomas of a home run. St. Louis won 6-2.

After attending a World Series game in Milwaukee, it was time to see one in St. Louis, so on October 19, Larry and I went south, hoping to find a couple of tickets to game six.

We assumed demand would be high, so after quickly finding two tickets just a few dollars over face value, we decided to do a little scalping. A small profit on each ticket could pay for gas and alcohol. It didn't happen. During the first inning, we got rid of our last two tickets, selling them for under face value. That's right, under face value for a World Series game. Really?

The weather that night was perfect, around seventy degrees when the game started. Sound too good to be true? Two rain delays and a switch in the wind direction from south to north put a big dent in our comfort zone. Maybe that's why we had to sell our tickets at a loss.

During one of the delays, while talking to the couple sitting next to us, we learned they were from Evergreen Park, the suburb two miles east of my place. Fifty thousand people at a game in St. Louis and the people next to me were almost neighbors. It's amazing how often this happens.

Anyway, I saw a World Series game in both cities. Not counting the media, I'd love to know how many people did what I did. And I'd love to know how many of them weren't from either city.

The Cardinals won 13-1 and went on to win the series in seven games.

'83 Phoenix

It's the end of March, so I rented a motor home for the trip to Mesa, Arizona, for Cubs spring training. This time it was Ted, Larry B., my brother Jim, and me—oh yeah, and a bottle of Brut aftershave. We were convinced Larry was using it as his daily shower. None of us ever needed any aftershave; all we had to do was walk back into the RV after Larry left it.

The traditions continued when we returned to the same campground and got to hang out at poolside with a bunch of seniors from Alberta, Canada. They still had a sense of humor.

Then it was game time, and like the previous year, we were able to park our motor home up against the right field fence at Hohokam Park. Remember, we had a spot.

Our friend Beatta hung out with us for a couple of games. She and her husband did the same thing the year before, but they had divorced since then. She decided to stay in the Phoenix area, and had a great story. For one week, she passed out flyers for a new cleaning service, and within six months, had people working for her. I'd love to know how she's doing.

For a change of pace, the four of us went to see the Phoenix Suns play the Utah Jazz on the 29th. We got our tickets outside the arena from a guy who told us they were at center court. He didn't lie, but there was a slight problem. The seats were located in just about the last row of the last level. The Suns won 115-107. The next day Grace, Ted's sister-in-law, joined us for a game and, of course, joined us on the roof.

Seconds after getting there, she plopped down on what she thought was a seat cushion. It wasn't; it was a square white vent for the RV's bathroom. It was never the same.

Before the game started, a handful of players were getting their running done in the outfield. The NCAA men's basketball tournament was going on, and we had our small TV propped up on the roof. Cub catcher Jody Davis was more interested than we were. He kept stopping and asking for updates because Georgia, his alma mater, was playing. I think it was the game Georgia beat North Carolina to advance to the Final Four.

One night, while heading back to the campground, we made a stop for some drunken munchies at a Dunkin Donuts. My choice was a box of Bavarian-cream donut holes. Walking out, carrying my little box of heaven, the bottom broke. My friends were laughing so hard they were almost in tears. I crawled around, almost in tears, trying to round up my food. They weren't on the ground that long, so they were pronounced OK to eat.

After our last ballgame and stops at a couple of bars, we decided to start our long drive home. It would be north to Flagstaff where, in theory, we would pick up Route 40 and start driving east. It's only 150 miles, but we never got there. After an hour or so, we pulled into a rest area and passed out, actually doing the responsible thing.

Our next stop was for gas the following night in Oklahoma City. We were also ready for a couple of drinks, but the neighborhood we stopped in wasn't exactly what we were looking for. After getting directions to a nearby campground, it was a quick nap followed by a hot shower. A couple of days of alcohol and warm weather in close quarters? Not pretty. After that, it was time to head home.

There was one more thing. Before leaving for Arizona, we purchased tickets to a St. Louis Blues hockey game, thinking we could stop there on the way back.

Didn't happen, but home safe.

'83 Europe Vic

On June 12, a year after our two honeymoons, Vic and I went to Europe for three weeks. Rome was our first stop, spending the first two days doing the usual tourist stuff. Remember, I was there in '72, but didn't see much because I was out of money and had to catch an early flight home.

The one thing that stood out during our stay was the time spent in Vatican City, which included a tour of the Sistine Chapel. It was impressive, but I didn't realize how muted the colors were because of the dirt and smoke that had accumulated on the ceiling over the years.

On day three, our last day in Rome, we got an early start and took a train to Ostia Antica, about twenty miles west of the city. Way back in the day, Ostia, which was located on the Mediterranean Sea, was the port for Rome because the cities were connected by the Tiber River.

Over time, its bay area silted up and changed the course of the river, leaving the ancient city almost two miles from the sea. We saw some great 2,000-year-old ruins at the old city and snuck in some beach time at the new one.

On the way back to Rome, we decided to find a park somewhere away from the congested tourist areas and do a picnic dinner. We headed to Trastevere, a neighborhood on the opposite side of the Tiber River, where we learned there was a lot less English spoken. After a short walk around the neighborhood, we found a deli.

Luckily, only six people were in the store so the wait in line was short, and luckily, only six people got to listen to me trying to place an order in Italian. I walked up to the counter and gave it a shot: "Due cento grammi" of some formaggio and "cinque cento grammi" of some salami. That's 200 grams of cheese and 500 grams of meat. So far, so good.

The problem arose when I tried to order mustard. Not knowing the word in Italian, I became the typical clueless American. I'll just add an *o*. Mustardo! Wrong, it didn't translate. "Mi dispiace." ("I'm sorry.")

This was the point where it became a community project. Of the six people in the place, not one of them knew what we wanted, but they all seemed to be talking to each other, trying to help us out. That's when an old man, who reminded me of my Italian grandfather, walked over and grabbed the Italian-English dictionary out of my hand. He gave it a quick once-over, mumbled something in Italian, then handed it back. Nothing.

I've traveled a lot in Europe, and I've put together trips for people who wanted to travel there. The one piece of advice I tell everyone is to try and learn a few words of the language spoken in the country you plan on visiting.

The average European can tell just by looking at you that you're an American, which means you probably only speak English. The important thing is the effort. No matter how badly you butcher their language, they will appreciate the attempt. And finally, when you do try, there's good chance you will make a fool of yourself. You gotta be able to laugh it off.

I was beginning to giggle, because it was apparent nobody on either side of the counter knew what we wanted. Vic and I were ready to accept the fact mustard wouldn't be on the menu, but that's when the owner's young son came to the rescue.

He had been standing off to the side taking in the whole scene when he disappeared from sight. After a few seconds beneath the counter, he popped up with a jar in his hand. "Questo [this]?" Yes, it was mustardo! Everyone was thrilled, but it wasn't mustardo, it was *senape*. That's the word for mustard in Italian.

The next day, we grabbed a morning train to Florence for a two-day stop, finding a hotel about a block from the Santa Maria Novella Station.

The summer crowds hadn't materialized yet, so the line into the Accademia to see Michelangelo's "David" wasn't bad. If you're traveling in Europe in the summer, expect to stand in line to get into most places, and not just for a few minutes. The line to see "David" during prime time is usually one to two hours.

After that, we got ambitious and walked almost four miles up some narrow walled roads past the Villa Medici to the town of Fiesole and its nine-hundred-year-old cathedral. We also saw some Roman baths and a Roman theater, with our final reward being a great panoramic view of

Florence. Later that day, we learned bus #7 would have taken us there in a few minutes, but it didn't matter; the walk was worth it. And it didn't deter us. We kept going, and discovered the Piazzale (plaza) Michelangelo. It's located on a hill in the Oltrarno district, which means the other side of the Arno River from the old city center. It's lower and closer to the city than Fiesole, so the view was more detailed. The walk from there, downhill and across the Ponte Vecchio Bridge, wasn't bad either. Ten miles was our estimate for the day.

Florence is a fascinating city. It's listed, obviously, in the book *1,000 Places to See Before You Die*. A no-brainer, but it's also listed in the book *500 Places to See Before They Disappear* because the city is prone to severe flooding.

At some of the historical sites, you can see how bad it got during the flood in 1966. Inside the city's cathedral, the water marks were about ten feet high. Another flood, almost as bad, hit the city in 1992.

We finished our first day in Florence at the Uffizi Gallery, where we saw works by Botticelli, Da Vinci, Michelangelo, Rembrandt, etc. So far, I've made it to the Uffizi, the Prado, the Louvre, and of course, Chicago's Art Institute. A stop at Munich's Pinakothek Art Museum would come in a few days.

After a one-hour train ride, most of day two was spent in Pisa and its Field of Miracles, which includes the city's cathedral, baptistery, and in the early '80s, the ability to climb to the top of the Leaning Tower. It's a strange walk, because you climb about three hundred steps up a circular stairway inside a tower that tilts to one side.

The next day, the 18th, we took a late morning train to Venice. Vic now worked for a travel corporation, so we were able to enjoy a few perks from her company. The first one was the Carlton Executive, a four-star hotel located on the Grand Canal. It was a short walk from the train station, and we got it for half price.

During our stay, we took a boat trip to the island of Burano, which is famous for its lacemaking. That was followed by the island of Murano, which is famous for its glassmaking. We toured a glass factory, stood there watching the process with everybody else, and like everybody else, left trying to figure out how they did it.

Back in Venice, we walked around seeing the usual stuff, including a stroll across the Bridge of Sighs. Aaaah! Then we got lost. Well, not really, we were on an island.

After two days in Venice, it was a train to Munich and a reservation at the Penta Hotel. We had a beautiful suite for three nights that included a buffet breakfast and a daily basket of fruit, cheese, and sausage. It was free.

We walked around the old town area, and after a stop at the Pinakothek Art Museum, ended up at the Hofbrauhaus, where we had a few liter mugs of beer. It was fun, but a little touristy.

The next morning was very sobering, but not because of the beer the previous night. We took a trip to Dachau, about fifteen miles north of Munich, to tour the World War II concentration camp. It's hard to describe the emotions we felt after seeing its crematorium, gas chambers, and a film containing actual footage from the war. It was rough, but it's a place everyone should see.

On a lighter note, after returning to Munich, we went to a McDonald's for lunch. When our delicious meal was over, we toured the Oktoberfest Fairgrounds, where I drank on a break during my semester in Spain. That was followed by a tour of its museum, then dinner at a Mexican restaurant. Yeah, I know, I was in Germany.

Our last day was spent wandering the city and relaxing in the Englisher Garten, a huge park that reminded me of Chicago's Grant Park.

The next morning, the 23rd, we checked out and used our Eurail Pass for a bus trip north on the Romantic Road, beginning in Augsburg and ending in Frankfort. In between were three medieval cities.

Nordlingen was first. We took a slow walk through and around the old, walled Roman city and toured its museum, where we learned a little bit about the city's history. Then it was back on the bus for a short ride to the next town.

Dinkelsbuhl was city number two. It was similar to Nordlingen, but smaller, so we were back on the bus in about an hour and on our way to Rothenburg ob der Tauber, which translates to "The Red Town over the Tauber River."

Rothenburg was another walled city. Time wasn't an issue, so we took the two-mile walk around it, then toured St. Jakob's Church, which has a rock crystal on display that supposedly holds a few drops of Christ's blood. Last call, before getting back on the bus, was the Medieval Crime Museum, which proved to be pretty interesting. It also proved to be pretty gruesome. There were some lovely ways to be put to death in medieval times.

Our day came to an end after a thirty-mile train ride from Frankfort to the town of Mainz, where we hooked up with Mark and Dawn, a couple from Minnesota we met on the bus tour. The girls stayed at the train station, sending Mark and me in search of a place to stay for the night. We were back a few minutes later, after finding a hostel that had a toilet and shower in each room for only about twenty dollars, and yes, the girls joined us.

The next morning, the four of us took a cruise on the Rhine River, ending up in the town of Koblenz, where the Rhine intersects with the Mosel River. It turned out to be one of the highlights of the trip because Dawn and I got to sit back and watch Joe Tourist (Mark) and Joan Tourist (my wife) go crazy with their cameras.

After docking, Vic and I found a room and snuck in a short nap, then met up with Mark and Dawn for dinner and a few drinks, actually a few bottles. Spatlese was the wine of choice.

The next day, we went our separate ways. I don't remember why, but Vic and I decided to stop in Zurich, Switzerland. It was pretty uneventful until we discovered a local street fest. Walking into one of the tents, we grabbed two open seats at a table inhabited by a bunch of locals. It turned out to be a great move.

We got to party with a group of Zurichers and, with the help of an Austrian oompah band, learned something called the chicken dance, which would soon make its way into American wedding receptions. As the fest was coming to a close, we started to say our goodbyes because it was time to catch a tram back to our hotel, but there was a problem. They had stopped running about thirty minutes earlier.

Our new friends then offered us a deal. Come back with them and continue partying at one of their homes, then they would drive us to our hotel when the festivities ended. It felt right, so we went. Zurich may have started slow, but being able to party with a bunch of locals all night was awesome. They got us home at first light.

Yes, we missed breakfast but somehow made our train to the town of Buchs, followed by a bus to Vaduz, the capital of Lichtenstein. We walked, very slowly, around the city and even slower when we tried to check out the medieval castle that overlooks the area. After that, it was back to the hotel to regroup. A big dinner, a little more walking, and we were done by 10:00 p.m.

It was another quick stop with a morning train to Lucerne, which is located on the shores of . . . Lake Lucerne. The highlight of this stop was the city itself, centered on its famous wooden covered Chapel Bridge. In 1983, you could walk across the bridge and see around 150 paintings, many of them dating back to the 1600s. Most of the bridge and many of the paintings were destroyed by a fire in 1993, but the bridge was quickly restored.

The only downer was the weather because the rain arrived about the same time we did. After a leisurely walk around the city, lunch was at a place called McCheaps. With a name like that, we had to check it out. It turned out to be a horrible imitation of McDonalds. Yeah, it was that bad.

The next morning was a three-hour train ride to the city of Locarno. Our room at the Hotel Rondinella was on the fourth floor, across the street from Lake Maggiore. Standing on our balcony, we spotted a place where we could rent a pedalo. They're little one- or two-seater boats that you pedal around the lake.

Back on shore, a thirty-minute hike got us up to the Madonna del Sasso Church. In hindsight, after all the pedaling, the funicular (cable car) should have been our choice. And yes, we were rewarded with another great view.

Locarno is located in a weird temperate zone. I looked it up, and found it has the lowest elevation and warmest temperature of any city in Switzerland. When you're down at lake level, there are palm trees. That's right, palm trees. Then when you look past them across the lake, you can see the snow-covered Alps—true story. I'll be back.

It's time to meet my Italian relatives.

Europe—Vic-Milan

Vic and I arrived in Milan on Wednesday, the 29th. The plan was to meet my mom's relatives on the 30th, so we used the first day to see what we could, not knowing what my cousins had planned. Our train got us there just before noon.

We found a room at the Hotel Cristallo, just a couple of blocks from the main station, then took a quick tour of the city. We kicked ass, seeing Sforza Castle, the Duomo (cathedral), and La Scala, Milan's famous opera house. There was even a quick stop at the Victor Emmanuel Arcade (mall). Yes, it was time for Vic's mini shopping fix. That's right, mini.

The Santa Maria della Grazie Church was next. It's where "The Last Supper," Da Vinci's famous painting, is located. It's on a wall of the refectory, a building attached to the side of the church, and it's where we learned a story about the painting that might qualify as a miracle.

There are pictures from World War II showing the devastation from the bombing of Milan. A good portion of the church and refectory had been destroyed, with only two walls still standing. Yes, "The Last Supper" was on one of them. After that, we took a gelato break.

With time for one more stop, we were able to tour an exhibit at the Da Vinci Museum of Arts and Sciences, where we saw a special presentation of his works and ideas. On the way back to the hotel, we stopped at a deli and got some food to take back to our room. This stop was uneventful, not like the one in Rome.

The next day, after breakfast, we met a couple of cousins who took us back to our hotel to get our bags and check us out. That meant I would be staying with family. If you remember, it almost happened in 1972.

After lunch, Nuccia (a teenage cousin) and a couple of other young relatives took us to see . . . you guessed it, Sforza Castle, the Duomo, La Scala, and the Arcade. We didn't have the heart to tell them we saw everything the day before.

Dinner that night was with a lot more relatives, and some of them were convinced Vic was the cousin. I really don't look Italian, so I could understand their confusion. After dinner, we all had a few drinks and talked, usually at the same time.

Before the trip, Vic and I listened to some Italian language tapes, hoping they would help us when we met my family. That, and my high school Spanish did help us understand a little bit, but we weren't really able to answer them. Nuccia did most of the translating until she lost her voice, so Salvatore, another young cousin, stepped up and finished the night.

When my uncle called to confirm our flight home, he learned it had been canceled, so on Friday, Nuccia and Salvatore took us to the Pan Am office to exchange our tickets. Our flight would be leaving on Sunday, not Saturday, which meant we got one more day in Milan, which meant we got one more day of home-cooked meals, pictures, and lost voices. They even imported a friend who spoke fluent English just to give my young cousins a break.

On Saturday, our bonus day, two of my uncles took us to San Siro stadium, hoping to find four tickets to see AC Milan play soccer. Milan has two pro soccer teams, similar to Chicago with its two pro baseball teams, but there is one difference. AC Milan and Inter Milan both play in Serie A, the same league. My relatives are AC Milan fans, which meant we were too. No luck finding tickets.

Now it's Sunday and time to leave, so Nuccia and my uncle Salvatore drove us to the airport for our rescheduled flight home. We knew something was wrong while watching the conversation at the counter. My uncle became very animated and very loud. He was being very Italian.

It turned out the airline failed to mention the rescheduled flight had been moved to Milan's other airport. Vic and I got our update while running out the door. Normally, the drive is about an hour. Our flight was leaving in ninety minutes, and we were just getting back to the car. The ride on the Autostrada was a riot. We made it with time to spare.

A year later, Nuccia and her friend Sylvia came to Chicago and stayed with my mom and dad. They were nineteen years old and got to sit in on some classes at Mother McAuley, a girls' Catholic high school a couple miles away. They had a lot of fun because they were treated like celebrities.

One night, we took them to a Blackhawks hockey game against the Pittsburgh Penguins. Sorry, that night they were the Penguinos.

One more thing: Before leaving for Europe, my uncle Charlie, who had married into the family, told us we were crazy to go to Italy. His theory was my mom's relatives were probably poor farmers with dirt floors and goats walking around inside the house.

For the record, we stayed in a fully furnished apartment in the same building as my Aunt Rosa and Uncle Salvatore. They owned it and had it waiting for their daughter, Nuccia, whenever she was ready to move in.

Also, Mercedes was my relatives' car of choice, and that's because the family business had done the pipe insulation work on the Pirelli Building, which, when finished, was the tallest building in the city. I couldn't wait to get home so I could tell my uncle how clueless he was.

One more thing: Every time I have visited my relatives, at least one dinner included rabbit.

'83 MLB All-Star Game

Vic's job was located in downtown Hinsdale, a suburb west of Chicago. The office across the hall from her was occupied by Charlie Comiskey, the former owner of the Chicago White Sox.

Old Comiskey Park was hosting the All-Star Game on July 6, and Mr. Comiskey was nice enough to provide the people in Vic's office with tickets to the game, which was fifty years to the day of the very first All-Star game. We also got tickets to the Old-Timers' game the day before.

Our seats were in the right field upper deck, where we were able to watch Fred Lynn's grand slam homer land just below us. The AL won in a rout, 13-3.

Thanks, Charlie.

'83 Cubs—Vic-Don

The story begins as I left Wrigley Field in my '78 Dodge Charger with Vicky and Big Don. She sucked it up and crawled into the back seat, giving Don easy access to the passenger-side bucket seat.

We were heading home after a 1:30 p.m. Cub game, so combine that traffic with the normal rush hour crowd. Yes, it was slow. We were creeping east on Irving Park Road on our way to Lake Shore Drive. That's where you head south through downtown on the way to the southwest suburbs.

While at a dead stop, Don jumped out of the car and ran across the street to a local bar. Actually, he didn't jump and didn't run; there's a reason he's called Big Don. Anyway, he was in and out of there in about a minute, getting us beer for the ride home.

We finally started moving but, because of the traffic, got stuck in an intersection as the light went from yellow to red. I didn't think anything of it, but the occupants of a Chicago Police paddy wagon did and pulled us over.

We stashed our beers in the console between the driver and passenger seats, and I stepped out of the car to talk to the officer. He told me I ran a red light. I disagreed, saying the light was yellow. He then told me my friend in the front seat was drinking a can of Budweiser. Didn't have an answer for that one.

About the same time, Don started to get out of the car to see if there was anything he could do, but he was quickly ordered to sit back down by the other officer. He was then told to open the console, grab the open beers, and dump them by the curb. The whole time, Vic sat quietly in the back seat. The look on her face said everything.

All this took some time and I hadn't been arrested or even issued a ticket, so I offered to buy the officers their dinner. When they accepted, I got back in the car and restarted our drive home. Vic and Don sat there, waiting to hear what happened. "You did what?" That came from my wife.

Turning south on to Lake Shore Drive, we all cracked open a beer—actually, just me and Don.

'83 BEARS IN BALTIMORE

In September, five of us rented a motor home for a road trip to see the Bears play the Colts. It was 1983, so our destination was Baltimore, not Indianapolis. The game was on Sunday the 26th, so we looked around for a college football game on Saturday somewhere on the way east.

Kent State jumped out. We figured it would be a lot easier to get tickets there instead of some of the Big Ten schools. What made it more interesting was their opponent. It was Northern Illinois U. The school's location also worked out because it was about halfway between Chicago and Baltimore.

We got there early and found a parking lot near the stadium. It was time to do some tailgating, but we got a strange look from the parking attendant when we pulled in. The empty lot explained his puzzled face. For some reason, tailgating wasn't very popular at Kent State, at least, not in that lot.

Our first thought was the majority of the fans were probably students who primed up in their dorm rooms, then walked over just before the start of the game. Our backup theory was we were sent to the "other" lot once they saw our Illinois license plates.

Pregame turned out to be the best part of the day. Once the game started, things went downhill fast with NIU getting their asses kicked 38-7. It was time to head to Baltimore.

We got to Old Memorial Stadium early Sunday. People tailgate there, and they have a sense of humor. We made friends with a group of Colt fans in the motor home next to us, even after unfurling our City of Chicago flag.

They also gave us some good information on the area, including the

Inner Harbor. The dad of the family told us it wasn't that long ago when you wouldn't feel safe there unless you were carrying a gun. Now, after the renovation, his daughters went there with their boyfriends.

The Bears got beat 22-19 in overtime. After the game, we hit the Baltimore City Fair, then a few places in Fell's Point. I would learn about the water taxis on my next visit to the city.

Quote of the night: "We need to leave now!" This came after Dave L. ordered a martini with a peeled grape and he was told it wasn't possible.

Six months later, in March 1984, the Colts packed up in the middle of the night and moved to Indianapolis.

'84 Phoenix

For the third year in a row, we went to Mesa, Arizona, for spring training. And for the third year in a row, we were able to park our motor home up against the right field fence at Hohokam Park.

At work one day, Vic mentioned to Mary, a coworker, that I would be in Arizona for spring training with my brother and four other friends. When Mary heard that, she lit up. Her husband, Joe was an ex-ballplayer, and they were good friends with Hall of Famer Frank Robinson and his wife. Whenever they were in the same city at the same time, they would hang out together.

Robinson had just become manager of the San Francisco Giants, so Mary told Vic when I met him to make sure I mentioned Joe and Mary said hello. We had a good laugh, figuring the odds of me meeting Frank Robinson were pretty slim.

The Giants' home during spring training is in Scottsdale, just a short ride from Mesa. On March 31, they were playing the Cubs at Hohokam Park. The routine was to warm up at their park, then hop on the team bus for the short drive to Mesa, ready to start the game.

Knowing the Giants would be arriving soon, I stuck a baseball and a pen in my pocket and walked around to the third base side where their team bus would pull in. Frank was the first one off, so I walked up to him from the side and said hello. He said hello back, with that look wondering who I was.

That's when I mentioned Joe and Mary and how they ordered me to say hello when the two of us met. He did a double take and asked how I knew them. As we continued walking, I told him the story I just told you. He was a great guy, and since we were talking, nobody stopped me.

Seconds later, here's his quote: "You know, you probably shouldn't be out here." Confused for a second, I took a look at my surroundings, then realized I was standing on the field next to the third base line. With that, I asked if he could sign a ball before I was escorted out. No problem, he signed it, shook my hand, then turned and walked toward the dugout, leaving me there all by myself.

Following him seemed to be the right thing to do, then I remembered my friends on the roof of the RV. Now, stopping and turning around seemed to be the right thing to do. They were all standing there with their mouths hanging open and their arms spread out. I gave them a long wave, then made my exit.

We were back in our spot Sunday, April 1, with the spot next to us inhabited by the same group of guys from the day before. Immediately after pulling in, they started asking us when we would be signing autographs. Everyone assumed it was because of me walking on the field with Frank Robinson the day before, but we were wrong.

It all made sense when one of our neighbors showed us a copy of the Sunday edition of the *Mesa Tribune*. There, on the front page of the sports section, was a picture of us on the roof of our RV.

Evidently, a photographer had positioned himself on the third base line in a lower box seat, waited until we were all facing the infield, then snapped the picture. It also included Cub outfielder Mel Hall, who left a few days after we did. He was traded; we just left.

After realizing our celebrity status, somebody walked the two blocks to a convenience store and brought back enough newspapers for everyone. I kept a copy and tried to get the picture reproduced when I got home, but nobody would touch it without a release from the *Mesa Tribune*. Remember, this is before camera phones.

A few more days of baseball and drinking and it was time to head home, but not before one more good bar story. The place we picked offered two-for-one Long Islands. For last call on our last night, four of us decided we would do the eight. They brought sixteen.

Good night.

'84 STL

It was June, and the Cubs were in St. Louis for a three-game series, so it was time for a few of us to head south. We made it for the night game on Friday the 8ᵗʰ, had a "few" beers, then returned to the park the next afternoon and picked up where we left off.

After a performance similar to the night before, we headed back to our hotel because it was time to cure the munchies. Pizza was our first choice but we weren't in Chicago anymore, so we got the yellow pages out and hoped for the best.

A place called I——'s jumped out because it had more locations than anyone else. How bad could it be? While Don called in the order, the rest of us headed to the hotel pool. When he walked over to tell us our dinner had arrived, a red flag went up. We have a great selection of pizzas at home, but none of them are ever delivered in fifteen minutes.

Not long into our "gourmet" dinner, Big Don, who is six feet tall and then about 300 pounds, set his slice of pizza down in mid-bite. It tasted like a burnt grilled cheese sandwich, so we left the rest of it for the maid. I hope she found it, because it was under the bed.

Even though Vic and I were divorced in '89, it didn't matter. Every time I returned to St. Louis, whether for a hockey game, a baseball game, or a visit to my daughter, somebody from her family would always bring up I——'s and tell me the delivery was just minutes away.

The other thing was the use of the word *pop*. I guess it's called soda in most areas of the country, so I would also be reminded of that. Dick, would you like a slice of I——'s and a can of pop?

In late 2013, a customer at the bar who was from Toronto, Canada, informed me the word *pop* was also used in his city. See, it's not just us.

'84 SHAW'S

A couple of years after we were married, Vic started working for a billboard company in Chicago. One of their biggest accounts was Lettuce Entertain You, a large restaurant conglomerate that covered most of the metropolitan area. A tiny portion of their monthly bill was paid as part of a barter account with coupons that could be redeemed at any of their sites. Once in a while, a few lucky employees were able to use them.

As a reward for the work she had done on a special project, Vic's boss told her to take her husband (that would be me) out to dinner that Saturday. His favorite place was Shaw's Crab House, and that's where the two of them decided we would go. All she had to do was call the restaurant and make a reservation, and he would take care of the rest.

After making the call, Vic learned Shaw's didn't take reservations, so she walked over to her boss's office to let him know. Ten minutes later, he walked over to her office to let her know the reservation for two was at eight o'clock. Dinner was free. All we had to do was pay for parking and tip the maître d' when we were seated.

At the restaurant, we got in a line winding toward the hostess desk. A few minutes later, we heard a woman tell the couple in front of us the wait for a table was a little over an hour. When we stepped up, I gave her our name and reservation time. Her reaction was a funny look while explaining the restaurant's "no reservation" policy.

Before we could say a word, a woman employed by the restaurant magically appeared and asked if we were Mr. and Mrs. Groth. She said not to worry because our table would be ready in just a few minutes. Then a waiter magically appeared to take our drink order. This is when we started to get a few looks from the people in line. Who was this couple?

The waiter quickly returned with our drinks and asked if we would be paying cash or starting a tab. As I started to answer, the same woman appeared and waved him away. We were really starting to like this.

The maître d' then took us into what was, of course, the VIP section. Walking to our table, we could feel the stares. It was pretty funny, because they were coming from actual VIPs. Anyway, I did as I was told and tipped him when we were seated.

During the appetizer course, we had looked over the wine list and we were ready to order a bottle as soon as our waiter returned, but before that could happen, our angel appeared again. This time, she brought us a gift: an ice bucket holding a bottle of Moet Champagne. She must have noticed the look on our faces, because she made sure we understood the champagne was also on the house.

We enjoyed a nice, leisurely, and delicious dinner. After dessert and one more drink, it was time to move on. We knew our dinner would be on the house, but we asked the waiter how much it was so we could leave him a tip. He refused to tell us, explaining he had already been taken care of, then told us to go out and enjoy the rest of the evening.

'85 Spring

After work, on the evening of March 4, Vic was making dinner and I was probably on the living room couch. She called out, asking me to come into the kitchen. All right. When I walked in, she calmly pointed to the floor. I looked down, saw the mess, and hoped it was because her water broke. Any other reason would have really freaked me out. That's what it was, so we headed to La Grange Hospital, about a thirty-minute drive from our place.

Christ Hospital was only three minutes away, but the plan was to go to La Grange because her doctor was there. We checked in around 8:00 p.m. Luckily, time wasn't an issue, because my beautiful daughter Stephanie wasn't born until 10:30 a.m. the next day.

Writing this brought back memories. One of them was something called an episiotomy, which, at the time, was considered a better solution than a Caesarian. The sound of the doctor snipping Vic's skin to make a wider opening was one of the worst sounds I've ever heard. She was drugged, so it didn't hurt her as much as it hurt me—just kidding. Anyway, we both toughed it out and made it through the day.

On June 9, Vic and I went to Wrigley and saw the Pirates beat the Cubs 5-1. It was noteworthy because of the person who came with us. It was Stephanie, our three-month-old daughter, making her first appearance at a Major League baseball game.

Farm Aid '85

On September 22, the first Farm Aid concert took place at the University of Illinois' football stadium in Champaign. Vic, her best friend Nancy, JD (one of my oldest friends), and I decided to rent a small RV for the trip. General admission tickets were $17.50 each, and we found a spot in the upper deck, near midfield, in maybe the third or fourth row. Easily, the best concert I've ever seen.

There was one downside. It was the rain; it never stopped. The university had covered the whole floor of the stadium with tarps. They were hoping to save the playing field from any damage it might incur from the thousands of people that would be on it all day. My guess is they never checked the weather forecast or never thought it would rain like it did, because covering the whole field covered all the drains.

We noticed the problem late that night. Do you know what you get when you combine the rain falling on the field with the water flowing down the stairs from the stands? That's right, an enormous wading pool. People had been standing in a few inches of water during the last half of the concert. It just confirms how good it was, because nobody left.

It was an incredible day of music, put together by Bob Dylan, Neil Young, Willie Nelson, and John Mellencamp, as a fundraiser to help family farms in the United States. A concert with just those four guys would be amazing. Now, here's a list of most of the other acts:

| Stray Cats | Foreigner | Blasters | Emmylou Harris |
| Lou Reed | Charlie Daniels | Don Henley | Roy Orbison |

Loretta Lynn	Billy Joel	Johnny Cash	Kris Kristofferson
B. B. King	Tom Petty	Bon Jovi	Waylon Jennings
Carole King	Beach Boys	Bonnie Raitt	Merle Haggard
John Fogarty	Hall & Oates	Van Halen w/ Sammy Hagar	

One of the highlights was Sammy Hagar and Van Halen playing together for the first time. During their rendition of Led Zeppelin's "Rock and Roll," Sammy Hagar stopped to watch Eddie Van Halen's guitar solo, pointed over to him, and yelled out, "The king, the king!" He also put a "z" at the end of Illinois.

Home safe.

'85 Bears and Hawks in Detroit

The Blackhawks were in Detroit to play the Red Wings at Joe Louis Arena on Saturday night, December 21. The Bears were in Detroit to play the Lions at the Pontiac Silverdome on Sunday afternoon, December 22. You know what that means. Nine of us (Jim H., Puddin, Kent, Chez, Larry B., Stu, JD, Ray "I'm OK," and I) piled into a motor home and headed there Saturday morning.

The Hawks beat the Wings 6-3. After the game, we talked about going across the border to Windsor, Ontario, for the ambience. That meant strip clubs. It wasn't a good idea because of all the drinking before and during the game, so we took a pass.

On Sunday afternoon, the Bears beat the Lions 37-17. That meant both teams won a road game in the same city on the same weekend. Pretty good, but getting home would be the top story.

When the game ended, we jumped on State Road 59, which would eventually merge with Interstate 96. The plan was to do our postgame tailgating in a moving RV, but an ice storm had moved into the area at the same time, lasting about three hours during our drive west. My top speed was around thirty miles per hour. We could tell it was freezing up just minutes ahead of us because the vehicles that had slid off the road still had their lights on and their motors running. To make things even more interesting, our defroster stopped working. Kent quickly came up with a solution and started up the generator.

Puddin (George) had taken a lot of shit because he brought a hair dryer on the trip, but quickly became a hero. With the generator running and the hair dryer plugged in, JD sat in the passenger seat and held it up to the windshield. It was defrosted and George was forgiven.

After about eighty slowly driven miles, we got to Lansing and took Interstate 69, which heads southwest toward Interstate 94. It warmed a few degrees, which was all we needed. When the ice began turning into slush, it was time for someone to peel my fingers off the steering wheel. As my first hand got free, it immediately rose up and ordered a very large Bacardi and Coke.

A few more hours and a couple of more drinks, and we made it home safe.

'86 Phoenix

It's late March, and our destination was Mesa, Arizona, for spring training with the Cubs. Yes, you've heard this before, but I skipped a year because Steph was born on March 5, 1985.

It was an RV again, but with a different group. There were two Nancys on the trip. One was my sister, and the other was Steph's godmother. There were also two Jims on the trip. One was my brother, and the other was a good friend who would become my roommate a few years later. Oh yeah, Steph was there with her mom and dad.

On the drive down, my one-year-old fell in love with my future roommate. He had never been west of the Mississippi River, so he stayed awake for most of the ride. Steph, who had just started walking, would stand and hold on to the couch, then stare at him for what seemed like hours. Her crush on him would continue.

We got down to Mesa, and just like the previous few years, we were able to spend a few days watching some ball games in our spot. Yes, it was up against the right field fence at Hohokam Park. I'm not sure, but this might have been the last year the Cubs allowed motor homes to park there.

It was pretty low-key this time, mostly baseball, not bars. Then home.

'87 PITTSBURGH

It's late June, so six of us piled into my station wagon and drove to Pittsburgh to see the Cubs play the Pirates. The weekend also doubled as a bachelor party for my brother, so Pops (John), my brother's best man, flew in from Florida. Arrival time was late afternoon on Friday the 26th for the night game.

The ticket for Friday's game also listed an Old-Timers' Game. The funny thing is nobody remembers seeing it. Tailgating before the real game was our top priority, so I guess that would explain the blank looks when I asked my friends about it.

Anyway, the highlight of the trip took place on Saturday afternoon at Beer World. It was a giant warehouse with stacks of just about any beer you could think of and any beer you didn't know of. If you had a craving, they had an answer. It was a little overwhelming for Big Don. Actually, the word was *orgasmic*. When he finally made it out to the parking lot, he lit up a cigarette. Yeah, it was that good.

Now I understand where all the empty bottles of Rolling Rock came from. Evidently, we went through over 150 of them tailgating before Saturday's game. Don't judge us until I tell you they were seven-ounce bottles. OK, go ahead and judge us. Also, my ticket says it was Centennial Cap Day, but nobody can produce one.

After the game, it was back to the car for more of those little bottles and to watch a great fireworks display over the park. When the show ended and everyone started leaving, we heard some tires squealing and horns blowing maybe fifty feet away. Somebody cut somebody off.

That's when we noticed two men getting out of their cars, jawing at each other. We didn't take it too seriously until we saw Big Don put down his handful of seven-ouncers and walk over to separate them. One had a wife and two young kids, so Don walked the single guy to his car and had him drive away. He then went back to the vehicle with the family and had them wait while he waved a bunch of cars through, creating a big gap between the two.

We congratulated Don on a job well done. Pops even used the word *heroic*. Don's reply: "I just saw a couple of scared kids. Where did you put my beers?"

Sunday was a hungover afternoon game, with our section infested with thirty to forty kids throwing a few beach balls around. It might sound cute, but to us, it was pretty annoying. We tried to be patient, but Don finally snapped, took out his pocketknife, and ended the life of the biggest ball.

All we heard was a young voice yelling, "Daddy, that big guy just stabbed my ball!" After that, the kids gave us plenty of space and nothing else was stabbed.

Then home.

'87 Cincy

The Cubs were in Cincinnati at the end of August so a few of us headed there for the weekend series, this time moving a little closer. We stayed at the Travel Lodge in Newport, Kentucky, conveniently located across the Ohio River from the ballpark. We didn't know it then, but it would become our lodging of choice for a long time.

This is also the town where we discovered Kelly's Keg, conveniently located across the street from the Travel Lodge. We didn't know it then, but it would become our bar of choice for a long time.

After Friday's night game, the bartender at Kelly's told us about a couple of places we should visit. One was the Oarhouse, a bar back across the river in Cincinnati, but we decided to put that one on hold until Saturday.

The other was a strip joint just a short walk up the street, so that's where we went. The highlight of the night, other than the obvious, was an announcement asking the guy in the baseball hat to sit in his chair and not on the table next to the runway. That would be me.

On Saturday night, we actually drove across the river to the game because the Oarhouse was on our schedule. After discovering Newport and everything we could do on foot, it would be the only time we drove anywhere after a game.

Anyway, we quickly made friends with the bartender at the Oarhouse. We knew this because after just one drink, she was showing us topless photos of her outstripping a male stripper at a friend's bachelorette party. She was also nice enough to direct us to a few places that would take care of our drunken munchies, but after listening to all the different places for chili, we went to White Castle.

Home safe the next day.

'87 BOSTON

On December 5, Vic and I flew to Boston to see the Blackhawks play the Bruins. So did Steph, who was almost three years old. Also on the trip were Nancy M., Jim H., and Larry B.

We encountered some turbulence over Ohio, and you could see people tensing up. Steph seemed to be the only one who didn't care. Her reaction as we were bouncing around? "Mommy, that tickles my tummy." We had a great time in Boston, except for the game. We lost 7-3, but on a positive note, I made my pilgrimage to Boston Garden. I would return in 2002 to see a game at Fenway Park.

And once again, Steph became enamored with Jim. The year before, it was in the motor home on the drive to Phoenix. This time, she would hold on to his leg as we walked around the city.

We had to make a stop at Filene's Basement so the girls could get their shopping fix. The guys stayed outside, and so did Steph, so she could be close to Jim. She also became our chick magnet. There is nothing like a cute little girl walking around in a white fur coat if you want to attract women. Oh wait, I'm married.

That was it for Boston—short, but sweet.

'88 NBA

On February 7, Chicago hosted the NBA All-Star Game at the Old Chicago Stadium. Four of us (Larry B., Fitz, Mike P., and I) got tickets that also included the NBA Slam Dunk Contest, which took place the night before.

We weren't sitting for the Slam Dunk Contest; we were standing in the first balcony behind one of the baskets. We got lucky because our end was where the final slams took place. Michael Jordan beat out Dominique Wilkins. We also got to see Larry Bird win the three-point shootout.

When it was over, we headed to Greek town for a few more drinks. Talking to a couple of women, we learned the Marriott Hotel on Wacker Drive was the headquarters for the NBA that week. Yes, it became our next stop.

Fitz and Mike had bought commemorative basketballs, so they used them to get some autographs in the hotel bar. Isiah Thomas, Dominique Wilkins, and Charles Barkley were a few of the signatures they got. Don't remember why, but no ball and no autographs for me.

We were standing again for the All-Star Game, where we got to see Michael Jordan score forty points and win the MVP award.

8/8/88

Yes, it finally happened! The Chicago Cubs decided to play a baseball game at night at Wrigley Field. It was inevitable, but it just didn't feel right. My dad grew up about a mile from the park, and I grew up walking up the railroad tracks from Grandma's house to see the Cubs play. And yes, it was during the day.

For this historic event, a handful of us decided we would be some of the coolest fans in attendance, so we rented a limo. When we finely got down to the park, there was a major traffic jam. And would you believe that it was all limousines? Everybody had one, but they just weren't as cool as we were.

I don't remember why, but we ended up with an extra ticket. My brother volunteered to stay outside the park and get rid of it. While we went inside, he got arrested for scalping. He had been downstate to see an old college buddy the weekend before the game, and missed the warnings about trying to scalp the Cubs tickets. Sorry, too late. What was really shitty was that he wasn't even interested in making any money. He was only asking face value for the ticket, but technically, just the resale of the ticket was against the law. I'm pretty sure that never happened before any other game.

Inside, we watched a guy named Harry Grossman push a button to turn on the lights. He was picked for the honor because he had seen the Cubs play in the 1908 World Series. There was a countdown, and before he pushed the button, he said, "Let there be lights!"

And now, finally, the game—it was the Cubs vs. the Phillies.

The first pitch was hysterical. This was before camera phones. Rick Sutcliffe's first pitch blinded everyone. There were so many flashes going off that nobody, including the home plate umpire, could have called it a ball or a strike.

Two pitches later, Phillip Bradley, the first batter at the first night game ever at Wrigley Field, led off with a home run.

In the bottom of the inning, Mitch Webster led off with a single. Ryne Sandberg was the next batter. As he walked up to the batter's box, Morgana, known as the "Kissing Bandit" somehow got on the field and started running toward Ryno. Security got her before she could get near him. It didn't seem to bother him, because a couple of pitches later, he hit a home run.

Two innings later, after being released from the neighborhood police station, my brother joined us. Ironically, he ended up paying a ticket scalper something over face value to get into the game. Justice was not served. His luck continued. He knew where we were sitting, so when he finally caught up with us, it started to rain. And boy, did it rain. Monsoon is the word that comes to mind. My brother saw a couple of batters, and that was it for the night. Three and a half innings, and the game was called.

So the first night game ever at Wrigley Field was called because of rain. Omen?

The next day—sorry, the next night, the Cubs beat the Mets 6-4.

'88 Bears

In the fall, Bill C., a guy who worked with Vic, invited me to a Bears/ Packers game on September 25. It's a great rivalry and tickets can be hard to come by, but what made it more interesting was its location. We were going to Lambeau Field in Green Bay. He had relatives in Wisconsin and they had a couple of extra tickets, so early Sunday morning, the two of us headed north.

For years, my mom would lecture me and my brother, telling us when we met Gary Fencik, who played twelve years for the Bears, there was one important thing to remember. We had to tell him how she had gone to high school with his dad at Gage Park on the south side of Chicago. The family always had a good laugh, thinking how slim the chances were of fulfilling her request.

Anyway, we got to Lambeau early and met up with Bill's relatives to do some tailgating before the game. They got there real early, so our home base was close to the stadium. Bill and I loved the game. The Bears won 24-6.

When it was over, we hung out with his cousins for a little while, two Bears fans in a sea of green and gold. Because we were driving home that evening, there wasn't too much celebrating, but just before hitting the road, we heard a voice behind us commenting on the friendly jerseys. We turned around to see Gary Fencik standing there.

Remember, we were close to the stadium and closer to the Bears team bus, so he walked over, hoping we had some beer we could spare. I told him we had plenty to donate, but there was a catch; he had to listen to my story. I quickly told him about my mom's lectures, then explained if she ever found out we met and I failed to tell the story, she would probably never speak to me again.

After a good laugh, I filled up a box with the extra beer, then stood for a few seconds, waiting for him to grab it. Instead, he asked if I wouldn't mind passing them out.

Walking up the stairs, I met Vince Tobin, the Bears defensive coordinator, who was sitting in the first seat. His reaction: "Where the fuck are you going?" I apologized and said Fencik asked me to pass out some beers to the guys. It only took him a couple of seconds to respond: "Yeah, that sounds like him. Go ahead."

I then proceeded to walk down the aisle, passing out beers to Bears. I don't remember any faces but do remember they all seemed to be thirsty. A minute later, I was leaving with an empty box.

At home that night, I told Vic the story. She told me to make sure the first thing I did the next morning was call my mom. I did, then told her how I met Gary Fencik in Green Bay. Of course, she had to know. "Did you tell him? Did you tell him?"

"Yes, Mom, I told him." She was so proud.

There's an interesting end to this story. While writing it, I learned he had retired the previous year and just happened to hop on the bus and travel with the team that day.

'89 WESTERN OPEN

In June, the Western Open Golf Tournament took place at Butler National Country Club in Oak Brook, a western suburb of Chicago. Bill C., who worked with Vic, somehow got hold of some tickets and gave me two for June 30. Yes, the same Bill who dragged me up to Green Bay the previous year to see the Bears play the Packers.

This time, it was me and my brother. We didn't do much walking, spending most of the day in, or just outside the hospitality tent situated between the fourteenth green and the fifteenth tee. The highlights from the day had nothing to do with golf. All we remember is the pretty waitress and the free food and drink.

'89 STL

The Blackhawks were in St. Louis for a game on October 14, so I ran a trip from Bootlegger's, where I used to work. I got a penthouse suite called Kelly's Corner, and we invaded the city via Southwest Airlines. Don't remember too many names, but I do have one picture from the suite. Mike P., a bartender, is the only one who looks familiar.

Cindy, my wife's sister, had gotten married that afternoon. The reception was in South County, St. Louis, about a twenty-minute drive from downtown, and Steph, my four-year-old daughter was the flower girl. When the game ended, Puddin (George) and I hit the road.

We commandeered one of the two rental vans, changed clothes in the parking lot, and went to the party. That meant everyone else had to jam into the other van for the ride to the bars near our hotel. It wasn't a long ride, so they managed, plus I got to see Steph. After a couple of drinks and a couple of shots of Jack Daniels with my brothers-in-law, George and I made it safely back to the city.

The most interesting part of the trip was the flight home, actually starting in the airport bar. Its special was two-for-one drinks, so we took full advantage of it. It got interesting when a beer drinker on the trip whom we'll call Finn decided rum was the way to go.

After quickly downing a few specials, he calmly threw up while standing at the bar. I was the only one who noticed because some of his puke landed on my shoe. He then walked away, looking for the nearest bathroom because what didn't land on the floor, or my shoe, landed on his shirt.

His plan was to put on the jersey he had purchased for his daughter, so he got a few looks when he took his shirt off and threw it in the garbage.

Not surprisingly, the jersey didn't fit him like it was meant to fit his daughter, but it was an emergency. While this was going on, people started boarding the flight. He was one of the last to get on the plane and the story had already made the rounds, so as he walked down the aisle, barf bags were raised in honor of his performance.

Unfortunately, he sat directly behind me and thought it was important to keep talking for most of the flight. That meant every time he leaned forward to say something, I was able to enjoy his nasty breath. Luckily, St. Louis is only forty-five minutes away.

After landing at Midway Airport, Finn disappeared. We found out later he walked home. He wasn't sure, which was a good thing, because it was about a five-mile trek.

And the Blues beat us 2-1.

'89 My Wrist

Vic and I separated in July, so I rented a house with Jim H. in Mount Greenwood, a neighborhood in the far southwest corner of Chicago. The bar at the end of the block was where a few friends and I got naked in 1973.

It's the end of November, and I was in the basement closing a couple of windows. We had left them open because of a mildewy smell, but it was getting cold. One was a little off center, so when I gave it a good push, my hand slipped and went right through the glass. It was serious. After letting my wrist go for a second, a spray of blood shot out across the basement floor. Yeah, I severed the artery.

Jim was at work, so I ran upstairs, grabbed a T-shirt, and tied it around my wrist while bleeding in the kitchen sink. Luckily, I grabbed a red T-shirt.

Since I had slowed the bleeding to a trickle, I ran next door to my neighbor's house, hoping they could drive me to the hospital. Unfortunately, the only adult was a babysitter who freaked out when she saw the blood. Once composed, she directed me across the street where a paramedic lived.

Being new to the neighborhood, I just assumed she knew the house. She didn't. The woman that answered the door sent me to the right house, where I found out the paramedic was at work. Luckily, his wife let me in, then called 911 while I stood dripping blood in her kitchen sink. After finishing the call, she ran to the bathroom to throw up.

She had described the problem as a cut wrist, so the Chicago Fire Department reacted as if it was a possible suicide. That meant an ambulance, a fire truck, and two Chicago police cars showed up. Yes, the whole block lit up because of the new guy.

The paramedic asked me a few questions about what happened, then said I seemed to be the calmest one in the place. That's right; it was my ass on the line. Anyway, welcome to the neighborhood.

I was checked into the hospital, then got to kill some time sitting on a gurney in the hallway. After a few minutes, I started to feel a little faint and was about to tell the nurse, when she walked over and had me lie down because I looked a little faint. Microsurgery was done the next morning. I don't know the exact totals, but it was around sixty stitches inside on the artery and another thirty on the skin.

After all was said and done, Vic's insurance paid for everything. When we divorced, she agreed to keep me on her policy while I figured out what I was doing, in exchange for the right to move out of state with our daughter without a hearing before a judge. It worked out for both of us.

Jokingly (?), my good friends couldn't believe putting my hand through a window was the way to end it all after my separation. I told them if I had really wanted to end it that night, all I had to do was sit down on the basement steps and stop squeezing. It would have been over in a couple of minutes. After that, I began charging one dollar to view the blood-soaked stairs and floor of the Memorial Basement. I showed them.

90's

'90 Phoenix

It's the middle of March and I got some vacation time at the last minute. My brother and his best friend Pops (John) were heading to Mesa, Arizona, for spring training, so joining them seemed to be the thing to do. With my vacation starting in a couple of days, it was impossible to get a cheap flight. With plenty of time but not plenty of money, renting a car was the way to go.

I hit the road around midnight, driving about six hours. After getting on the highway, a couple things jumped out at me. The rental didn't have cruise control or a cassette player; that's right—cassette player. Remember, it's 1990.

It turned out to be a blessing when I realized what would have happened after setting the cruise control and popping in a tape. It's called nap time. Having to keep my foot on the gas pedal and constantly searching for another radio station probably saved my ass.

Anyway, I pulled over about an hour west of St. Louis, grabbed a couple of hours of sleep in the car, then continued west. The drive wasn't bad, especially through Oklahoma. There were five or six vehicles that hooked up and took turns leading the pack. We did it in record time.

At the last exit, everybody beeped, waved, and went their separate ways. I made it to Tucumcari, New Mexico, late that night, found a cheap motel and took a four-hour nap, alone.

Somehow, I was up and on the road at first light. After crossing into Arizona, it was Route 191 south to Route 60, which angles southwest, eventually ending up in Apache Junction. During the drive, my thought was I must have taken a wrong turn, not expecting to see lush, green forests in Arizona. A few more miles west got me to Mesa, where the Cubs have their spring training facilities.

When I arrived at my brother's hotel room, the two of them were leaving to see a NCAA basketball tournament game. They looked at me, then looked at their watches. They expected to see me in the early evening not the late morning. I had averaged almost fifty miles per hour, including six hours of downtime. After a nap and some pool time, I met the two of them for a few drinks.

On March 12, I went to the *Mesa Tribune* office to see if they could help me out. Remember the '84 trip? On April 1 that year, the *Tribune*'s Sunday sports section ran a picture of some guys watching the Cub game from the roof of their RV. That was us.

At home, it wasn't possible to get the photo reproduced. No camera shop would touch it because of copyright laws. Now, with camera phones, it isn't even an issue, but it was back then. A few minutes later, after telling my story and showing them the photo, I walked out with a letter releasing it to me.

And speaking of motor homes, one thing we noticed at our first game was the lack of them in right field. In the early '80s, we lived there. After asking a few people, we learned the Cubs had to put an end to it. People became assholes and ruined it for everyone.

Three whole days and it was time to head home. I made pretty good time, but nothing like the way down. I was gone for eight days and drove around 3,700 miles. When I returned the car to the rental company, an employee did a quick once-over and pronounced it OK, then checked the odometer.

"Where the hell did you go?"

'90 MLB All-Star Game

On July 10, Wrigley Field hosted the MLB All-Star Game. The festivities started the previous night with the Old-Timers' Game and the Home Run Derby. My brother and I had tickets for both nights. The Old American Leaguers won their game 10-0, but the home run contest had a better outcome.

There were eight players entered in the Derby and they hit five home runs; not by each player, that was the total. Yeah, the wind was blowing in. Mark McGuire hit one, and so did Matt Williams. Ryne Sandburg hit three of them, which was good enough for the win.

The next night, the only highlight was Ernie Banks throwing out the first pitch. After a boring Home Run Derby the night before, we got to watch a long, boring baseball game, worse if you were a National League fan. The American League won 2-0, scoring two runs in the top of the seventh, just before a ninety-minute rain delay. The game ended just before midnight. Yawn.

'91 NHL All-Star Game

On January 19, the NHL All-Star Game took place at the old Chicago Stadium. I was only working a few hours a week and collecting unemployment, so there wasn't much money to spend on luxuries.

I had attended the MLB All-Star Games at Comiskey Park in '83 and Wrigley Field in 90, and the NBA All-Star Game at the Stadium in 1988. My roommate kept urging me to get a ticket, explaining I would be one of a handful of non-media people who had been to all four games. I took his advice and scraped up a few dollars.

There was some controversy leading up to the game because it took place right after the start of the Gulf War. Some people, including Wayne Gretzky, thought the game should have been canceled, but that would have been a mistake because it was scheduled to take place in the perfect spot. If you've never heard our National Anthem at a Chicago Blackhawks game, you're missing something.

My seat was on the main floor but set back underneath the overhang of the first balcony, and yes, the place rocked. It was the loudest and most emotionally charged anthem ever, but it wasn't until I got home and watched a tape of the game that I saw all the American flags and banners supporting our troops that were hanging from the first and second balconies. It was incredible. Check it out online.

There was one other controversy, although mainly in Chicago. John Muckler of the Edmonton Oilers, who was the coach of the Campbell Conference, snubbed our goalie, Ed Belfour, who was the best goalie in the league at the time. Instead, he picked Bill Ranford, who played for—you guessed it—the Edmonton Oilers.

The Campbell Conference won the game 11-5, but Gretzky and Muckler can . . .

'91 Boston and Pittsburgh

On Saturday, February 9, four of us had tickets for an afternoon game in Boston to see the Blackhawks play the Bruins, but there was a problem. It's called fog. By the time we took off from Midway Airport, it was too late to make the game. Not the worst thing for me because I had already made my pilgrimage to Boston Garden in 1987 with Vic and Steph. Sorry for the other guys. And we lost, 5-3.

After a bar crawl that night, it was an Amtrak train to Hartford on Sunday for a game against the Whalers. Once on board, we found the bar car and picked up where we left off the night before.

Andy ended up sitting next to a woman who was eating a cinnamon roll the size of a medium pizza, so it wasn't long before he started quizzing her. Her response? "Quit bothering me and go back to your Bloody Mary." He did as he was told.

We lost that game too, 3-1.

Six weeks later, the Hawks were in Pittsburgh on March 23, so I put together a trip from McMahon's. Our seats were on the first level but under the balcony just a few rows from the back wall. It's where we got to listen to a barrage of crap from the hometown fans sitting behind us.

When the first period ended, it was time for a beer run so Roger (bar owner), George (bartender), and I got up and walked back toward our "friends." All three of us are over six feet all, and none of us are skinny, and that's when it got real quiet. It didn't take long to figure out why. The guys who had been dishing it out were all about Napoleon's size. We went and got our beers, joined them for most of the second period, and became best buds. They even bought us a round.

After the game, we hit a few bars. I don't remember much, except for a bar with a boxing ring that was used as a dance floor. If anyone from Pittsburgh reads this, let me know if I was hallucinating.

And we actually won that game, 7-5.

Movie Extra '91

In April, I got called to work in a movie named *Gladiator*. No, I didn't have to wear a toga; it was a boxing movie starring Cuba Gooding Jr. My one day of work was at an old abandoned warehouse on the west side of Chicago, which was used for most of the boxing scenes. Nothing too exciting—I was one of many sitting around the ring.

At the end of the day, I was offered a week of work. Yeah, I was that awesome, but was leaving for Spain in a couple of days and had to turn it down. Did I miss my big break? Don't think so.

In November, I got some work as an extra in the movie *Hero*. It was about a homeless guy played by Dustin Hoffman, who saved a bunch of people from a plane crash in the Chicago River. It also starred Geena Davis, Andy Garcia, and Suzy Cusack—and me.

My first day of work was at the Chicago Criminal Courts Building on the near southwest side of the city. I was paired with a woman dressed in a business suit, carrying a briefcase. Yeah, she was my attorney, my pretend attorney.

Our starting point for the scene was down the hall and around the corner from the action. After the first few takes, we would hear somebody yelling, "Cut!" and this was before we ever took a step. My partner finally went up to one of the production assistants and asked if was possible to move us to a spot where we would have something to do. A few takes later, our wish was granted. Our new starting point was right next to director Stephen Frears. We could look over his shoulder at the monitor used to review each take.

Just before he would yell, "Action!" one of the production assistants would motion to us to start walking down the hall toward Dustin Hoffman and his attorney, played by Suzy Cusack. We would pass by them as they spoke their first lines, so I was looking forward to seeing myself in the same scene with Dustin Hoffman. It didn't matter if I was walking away from the camera. I was in the same scene with Dustin Hoffman. In the final cut, you can see my left arm. Apparently, Dustin and Suzy were more important than me.

The scene seemed pretty simple, but it took all day to get about twenty seconds of film. At the end, Dustin Hoffman walks out of the building through the revolving doors while ranting and waving his arms. After about a dozen takes, he caught his foot, the door came to an abrupt stop, and so did he, slamming into it. You could see the whole crew tense up waiting, I'm assuming, for him to explode. Exactly the opposite happened. For the first time all day, he came out of character, started laughing, and blurted out, "What a fucking moron." That was followed by a big laugh from the crew, followed by a big sigh of relief from the crew.

My other day of work was a night shoot outside the Drake Hotel in downtown Chicago. It was a crowd scene, with everybody staring up at a ledge on the tenth floor, where Dustin Hoffman and Andy Garcia were sitting. They weren't really on the ledge; we were acting.

There was also a camera looking down, filming us looking up. In the movie, some of those faces were superimposed on the big screen. A good friend of mine called me after watching the movie, sickened by what he saw. Amazingly, my face made the final cut. To this day, I have not had one request for an autograph.

'91 SPAIN

In April, I went to Spain with a friend, Scott, and Ursula, a woman he worked with. She knew somebody who knew somebody, so we got a great deal on a timeshare in the resort town of Nerja on the Costa del Sol. We flew to Madrid and spent our first two days there.

On our last night, while hanging out in a meson (bar) near the Plaza Mayor, a young twenty-something girl came over and asked for my help. When her girlfriend got up to go to the bathroom, an overzealous Spaniard decided it was time to make his move. She wasn't interested, but he was. Looking around for some help, she spotted me and the Dockers pants I was wearing. I had to be an American.

I live most of the year in jeans or shorts, so the odds of me wearing Dockers were astronomical. I think it was fate. Her girlfriend joined us and after a few minutes, we discovered all of us were on the same train the next morning down to the coast.

The girls were from Seattle, were Yale Med School students, and they had picked the beaches of southern Spain for spring break. They were staying just outside of Malaga, about a thirty-minute drive from our place.

On our first full day, Scott, Ursula, and I rented a car and took a quick trip to Sevilla. It was my first time back since the fall of '72 during my semester of school in Spain. We walked around my old neighborhood, El Barrio de Santa Cruz, and I found the hostel that was my dorm for three weeks. The orange tree on the second-floor courtyard was still there.

The girls joined us for a couple of day trips and stayed at our place both nights because of the convenience. On day one, everyone went to Gibraltar except for me. I had to call in sick. The next day, another short car trip got our group, including me, to Granada, where we walked through the

Moorish Quarter and toured the Alhambra. With spring break coming to an end, the girls had a few other things to do and left the next morning but not before one of them took advantage of me.

Two months later, after finishing their semester in Connecticut, they were driving back home to Seattle. Chicago was on the way, so they stayed with me for a couple of nights and got a brief taste of this great city, including of course, some Chicago pizza. And . . . yes.

We kept in touch for maybe a year or so, then in a short period of time, both girls got engaged then married.

As of this writing, Washington is one of the four states I haven't visited, so I might have to look them up.

'91 Gambling

On June 29, we had a bus trip from McMahon's to Davenport, Iowa. This was before Illinois had casinos, so we drove across the Mississippi River and boarded a riverboat to do some gambling.

The day was hot and horribly humid, and we were on the river, literally. Back then, the boats actually left the dock and sailed up and down the river for two to three hours. Walking off the boat around 10:00 p.m., I remember seeing a sign showing the temperature. It was still ninety degrees.

The trip was pretty uneventful. There were no big winners or losers, but there was the cat. The story was Billy B.'s wife found a stray cat in the parking lot and took it on the bus for the ride home. It might have happened.

Those few hours in Iowa must have made an impact, because a couple of weeks later, I helped put together a bus trip for thirty to forty people to Kenosha, Wisconsin. This time it was a dog track, which had opened about a year earlier. Now we had another place to gamble.

It was a nice Sunday afternoon outing with two stops before we got there. The first one was the Goose Island Brewery on the west side of Chicago for a quick tour and a few beers. The second one came after crossing the border into Wisconsin. It's Kenosha's famous Brat Stop. You can't just drive by it.

On the ride up, Roger would ring a cowbell every fifteen minutes. When you heard the bell, it was time to get up and change seats. Don't know why, because everybody on the bus knew everybody else.

We spent a few hours losing our money then left the track and headed west on Wisconsin's Route 50. It was time to find a local bar, invade the place, and spend our last few dollars. We found a place in the town of Bristol and, in about sixty seconds, turned the bar's quiet Sunday afternoon into a full-blown party. The owner loved us and told us we were welcome back anytime. The invasion lasted about three hours.

When it was over, we boarded the bus and watched as the driver turned west coming out of the parking lot. We needed to go east. Luckily, a few relatively sober people caught the mistake. Once alerted, he took the next available turn, but it was a residential street and a dead end. After five or six three-point turns, we headed east and made it home without any more cowbells.

'91 Seven Days

On the morning of August 14, Big Don and I hit the road. Our plan was seven stops in seven days, hoping to see all six Cub minor-league affiliates, finishing up in Iowa at the Field of Dreams.

Day 1: 525 miles to Jamestown, New York. At the time, it was an affiliate of the Montreal Expos. We got to see the Geneva Cubs play there along with around 2,000 other people. The Cubs lost 7-4.

The highlight of the day was Captain Dynamite. Over the years, minor-league teams have always run promotions to get people into their parks. This one happened to be a seventy-year-old man who blew himself up for a living.

Before the game, a box that looked like a coffin would be set up near second base. He would then climb in and set off some dynamite, which usually knocked him out for a few seconds. After coming to, he would get up, wave to the crowd, and stagger off. Once the ground crew cleaned the area, the umpires would give the OK to play ball.

At each game, we would buy a program to help us remember where we were and what we saw. A couple of innings in, I noticed the Captain sitting down the third base line in a lower box seat, so I grabbed my program and a pen and headed over to get his autograph. He was happy to sign it, but there was a problem. It was what he did for a living. C . . . a . . . p . . . etc. It took him about a minute to scribble his name with his shaky hand. I didn't know whether to laugh or cry.

Don and I learned a few things in Jamestown that would carry over through the rest of the trip. Small-town America is great. Things are cheaper, the people are awesome, and there are always good local bars. We found the Cherry Lounge.

Day 2: 440 miles to Huntington, West Virginia. Our drive was quickly followed by a milkshake and a nap. Refreshed (sort of), we went to see the Huntington Cubs play the Martinsville Phillies. This time, only about two hundred people joined us. For $3.25, we got a seat in the grandstand, and during the game, a foul ball bounced through the empty seats, ending up in Don's lap. He looked around, found a young boy and his dad sitting a couple of rows behind us, reached back, and handed them the ball. They both were thrilled.

Day 3: 275 miles to Winston-Salem, North Carolina. Don was having some car problems and we were on a tight schedule, so we left it in Huntington, got a rental, and continued on. The WS Cubs lost 9-5 to the Salem Buccaneers. We were now zero for three, with the highlight being a picture of me and Slugger, the Cubs' mascot.

At the game, some locals told us about a place called Shooter's. We found it, then learned it wasn't a bar. It was a private club, but there was an option. We could pay their annual fee, or the $3 daily cover charge. At the time, hard liquor wasn't sold in the town's bars, so a private club was the way to get around it. We gladly paid the cover.

Walking in, we immediately saw an enormous chalkboard with the names of somewhere between 300 and 400 shots. Neither one of us are shot drinkers, so we didn't put much of a dent in it. It was beer for Don, rum for me, then safely back to our room, where I did a little shopping in our hotel's kitchen.

Day 4: 80 miles to Charlotte, North Carolina. The Birmingham Barons scored all eleven runs in the second inning, beating the Charlotte Knights 11-5. We were zero for four. It was a quiet night because we had a long day ahead of us.

Day 5: 850 miles to Peoria, Illinois. We were hoping to see the Peoria Chiefs, and luckily, it was a night game because we still had to drive back up to Huntington to pick up Don's car. We got to the repair shop and waited our turn while the mechanic chatted away with his buddy. "Excuse me, we're on a mission!"

After the long drive, including a strong rainstorm in the Lexington, KY, area, we made it to the game in the third inning. Attendance was just under 5,000, making it the biggest crowd so far. Guess what? Peoria lost to the Clinton Giants 10-6, which meant we were zero for five.

Day 6: 265 miles to Des Moines, Iowa. It was last call to see a Cub team win a game, but it didn't happen. The Omaha Royals beat the Des Moines Cubs 4-3. That's right, zero for six.

There was one highlight. Maybe not the right word, but this is what happened. The seats for our final game were in the tenth row, even with third base. There were only a handful of fans between us and the field, so we had a perfect view of the Cubs' third baseman fielding a bad hop ground ball with his groin. He got a couple of minutes to regroup, then when the next batter stepped up, I yelled out, "Lay down a bunt!" Don and I cracked up, and luckily, so did the people around us. We didn't realize how far my voice carried until the home plate umpire called time out because he was laughing too. Oh yeah, there was a dirty look from the third baseman.

Day 7: 180 miles to Dyersville, Iowa. It's the home of the Field of Dreams, where I got a great picture of Don walking through the corn. Even if you haven't seen the movie but you're a baseball fan, make a trip to Dyersville.

Simply put, it was Iowa corn, the field in the corn, Don standing in the corn, no corn dogs, and mercifully, no cornhole!

After almost 3,000 miles, we spent $86 on gas, averaged $46/night for a hotel room, and drank for cheap in the local bars.

Home safe and (relatively) sober.

'91 Dad-NY

In early September, a few months after my mom died, my dad took his own road trip to New Jersey to see his old friend Joe. Over the years, that's how our family knew him. It was Joe from New Jersey. Their friendship went back to World War II, when they served together in the US Army.

When my dad's stay was over, his plan was to drive to Cooperstown in upstate New York to go to the Baseball Hall of Fame. I thought it would be fun to drive out and meet him, so with a few free days, I got in my van and hit the road, sleeping in a truck stop parking lot overnight. We met the next day, spending most of the afternoon at the hall. When we were done, my dad started his drive home. I got a motel room in the area for the night, found a local bar for a couple of drinks, then started my drive home the next morning. It was long, it was leisurely, but it wasn't direct.

I went north, picked up Route 20, then headed east, eventually finding my way to Vermont, followed by New Hampshire, ending up in Maine. In each state, I made a point of pulling over, getting out of my van, and touching land. Anal? Probably. Then it was time to head south.

The routine continued in Rhode Island and Connecticut, ending my driving tour in Delaware. Yes, I passed through New Jersey, but no, I didn't stop to see Joe. It was time to go west, finally running out of gas in Indiana. After a short nap, it was home safe.

Getting the chance to drive out to Cooperstown and tour the Baseball Hall of Fame was a lot of fun. Doing it with my dad was the best.

'91 New Orleans

On October 27, the Bears were in New Orleans to play the Saints, so I helped put together a trip there from BJ McMahon's. Seven games into the NFL season and the Bears were doing OK with a 5-2 record. The Saints were undefeated. It was gonna be fun.

We didn't stay in the French Quarter, but we were close. A ten-minute trolley car ride down St. Charles Avenue brought us to the Avenue Plaza Hotel, strategically located next to Igor's, a twenty-four-hour bar, restaurant, and Laundromat. It turned out to be a great spot. No matter what hour of the day, you could walk into the bar, find someone from our trip eating or drinking, and quickly catch up on what was going on. By the way, it was almost always drinking and never doing laundry.

You can see the place in the movie *The Pelican Brief.* There's a scene with Julia Roberts and another woman having a conversation while sitting on a couple of washers/dryers in a small laundry room. When they're done, they get up and walk through a bar and out the front door. That was Igor's.

During our time there, we saw something we had never seen in the Chicago area. It was police officers, in uniform, drinking at the bar. There were a few Chicago cops on the trip, so it didn't take long for them to bond.

To nobody's surprise, a small group of us were driven to the game by the New Orleans Police. The caravan raised some eyebrows when the cars pulled up to the Superdome, probably because a bunch of guys wearing Chicago Bears jerseys piled out. Normally, we would have been heading into the cars, not out of them.

One of the girls who worked at McMahon's had been to New Orleans quite a few times with her family. Over the years, they had become good friends with the owner of the Tropical Isle, a bar famous for its Hand

Grenades. At the time, there were two of them. Basically, it was a Tropical Isle at either end of Bourbon Street, and yes, most of us sampled the grenades.

A couple of high (low) lights involved Wendy, one of the girls on our trip. The first one was at Pat O'Brien's. While sitting outside with George and Bob/Amy, she pointed to an older woman and commented on her wig. When nobody else thought it was fake, it was time to prove them wrong. She walked over, grabbed the woman by the hair, lifted it up, then quickly dropped it back down. Now it was time to say, "I told you so," and luckily, everyone involved had a sense of humor.

Next was when she was arrested for disorderly conduct against a police department horse. She claimed it tried to bite her, so she punched it. The story we got was she attempted to grab the horse by its.... so we're thinking it was well within its rights to go after her. Anyway, she went to jail.

While George was trying to get her out, she was able to spend some quality time with a few not-so-lovely ladies. You can guess which ones wanted to become her BFF. Her bail was set at $500, but George returned with a badge and a gun from one of the Chicago cops, demanding a rebate. Amazingly, they got half of it back, then were able to get Wendy legally out of the parish (county) and the state.

Is anyone wondering about the game? The Bears pulled off the upset, scoring with a minute to go, beating the Saints 20-17. Oh yeah, I have a ticket stub from Saturday, the 26th, also from the Superdome. It was a preseason basketball game between the Bulls and the Denver Nuggets.

September's '90s

In the early '90s, I picked up a night at Septembers, a bar and grill in Chicago's south Loop, recently purchased by Jim H., my roommate until '91.

We quickly discovered the Chicago Restaurant Show, held at McCormick Place, about a mile east of the bar. It quickly became an annual tradition because our bar would get a few tickets every year. That meant it was time to invade the show.

Any company that sold food or beverages was welcome to set up camp and put out samples of their products. Once inside, everything was free. If you returned to the bar sober, without any sauces splattered on your clothes, you didn't do your job. Hiram Walker was our favorite. They would set up a couple of banquet tables to display their flavored liquors, so it became a nice slow walk while sampling each one.

We never had enough tickets for everyone, so a few of us would wait outside, approach the people who were leaving and offer them a few dollars for their ID/ticket. Remember, this was the early '90s, so security at the show was not a big issue. Had someone looked closely at my ID one year, they might have noticed I was a young Korean college student.

When you saw something at one of the booths that interested you as a bar or restaurant owner, they would swipe your card. That information would then be sent to the address you signed up with, so we made a point of swiping "our" cards at every opportunity. My guess is some of the people we bought our cards from are still getting stuff in the mail.

One year, while hanging out in the Miller Beer area, we watched some wild and crazy-looking guy painting on a huge, maybe 7' by 5' canvas. He had Beatles music playing, and he would throw paint on the canvas and either smear it around with his hand or stick two or three brushes between his fingers and paint away. We stood there for a couple of minutes trying to figure out what he was doing, when a portrait of John Lennon began to take shape—awesome.

We were back a year later, and it was the same routine. There was a lot of alcohol, some sauces on our shirts and the guy in the Miller Beer area. This time, it was music by the Rolling Stones. We remembered his performance the year before, and stuck around to see what he was up to. After four or five minutes of flying paint and blaring music, he abruptly stopped. The music did too. He then stepped back and took a bow.

Everybody stood there staring at the canvas, and everybody had a blank look on their face. Our crazy rock 'n' roll painter gave the crowd a few seconds, then stepped up and spun it 180 degrees. It was a portrait of Mick Jagger, similar to the one he did of John Lennon the year before, only this time he did it upside down. The crowd loved it. Another awesome.

The bar was also close to Columbia College and the American Youth Hostel, so our crowd was on the young side, especially as the night went on. One group from the college was into swing dancing, with one of the girls eventually opening a dance studio.

She and I were dancing in the bar one night, and things seemed to be going pretty well; at least, that's what I thought. At one point, she looked up and told me how sweet I was. All right! Then she told me why. I reminded her of her dad. Oh, well.

Maybe a month later, I came into work and the same group was there. This time, there was an older guy with them who had a little gray in his beard and was wearing a baseball cap. Now I get it.

One more thing: a girl who will remain nameless and I had the honor of christening Booth One.

That's all.

'92 Toronto

During my annual New Year's Day BBQ, a few of us from McMahon's decided to get a group together to see the Blackhawks play the Maple Leafs. The game was in Toronto on Saturday, February 29. I had started putting together trips to Europe for a few friends, and that's how I met Diane. She was a travel agent who worked in an office just a block from the bar and had booked my flight to Spain '91, so I started sending her my airline business. She's the one who booked my group of forty-six on Amtrak and put in a request to double stock the bar car. If they had only listened . . .

There were a couple of problems on the ride north:

1. Because of a snowstorm and snowdrifts on the tracks, the train broke down in Ontario in the middle of nowhere. We sat there for almost three hours and proceeded to clean out the bar. As we neared Toronto, the story making the rounds was one can of tomato juice was the only beverage left.

2. We had a few young drunks on the trip. Amtrak had tried to help the rest of the passengers by giving us our own car, but the boys wandered off to a couple other cars and evidently annoyed the hell out of the people in them.

That's when a conductor came over and explained to me and Roger if there were any more problems, they would throw them off the train at the next stop. He then stood there, waiting for our rebuttal. We looked at each other and said, "No problem, we're sick of them too." The look on his face was priceless. We know he didn't see that one coming.

Since we had our own car, a little decorating took place. Blackhawk stuff went up on the walls and so did some centerfolds. After all their hard work, a couple of the young guys climbed up into the overhead luggage compartments and went to sleep (passed out). Looking back, I'm amazed nobody messed with them.

But easily, the highlight of the trip was Kevin D. He went into the bathroom and, with the help of a friend and a roll of toilet paper, wrapped himself up like a mummy. He then proceeded to walk, quite stiffly, down the aisle of our car—yes, only our car. For good or for bad, this was before anyone had a camera phone. We finally made it to Toronto, checked into our hotel, and made last call.

Back in '92, the city had two Hard Rock Cafes. One was in their ballpark and the other one, the original, was on Young Street. I made it to both of them, but my best stop was the CN Tower. Up in its sky deck, there are two great views. One is looking out across the city. The other is looking straight down around 1,200 feet through a two-inch glass floor. Wow!

The game was at Maple Leaf Garden. For you youngsters, Toronto is one of the original six teams in the NHL. I've been lucky enough to make it to four of the six, attending games at the Montreal Forum, Boston Garden, Toronto, and of course, the old Chicago Stadium. The two I missed? Madison Square Garden in New York and the Olympia in Detroit.

At the end of the game, a young usher came up with one of the better lines about old-time hockey, telling us how his small group of friends would travel to different cities, just like we did. He described the Forum in Montreal as a kind of shrine to the game, but their best real hockey experience was at the Chicago Stadium. They got it right.

By the way, the Hawks blew a three-goal lead, losing 6-5 in overtime.

On Sunday afternoon, we headed to the train station for our hangover ride home. I was honored when two Canadian Mounties met me there, but it didn't take long to figure out why and it wasn't exactly an honor.

They had been briefed about our behavior on the way north through Canada and wanted to make sure it didn't happen again on the way south. As I remember, a few moons appeared in the train windows as we crossed the border into the United States. The only sound was around forty beer cans being opened. Not forty-six, some of the group were still too hungover.

Thankfully, the ride home to Chicago's Union Station was uneventful.

The problem arose when I got off the train, leaving a large envelope with all the trip information in the pouch on the back of the seat in front of me. It wouldn't have been so bad except my passport was in the envelope and my flight to Munich, Germany, was leaving on Tuesday evening.

It wasn't until Monday, while packing, that I realized it was gone. Luckily, downtown Chicago has a passport office, which I went to early Tuesday morning. Assuming everything went smoothly, they said my replacement would be ready around 3:00 p.m.

My dad dropped me and my bag off at the office later that afternoon, and just liked they promised, my passport was ready. It was four o'clock, not three o'clock, but close enough. I hopped on an el train and made it to O'Hare Airport for my six o'clock flight.

And here's the rest of the story. The envelope was from the travel agency I was affiliated with and, amazingly, was waiting for me in the office when I returned home. A college student on her way back to Michigan found it in the pouch and returned it, passport included. I wrote a letter thanking her for what she did, and I may have asked her also to marry me—still waiting for a response.

'92 Europe

It's Tuesday, March 3, and I was on my way to Munich, Germany with my replacement passport. Jim and Carolyn, married the year before, and our friend Scott were flying out a day later. That meant I was responsible for picking up the rental car, which I was able to do all by myself. We got a Volkswagen Jetta that kicked ass.

I did most of the driving and had a blast, especially in Germany. If you're going 90 mph on the Autobahn, Germany's highway system, don't even think about getting in the left lane. If you do, keep an eye on your rearview mirror. What might look like a dot will be on your ass, flashing its headlights a few seconds later. That's because it's probably doing around 125 mph. Things have changed a little bit since this trip, with speed limits put into some of the areas prone to accidents.

Anyway, I picked the three of them up at the airport the next morning. Carolyn was first, laughing and shaking her head. It all made sense when I spotted Jim and Scott. Both were drunk.

Unfortunately for them, our first stop was Dachau, a World War II concentration camp about a twenty-mile drive. After touring it with Vic in '83, I knew what was coming. It's very interesting but also very sobering, which meant it was nap time for Jim and Scott during the two-hour drive to Salzburg, Austria. On the way, we made a quick stop in the town of Melk to see its 1,000-year-old Benedictine Abbey, but I doubt they remember ever being there.

We arrived in Salzburg in mid-afternoon. While Scott and I hiked up to the top of a hill that overlooks the city, I kept waiting to see if the walk would kill him. It didn't, so we were rewarded with a great view, plus one of the oldest medieval castles in all of Europe. That was pretty much it for Salzburg, but there was one more highlight: no *Sound of Music* tour.

Vienna was next. We spent most of the day walking around the city center inside the Ringstrasse (Ring Road), about a three-mile road that encircles it. Then it was time for some refreshments, followed by more refreshments, followed by me becoming the Ugly American at our last stop.

When a Gypsy woman came in selling flowers, I thought it would be pretty cool to buy a rose for every woman in the place. There were some nasty stares from a few of the men, but when everyone realized it was just in fun and I wasn't trying to hit on their women, the mood lightened. Phewww!

As the night was coming to an end, we all left the bar but, strangely, not together. Jim and Carolyn ended up at the train station, where they discovered a wiener stand that was still open. Scott and I went off in two totally different directions.

A couple of minutes later, he noticed a woman who appeared to be following him. He ignored her, thinking she was a *hure*—that's German for whore, but he was wrong. It was a woman who worked at our last stop and had a gut feeling Scott was drunk and lost. She caught up to him, then got him home safely. I'm pretty sure my walk was uneventful.

The next morning started with a 300-mile drive to Venice. We did the typical tourist stuff, except for the gondola ride. It's expensive, so unless you're about to propose marriage, take the vaporetti (water-buses). Almost forgot—we did let out the traditional "aah" crossing the Bridge of Sighs.

Milan was next, another quick stop where I became the tour guide for the day. In '83, Vic and I were there for three days and got to spend a lot of time with some of my mom's relatives. This time, it was only a couple of hours.

Then it was time to head to the Swiss town of Locarno. It might be in Switzerland, but the culture, food, and language in that part of the country are all Italian. Remember, this is where Vic and I spotted palm trees with the snow-covered Alps in the distance. This time, the picture I took also included a Swiss flag flapping in the wind.

From there, it was about a three-hour drive to the town of Tasch, followed by a fifteen-minute train ride up to the auto-free city of Zermatt. We did a quick walk around the town, with the highlight being lunch outside with the Matterhorn in the background.

That was followed by another three-hour drive, this time to Geneva, leaving us just a few hours of daylight. All I remember is a walk around the old town while looking for a couple of hotel rooms because we were leaving for Munich in the morning.

After getting up, we changed our plans and took a 400-mile drive north, stopping in the town of Koblenz, where the Rhine and Mosel rivers meet. After a quick walk and a few photos, it was time for a few beers, crashing somewhere near Frankfort.

Munich was our last stop, so before the drinking started, Scott and I took a tour of Olympic Stadium. It's where he got a picture of me getting ready to take a corner kick. Only after the fact did we notice the signs telling people to keep off the field. I guess it's time to find a beer hall.

After a quick walk through Marienplatz, the city's main square, we made it to the Hofbrauhaus. There are two great pictures from that night. One is of Carolyn drinking from a one-liter beer stein while holding a pretzel as big as her head. The other is me on stage, kissing the accordion player. It was a woman.

Home the next day. Auf Wiedersehen.

'92 Camden Yards

On April 6, the Baltimore Orioles opened the season at their new ballpark, Camden Yards. Notice, I said ballpark, not stadium. It was the first place that tried to bring back the look and feel of the old parks. The White Sox opened Cellular Field, their new stadium—that's right, stadium—the year before. No comparison.

Remember, I was doing some work with Diane, the travel agent across the street from McMahon's. She had been Ed Farmer's travel agent for years. He's an ex-ballplayer from the southwest side of Chicago and, as I write this, an announcer for the White Sox. Near the end of his playing career, he got picked up by the Orioles and, while he was there, learned they were looking for a new travel agent. We never found out how, but he was able to put in a good word for Diane, and they hired her. It coincided with the opening of the new park, so as their travel agent, she was given four tickets to the first game. She couldn't use them, so she handed them to me.

I drove to Baltimore with Big Don, and my brother flew there, which meant we had an extra ticket. Jim, my old roommate, had an aunt and uncle that lived in the Baltimore area and were big baseball fans but, because of the demand, were only able to find one ticket. That meant Jim's aunt joined us for the game and made her husband sit by himself. She was a lot of fun, and she knew her baseball.

A special thanks goes out to the Orioles ticket office. Our seats were in the first row, club level, with waitress service. President Bush was one of many dignitaries on the same level. He threw out the first pitch that day, but he still wasn't allowed to sit with us. The Orioles won the game 2-0, with Rick Sutcliffe throwing a five-hitter.

The next day, my brother flew home. Don and I drove to Philadelphia and found a couple of tickets for the Phillies home opener. The baseball schedule was good to us because they were playing the Cubs. Greg Maddux was the winning pitcher as we beat them 4-3.

On April 8, we left Philadelphia and drove to Gettysburg. I wouldn't call either of us a huge history buff, Don more than me, but we were both interested in the Civil War. It turned out to be a great stop, with one of the highlights being a picture of me sticking my head into the barrel of an old cannon. Fortunately, there were no ghosts around to light the fuse.

Home safe.

Movie Extra '92

In May, I worked as an extra in the movie *Rookie of the Year*. It's the one where the young kid pitches for the Chicago Cubs. The scene I worked on was the press conference where the boy is introduced to the media. As he walks out of the kitchen into the pressroom, you can see my back while I'm pointing a camera in his direction. Don't blink.

Then during the press conference, every time someone stands up to ask a question, look closely at the back of the room. There are three guys holding cameras. I'm the one on the left.

It became a good sleepover movie for kids, and my daughter was in third grade at the time. She loved the fact she could yell out to stop the movie so everyone could see her dad.

I was divorced at the time and working nights as a bartender, so I would pick Steph up from school a couple of times a week. After the movie made the rounds, some of the moms told me what a whole new respect they had for me. They never knew I was this big-time actor. Yeah, I made $50 a day and got a hot meal.

A month later, I worked as an extra in the movie *Rudy*. It was a crowd scene filmed at St. Rita High School's football stadium on the southwest side of Chicago, which filled in for Notre Dame's football stadium. I even saw the real Rudy, who had a bit part in the movie, sitting a couple of rows in front of me.

Then in the fall, I got called to work on *The Untouchables*, the TV show, not the movie. My role was a stand-in for Agent Malone, played by John Rhys-Davies, a big bearded guy about my age. They called me back an hour later to make sure I could drive a stick shift.

I remember shifting gears in driver's ed at Bogan High School on the far southwest side of Chicago in the late '60s, but never since then. All I could envision was me stripping the gears on some vintage 1930s car, so I had to turn down the offer. Whenever I've told the story, somebody always stepped up, saying they could have taught me in just a few minutes. Where were you that afternoon?

A few months later, while working at Septembers, a guy walked in wearing an *Untouchables* jacket. I had to ask, was it from the movie or the TV show? He had gotten his jacket while working in production on the TV show, so I told him my story.

He raved about what a great guy John Rhys-Davies was, and how he would invite members of his stand-in's family to the set. He also thought John would have been happy to teach me how to handle the transmission. My guess is I still wouldn't have been allowed in the driver's seat of one of those vintage cars, but it was nice to hear.

'92 Christa's Honeymoon

Christa (a friend of a friend) and her husband Jim got married in the spring and asked me to put together their honeymoon. My pay was based on a small percentage of the hotel bills, plus the tips I would give them on what to do and what to skip. It was easily the most expensive trip I ever organized. The first few days of their trip started in Paris, and when it came to finding a room, Jim insisted on staying at a five-star hotel. Christa and I talked him out of it.

My first tip was to take a pass on the five-star hotel. I was working on commission, but still couldn't book them in such an expensive place. They were there to see Paris, not their hotel room, so Jim settled for a four-star hotel, which was about half the cost.

Working with Diane again, I did something for this trip nobody in their office had ever done. I booked Christa and Jim on the Orient Express, one of the most expensive train rides in the world. Dinner is a black-tie affair, prepared by a gourmet chef, so it's basically a five-star hotel on wheels. Jim got his wish after all.

Their destination was Venice, with the train leaving in the early evening. This is not the way to travel if you're in a hurry, so a few hours after their five-course dinner, it was time to settle in for the night. The next morning, after a leisurely breakfast, they spent a leisurely ride winding through the Alps and the Simplon Pass. Arrival in Venice was around 3:00 p.m.

It's a great ride but also an expensive one. They saved money in Paris, staying in a four-star hotel, but spent enough money on the train tickets to cover a few days in a five-star hotel. Twenty hours on the train, including travel insurance, was about $1,700/person, and remember, it was 1992.

They roughed it in Venice, staying at a three-star hotel. It wasn't too rough; they were right on the Grand Canal, and when they left, it was in a Lamborghini I had waiting for them. It was time to drive through the Italian countryside to Florence.

They spent three days there, seeing a couple of Tuscan towns, finishing their honeymoon on a high note, literally. It was in a hot-air balloon that took them over the countryside just outside of Siena, landing in a field for a champagne breakfast.

After everything they saw and everything they did, the balloon ride I booked got their vote as the highlight of the trip.

'92 BELFOUR

During the summer, I was bartending on a Friday night at McMahon's when a guy came in and sat down at the bar. We instantly recognized Blackhawks goalie Ed Belfour.

He had attended a charity function hosted by teammate Chris Chelios at an ice rink in Hickory Hills, a suburb a few miles west down 95th Street from our place. When it was over, he asked Chris if there were any good bars around, so Chelios sent him back east into Oak Lawn and told him to take his pick. We think he stopped at our place because of the big green awning that runs the length of the building.

It only took a few minutes before somebody came up and asked for his autograph. His response: "Sorry, I'm Joe Smith, in for the weekend from Michigan." After two more requests, I leaned over and said he could move down to the corner of the bar, by the entrance to the kitchen and out of the sightline of most of the people. He thanked me and said he was OK, which also kind of confirmed who he was.

As it got nearer to closing time, I invited him to stay and hang out for a while after we closed. I think not making a big deal out of everything was the deciding factor. He took us up on the offer and moved down to the corner.

You have to remember this was before everyone had a cell phone and if you did, it probably wasn't equipped with a camera. There were two bartenders, two waitresses, and a couple of friends who stuck around after closing, and not one person asked for an autograph. We think he loved that because he stayed for a long time. Great guy.

'93 STL

On Saturday, January 9, the Blackhawks were in St. Louis, so thirty mentally challenged patrons from McMahon's boarded a morning flight. Arriving at Lambert Field, we picked up two fifteen-seater vans. Roger and I were the designated drivers.

And of course, we picked the day St. Louis got hit with a big snowstorm, big for St. Louis. The final total was five to six inches, which isn't bad for someone from Chicago. It's not too common there, so the city was at a near standstill.

We stayed at the Embassy Suites, in the city's bar/restaurant area known as the Landing. From there, it was about a fifteen-minute drive, in good weather, to the Checkerdome Arena. It took a little longer that night.

Because of the snow, the general consensus was to forget the vans and have everybody pile into some cabs. That meant no more responsibilities for the two drivers, which meant we could drink or, actually, drink a lot faster.

As it got closer to game time, while sitting in the hotel's lobby bar, we kept hearing horror stories from people trying to find a taxi. Getting one was hard, so getting seven or eight was out of the question. Hearing that, Roger and I quickly matured because we were suddenly the group's drivers again. I think we never officially stopped drinking, but did slow down to our original pace.

Our vans weren't equipped for winter weather, so we crushed some empty beer cans and used them to scrape the windows. The drive was easier than we had anticipated because the majority of vehicles with Missouri license plates seemed to be everywhere but on the road.

After the game, which we lost, 4-1, Roger and I got everyone back to the Landing, then put the vans away. We caught up with some of our group just in time to do some "oh my god" shots. They're made with 151 rum, so after one sip, mine went down the beer drain.

The bars were closing, but we weren't done yet. The Embassy Suites balconies are inside, so Roger, Kirk, Mo, and I grabbed a drink and sat down outside my door. A few minutes later, we got to witness Dan tiptoeing to Trish's room for what he thought was a secret rendezvous. Little did he know. Anyway, it was the right move. They're still together.

Mo called it a night. Then there were three. Not exactly, the cooks had shown up to start preparing the free breakfast. The grill was in the hotel's atrium, so we went down before it opened and did some begging. The first food off the grill didn't go into the serving trays; it went on our plates. A quick meal, a short nap, and it was time to head to the airport.

And here's something I learned years later. While waiting in the hotel lobby before the game, Kirk ran up to his room. After a couple of minutes talking to the maid working his floor, he received her special room service.

'93 CINCY

Did someone mention Kelly's Keg? I guess that means we're going to Cincinnati because the Cubs are there in late April. And yes, we stayed at the Travel Lodge in Newport, Kentucky, directly across the street from, that's right, Kelly's Keg.

We love the location. Once your vehicle is parked in the motel lot, everything else can be done on foot, with the exception of the Oarhouse in '87. Basically, it means drinking, followed by our traditional stop at White Castle, or maybe some Dixie chili or maybe some Skyline chili or maybe some Gold Star chili, or . . .

This trip, we discovered a Hooters restaurant just down the shore (locals call it the Levee), but its location was a little different. It shared a large beer garden with a bar/grill called Remington's, but it wasn't on land, it was on an enormous barge attached to land.

At the time, Hooter's only served beer and wine, but everything worked out fine. Sitting in the middle of the beer garden, there were boobs to the left and Bacardi to the right. God bless America.

On Saturday afternoon, we picked the water taxi as our mode of transportation. It's a quick one-minute trip across the Ohio to Ohio. As we neared the Cincinnati side, the boat started a slow turn so it would come up to the shore broadside, providing an easy exit for its customers.

A guy sitting near us reached out for a rope, thinking he could help the pilot moor the boat. Instead, he fell overboard and got pinned against the shore wall. He survived because two friends scrambled to pull him out of the water, but not before he got a nice bruise on the side of his head. All things considered, he was pretty lucky.

The Cubs took two out of three that weekend.

Movie Extra '93

In the spring, I ended up in Stateville Prison in Joliet, Illinois. Don't worry; it's not as bad as it sounds. I got some work as an extra in the movie *Natural Born Killers* on what turned out to be the last day of filming there.

The only way to get into the prison, not counting the usual stuff, was to go through an FBI check at a hotel in downtown Chicago. All the extras were required to do it about a week before they were scheduled to work, and somehow, I was given the OK.

Arrival time for the shoot was just before sunrise, only getting us to the outer wall. That's where a large tent had been set up for a delicious breakfast of coffee and donuts before checking in.

Going through the checkpoint, I was handed my picture ID that was taken the week before and was instructed to wear it around my neck and under my shirt. I was also given a hospital bracelet to wear around my ankle and under my sock. After that, it was time to become a prisoner when they handed me a uniform.

A guard then explained if anything strange happened during the shoot, it was important to be able to prove I wasn't part of the regular population, and do it quickly. The ankle bracelet was the backup plan in case I lost my ID. This all came about when they tried to use inmates as extras, but the riot scenes were a little too realistic.

If you saw the director's cut, you might've seen me. The movie was originally given an NC-17 rating because of the scene I worked on. The warden, Tommy Lee Jones, is caught on the wrong side of the bars during a prison riot and pulled down into a crowd of us convicts. Seconds later, somebody holds up his arm as a trophy. Seconds later, somebody holds up his leg. Finally, his head appears on a broomstick. To get the rating lowered to an R, the decapitation was deleted.

After each take, I would walk back to my starting point, passing director Oliver Stone. The scene was intense, and some of us heard the production assistants talking about how crazy the extras were. They actually started worrying about a repeat of what happened with the real inmates.

Moviemaking is not a glamorous business, especially for an extra. It's long hours with a lot of sitting around, waiting for scenes to be set up. Overtime pay didn't kick in until we were on the clock for twelve hours. At least, that's how it was in the '90s.

By chance, I happened to know Statesville's recreational director, who was a customer at McMahon's. While sitting in the auditorium, waiting for the next scene to be set up, I decided to walk over to one of the guards and ask if he was working. His response: "Go back and sit down." Yes, sir.

When my work at the prison was done, the plan was to go to McMahon's still wearing my uniform with the fake blood on it, but it didn't happen. I was in demand.

Before clocking out, I was requested to work on one more scene. It took place in front of the prison, so I magically changed into a cable guy walking through the front door, carrying a large coil of wire. A good actor can do that. If you look closely, you still can't see me.

To do that scene, I had to leave the prison interior. While officially checking out, I realized the guy in front of me was Tommy Lee Jones doing the same thing. Earlier in the day, his name came up while we were sitting in the auditorium. A couple of extras had worked on another movie with him and said he was not the kind of guy who liked to be bothered.

After hearing that, it was refreshing to watch him calmly standing in line like everyone else. As the guard looked at his picture ID, I wanted to yell out, "Hey, it's Tommy Lee Jones. He's a big star, and he's been here for two weeks." I decided to keep quiet.

That one day at the prison was very sobering. Believe me, you don't ever want to end up there. It was bad enough as an extra.

'93 Sox Playoff Game

Diane, the travel agent I worked with, was still employed by the Baltimore Orioles as the '93 season came to a close. The Orioles didn't make the playoffs, but like every team, they were given a small allotment of tickets even if they didn't qualify.

The White Sox did qualify, so the Orioles sent Diane some tickets, and just like the year before, she gave them to me. The game was on October 5, against the Toronto Blue Jays at US Cellular Field. I'm not a Sox fan, but I do love connections.

The seats were in the upper deck, looking directly down the third base line. They reminded me of the Cubs tickets my brother and I had at the time. Our seats were in the second row of the upper deck, with the same sightline, but were about a block closer than the ones at Sox Park. I love Wrigley Field.

Toronto won the game 7-3 and went on to win the series 4-2.

'94 DC

The Blackhawks were in Washington DC to play the Capitals on Saturday, January 8. I put together a trip from BJ McMahon's, leaving on the 7th. Of the thirty tickets, I drove there with Kelly P. The other twenty-eight flew on Southwest Airlines.

We stayed at the Dupont Plaza Hotel, located in . . . the Dupont Circle. It's a good area to stay, especially with an entrance to the subway just outside the front door. After checking in, we learned the Circle was commonly known as the fruit loop, because of the area's large gay population.

First on our agenda was finding a local bar. A short walk from the hotel got us to a place called Childe Harolde, so it was time for a Chicago invasion. We met Roland, the bartender on duty and quickly made friends.

I had set up a group tour of the White House through the office of Sen. Paul Simon of Illinois, so a quick cab ride got me to the Senate Office Building. Walking in, his secretary immediately asked if I was Mr. Groth, here to pick up the tickets for the tour. I actually felt important for a few seconds.

Unfortunately, it was scheduled to begin at eight o'clock on Saturday morning. Because of the damage inflicted the night before, more than half of the group missed the tour. Of the thirty people, only twelve made it and I wasn't one of them.

Childe Harolde wasn't the only bar we visited. Somebody found a place called the Brickskeller, another short walk. It was different because it only had one beer on tap, which changed every month. It also had a menu of over five hundred beers in bottles, listed by country. They were stored in a large cellar and were sent up to the bar via a dumbwaiter. We would be back.

The highlight of the trip actually took place in our hotel lobby. The Dupont Plaza had a tradition where people, mainly celebrities, were allowed to sign and date the lobby ceiling. Somehow, we qualified, so BJ's name and the date made it up there.

There is one other thing, although it's not exactly a highlight. It's my roommate getting hit on by a guy. Remember, we were in the fruit loop. They're still together. Just kidding.

The game was Saturday night. We lost 4-1.

'94 V-B-P

Vienna, Budapest, and Prague, in that order. My good friend Maria and I landed in Vienna on March 25, and we would spend three days in each city.

On our first day, we took a tram ride on the Ringstrasse. Remember, it's the road that circles Vienna's Old Town. It might have been public transportation, but it reminded us of the Hop-On/Hop-Off buses in other major European cities. The trip is about three miles, so we grabbed a seat, took notes, and got a good feel for the city.

We spent two days seeing some of the major sites, which included Belvedere Palace, Hofburg Palace, St. Stephen's Cathedral, the City Museum, and Schonbrunn Castle. We also went to an open-air market where Maria bargained for some absolutely adorable Easter eggs. Really? I took a pass.

There is one thing we missed. It's called the Sacher torte, which might be the most famous dessert cake in the world. This was my second trip to the city, and I still haven't tried it.

On our last day, we took a train out to Vienna's wine region, met some great people, and got to sample a few different local wines. Based on how long it took to find the train back to the city, we may have sampled more than a few.

A flight to Budapest was next. It's a city cut in half by the Danube River, with Buda being the hilly west side and Pest the flat east side. From the airport, we took the subway into the city, but it took a while to figure out where we were going because of the language. We both have some ability when it comes to foreign languages, Maria more than me, but Hungarian was really tough. It comes from the Magyar people who migrated west to Hungary from Asia. The only other European country with a similar language is Finland. Bored yet?

We made it to the city center, and while we walked up the subway stairs to the exit at ground level, a man came up to Maria, said something neither of us understood, then grabbed her bag. It was scary for a couple of seconds until we realized he was just being a gentleman who wanted to help with her luggage. It didn't make me look very good.

Again, it was two days of the typical tourist stuff. We took the short ride up the hilly west side on a funicular (rail car) where we saw the Fisherman's Bastion, Matthias Church, and Buda Castle. We thought about taking the 300-foot walk, but not for very long. The icing on the cake was the view of the Chain Bridge and the Parliament Building on the other side of the river.

Budapest is famous for its hot springs and mineral baths, and one of the most famous spas is located in the Hotel Gellert. We spent most of our last day there, either getting a massage, lounging in a sauna, soaking in one of the thermal baths, or swimming in one of the pools. It was awesome.

Refreshed, it was time to go to Prague, where we encountered another tough language. Our hotel's subway stop was Krizikova, whose name looked a lot like every other subway stop. The reason we remembered it was because of a Chicago Blackhawk player named Krivokrasov. Whatever works.

Prague is similar to Budapest because it is also split in two, this time by the Vltava River, and again, one side is hilly and the other flat. The main connection is the Charles Bridge. It's pedestrian only and famous for its artists, musicians, and tourists.

On the hilly side but near the bridge is a Jewish cemetery with gravesites running from the 1400s up to the 1780s. Because land was limited, people were buried on top of each other. We learned the bodies were piled ten to twelve deep.

We picked a good time to go to Eastern Europe. The Berlin Wall had come down in 1989, so capitalism was still pretty new. In Prague, everything seemed cheap, especially food and drinks. A big plate of pork with dumplings and sauerkraut and two or three Pilsner Urquells thrown in for good measure cost only a few dollars.

On night number one, we went to the State Opera House in historic Wenceslas Square and saw *La Traviata*, the first and, so far, the only opera I've seen. It was in Italian, of course, with Czech subtitles on a screen above the stage. I had a much better chance of understanding Italian than I ever did with the Czech language, but it didn't matter, I'm glad I went.

The next day, we checked out St. Vitus Cathedral and Prague Castle, up on . . . Castle Hill. Then it was back down to the Old Town Square, and the town hall's tower, where we saw the astronomical clock that was built around 600 years ago. On the hour, disks would spin, Roman numerals would appear, and I think there was some zodiac stuff. We didn't get it and I can't imagine people 600 years ago getting it, but everybody around us seemed to think it was pretty cool.

After that, we walked into a ticket office, curious to see what was going on in the city and learned Sparta, Prague's pro hockey team, was playing Pardubice in a playoff game that night. Remember I told you how cheap everything was? Twenty dollars got us two tickets in the tenth row at center ice. That's right, for a playoff game.

Entering the arena, we saw a line of tables with people selling/trading vintage cards from European hockey and from the NHL. Arriving just before the start of the game, we looked forward to checking it out at the first intermission. Unfortunately, everything was packed up and gone when we went back.

During the first period, it felt like people were looking at me and talking about me. Maria figured it out when she realized the blue US Soccer windbreaker with red trim I was wearing exactly matched the colors of the visiting team. After explaining to the people near us we were from Chicago, not Pardubice, we all had a good laugh. Luckily, a few of them understood English.

My favorite memento from the trip was a *pomlazka*, which I purchased at an outdoor market. It translates as an "Easter whip," made of twigs from the pussy willow tree, and it is used on Easter Monday by the men and boys of the city. They either chase the women/girls through the streets or go door to door so they can whip them on their legs.

The tradition says when the girl is whipped, it will give her one year of health, youth, and beauty. She then hands the boy a colorful ribbon to tie to his whip. I have five ribbons on mine, but so far, nobody has tried to tie anything to my *pomlazka*. Case closed.

Then home.

'94 Denver

On April 21, Big Don and I drove to Denver to see the Cubs play the Rockies. It was Colorado's second year in the majors and the second of only two years for Mile High Stadium as a baseball venue. My brother flew in from Chicago and his good friend Pops did the same from Florida. Remember, it was April, so our main concern was snow. Luckily, it didn't.

We got tickets to the Friday and Saturday games through a friend of a friend who managed a truck terminal in the Chicago area owned by the Rockies owner. Arriving at the park, we stood in line at the will-call window, then were given replacement tickets. The date of the game was written in ink, which was a little strange, but we were shown to our seats. They were in section 116, twenty rows off the field even with third base.

Here are a few interesting things from the trip:

First of all, I got carded for beer. My wallet was in my van, not my pocket, so the vendor hesitated. I was born in 1951; it's now 1994. You do the math. After I explained I was old enough to be his father, he poured me a drink.

This would be our only trip to Mile High, so early in the game, my brother and I took a walk around the stadium. We eventually made it to the last row of the upper deck, way down the right field line, but it took a while because we had to stop a couple of times to catch our breath. Remember, we were in Denver, and the air is a lot thinner up there. To add insult to injury, a couple of seniors, probably doing their daily walk, passed us by, and they weren't even breathing hard. Ouch!

Once we got there, it was time to sit our asses down for a couple of innings. Attendance for Friday's game was around 55,000, but I remember there being a lot of room in the upper deck. Later, someone reminded me it was built as a football stadium with a capacity of about 80,000.

Anyway, this at-bat will give you an idea how far we were from home plate. Somebody laid down a bunt, the ball started to roll down the third base line, and then we heard the ball hit the bat. Yeah, pretty far.

We were back Saturday, with the exact same seats and so were a lot more fans. Attendance came in at just under 70,000.

We were leaving the next morning, so Don and I actually behaved that night, getting up early to start our 1,000-mile drive. I was the first one behind the wheel and was in the zone, driving the whole shift. It wasn't as bad as it sounds, because it gave me something to do. Don had a tougher time just sitting there but did make a major contribution early in the trip.

Based on our speed, and with no breaks (not brakes), he figured we could make last call at our bar in Oak Lawn that night. The first stop for gas reminded me of a pit stop at a NASCAR race. It was pay the cashier, pump the gas, take a piss, and grab some Gatorade. Don't ask me who did what. After the McDonald's drive-through, we were back on the road and made last call, averaging around seventy miles per hour.

It reminded us of the drive home from the south rim of the Grand Canyon in 1982. This time, the calculations were a lot easier and the drive was a lot shorter.

The Cubs won 9-2 on Friday and lost 8-2 on Saturday.

'94 World Cup

On June 17, Chicago hosted the opening ceremonies and first game of the 1994 World Cup Soccer Tournament. It was Germany against Bolivia at Soldier Field, and Big Don and I had tickets.

The World Cup is a big deal everywhere on the planet. In '94, it still wasn't a big deal in the United States, so having it here was kind of a gamble. To give you an idea how important it was, President Sanchez de Lozada of Bolivia and President Kohl of Germany were in attendance, and President Clinton made the opening speech.

Things went downhill after that. Oprah Winfrey, who was the master of ceremonies, fell off the podium. And for some reason, Diana Ross was chosen to do a ceremonial penalty kick. The plan was for fireworks to shoot up from the temporary goal, but her attempt missed and the net collapsed. We're still waiting for the fireworks.

Oh, and Germany beat Bolivia 1-0.

Chicago hosted three more games. I attended all of them, this time working security. My job was checking tickets and checking bags. No metal detectors—life was simpler then.

I tried to learn a few words of each language that would be spoken at the games, hoping to point people in the general direction of their seats. I've traveled a lot in Europe, and the perception there is the average American only speaks English, so being able to say some basic words like "left," "right," or anything else would help them and make me look good.

One other thing; It was the German women. We would ask them to open up their waist/fanny packs to make a quick check, and all we saw were $50 and $100 dollar bills. Please zip up. Danke Schoen.

I did OK with German and Spanish. Greek wasn't a problem because it seemed like they all spoke English, but Bulgarian, not a clue.

'95 ITALY

In late February, I went to Italy with my daughter and my sister, Nancy. Steph was nine years old, turning ten the day after we got home.

Our first stop was Florence, where we saw some amazing art, including Michelangelo's "David." The timing of our visit was great. Remember what I told you about traveling in Europe during the summer. Plan on standing in line. In February, we were able to walk right in to the Accademia Building.

We also took a quick train ride to Pisa to see the Leaning Tower. When I was there with Vic in 1983, we were able to walk up to the top of the tower. We weren't so fortunate this time, because the stairway had closed in January 1990 for about ten years. I also tried to get the traditional tourist photo with Steph holding up the tower. She was so close.

Venice was next. Our timing wasn't as good as Florence because we arrived during Carnevale. It's similar to New Orleans during Mardi Gras, but not nearly as crazy. We got lucky and found a room in the town of Mestre, the last train stop on the mainland, and it brought back memories. It was the stop I almost got off at, traveling through Italy after my semester of school in Spain in 1972.

It's a great time to be in Venice, especially if you're lucky enough to get a room in the city and not traveling with your sister and nine-year-old daughter. Since we were staying in Mestre, our time was limited to daylight hours. I was mature and took a pass on the nighttime stuff, but we still had a lot of fun. People dress up in elaborate costumes and mysterious masks from the time of Casanova and stroll through the city. Steph had a blast walking around and taking pictures.

Our last stop was Milan. The plan was to stay with relatives from my mom's side of the family, so at dinner the first night, a cousin explained, in English, the sleeping arrangements. Because everybody lived in condos, nobody had a place big enough for the three of us. Their solution was each of us would stay with a different family.

Vic and I had been divorced for a little over five years, and now, our daughter was in Italy, staying with people she just met. And remember, this was before you could pick up a cell phone and call anywhere in the world.

I told Steph we would talk about it after dinner. Her reaction was a funny look, telling me she would be fine staying with Aunt Rosa and Uncle Salvatore. Their daughter, Nuccia, who stayed with my mom and dad in '84, was living at home at the time. She was about twenty-eight years old and spoke English, which gave Steph somebody to communicate with. It was family; she never blinked. Me at that age? I probably would have peed my pants. To this day, I love telling the story.

Nuccia was also our tour guide for a couple of days, and she made sure we didn't pay for anything. I was even overruled trying to buy a newspaper.

One night at dinner, Salvatore, another young cousin, was trying to describe the different dishes we were eating. He was having trouble with one of the meat entrees so he raised his index fingers above his ears. They looked like horns, so our guesses were bull or goat. Nothing.

Then he blurted out, "Roger" a couple of times. Immediately out of my daughter's mouth: "Roger Rabbit?" Immediately out of Salvatore's mouth: "Si, si, it is rabbit." That's when Steph turned to me, wanting to know if we were eating Roger Rabbit. Yes.

She stopped for a second to take it all in, then calmly returned to her meal. Over the years, she's gotten a lot more selective with her eating habits, but that night was pretty awesome. There's also a picture of my nine-year-old drinking a glass of wine.

Home the next day.

Boat-I Summer of '95

What time is it? Boat time, whuh! Destination: Utica, Illinois. It's a town on the Illinois River, about an hour and a half from Chicago's southwest suburbs. The reason was our group's first houseboat vacation. Departure was from Starved Rock Marina, about a mile from the town.

It's a weekend trip where you board the boat on Thursday evening but can't leave the dock until the next day. That's because houseboat school takes place on Friday morning.

We got to the marina in the late afternoon, loaded our stuff on the boat, and took the short walk into Utica. That's right, no driving.

The plan was drinks and dinner, followed by more drinks. As we walked into town, Duffy's Bar & Grill was the first stop on what would become a mini-bar crawl. The big surprise of the night and, actually, the trip, took place when Dan bought dinner for all nine of us. His wife, Trish, was the most surprised one in the place.

Next in line was a bar called Blind Pig Pub, the town's blue-collar/ biker bar. We were only there a few minutes, when Mo's first shot on the pool table went bouncing across the floor. We stood out from the regular crowd just by walking in, so this didn't help. Somebody in our group actually overheard some comments about us being the "Beemer crowd." That got a good laugh, since we couldn't have bought a BMW if all nine of us chipped in.

I'm not a pool player, so I settled in at the bar, coincidentally, next to a hot blonde. Her boyfriend showed up a few minutes later and immediately asked the bartender for a Magic Marker. I'm guessing he needed to mark his territory, because he unzipped her jeans, pulled them down to the tree line, and wrote "Fuck me 'til I quiver" across her lower belly. Part of me wanted to take a long look (you know where), but the rest of me said no. I didn't need to get my ass kicked by some biker dude.

Next stop was a bar called Cousin Junior's, arriving in time for last call. One and done, so our bar walk totaled three places—quality, not quantity.

Back on the boat, we were scarred for life after witnessing Dan's (sexy?) pole dance. We all would have passed out with that image in our brain, except he decided to go up on the top deck and take the slide down into what he thought was deep water. It wasn't deep, but the bottom was soft, so crawling out of the sludge, he never looked cuter.

On Friday morning, he walked around in a daze, wondering where all the dollar bills came from, and where all the mud came from. While that was going on, the rest of us attended Boat School and got the OK to start our trip.

After breakfast, which eventually took place around noon, Mo began the first of two traditions that would continue on every boat trip. Walking out to the front or back deck became an issue because she just couldn't get it in her head it was important to slide open the screen door first.

Somebody came up with the idea of putting different-colored tape on the screens, but it only worked about half the time. We finally decided to leave the doors open and take our chances with the bugs. The other tradition was her stomach. 'Nuff said.

Interesting things would keep happening. It started when Otis (Sean) tipped over the untippable Jet Ski before he even pulled away from the boat. Then after getting on the river, he proceeded to run out of gas, so just a couple of hours into our trip, we had to call the marina and have them make a gas run. As the day went on, the smell coming from the bathroom continued to get worse, but with the sun going down, it was time to beach the boat. We headed to a place called Bull's Island, but remember, it's the first day of our first boat trip. Thankfully, some people on land sensed we were clueless and helped guide us to the shore.

Now on land, we gathered up some firewood, got a bonfire going, and relaxed on the beach for the rest of the night. The party officially ended at 3:33 a.m. The final naked count was five.

On Saturday, we got up and continued where we left off, dropping anchor in the middle of the river so we could try using the Jet Ski again. Our other plaything was the waterslide, and two scary things happened that included it.

Again, it was Sean who made a rookie mistake when he decided to ride down the slide before anyone had a chance to pour water on it. The noise of skin on slide was something none of us will ever forget. He never even made it to the water. Ouch!

Mac was next, and this is where it got serious. After hearing Sean go down the slide, he waited until it was wet. The ride down was smooth, but remember, we were on a river, so there was a current. Coming up out of the water, he was already a good distance from the boat, so one of the guys hopped on the Jet Ski and reeled him in. Thank God there was gas in it.

The mood lightened shortly after that when drunken Brenda slipped on the wet floor and did the splits. Everyone winced, with a few groans thrown in, but started laughing when she popped right up and declared, "I'm peachy!"

After slaving over a hot fire, JD, our master grill boy, needed a break, so I stepped up. Seconds later, somebody took a picture because of my outfit. I was wearing an apron—yes, just an apron. My butt got some decent reviews, but the best reaction was from my ten-year-old daughter as she flipped through the pictures from the trip: "Dad, you're so gross." Then she calmly returned to check out the rest of them.

The bathroom problem continued all day Saturday. Our guess was the marina's staff had been too busy or too lazy to empty the holding tank from the previous rental. Maybe they thought we would piss in the river. They were right, because the holding tank was full.

We were up early Sunday, returning to the marina so the boat could take a dump. With that done, we returned to our spot and got comfy. That's when we discovered comedian John Valby.

Somebody had given Trish a tape of his routine at a college campus, so she brought it with and threw it on. He was easily the most disgusting comic any of us had ever heard. We would listen to him for about an hour, laugh for about an hour, then our hangovers would magically disappear.

Back in the day, Redd Foxx was known as a pretty filthy comedian. JD and I saw him live in Las Vegas in 1977, but he wasn't in the same league as J.V. Every time we thought he couldn't get more disgusting, he did. My all-time favorite line: "My daddy refills cream donuts."

Our first boat trip was coming to an end and it was time to head back to the marina, but we were delayed when a strong storm came through the area. It rained so hard a couple of us showered on the top deck. One more interesting thing: There's barge traffic on the Illinois River and after we dodged a couple of them, a cabin cruiser flew by, then crossed in front of us. Seconds later, somebody spotted its large wake. When it hit, it was about two feet higher than our front deck.

Dan happened to be walking from the back of the boat, saw the wave, and got the sliding glass door closed in the nick of time. Everything, including the gas grill, a couple of beer coolers, and a couple of people began to float around the deck.

Dive! Dive! Utica, we have a problem! The front of the boat tilted down because of the weight of the water, so everyone inside started running, now uphill, to the back of the boat, hoping their weight would level it out. I didn't think it was possible, but we almost sank a pontoon boat.

Making it to the marina, we headed to the bar. Remember, we were feeling OK because of the Valby hangover cure, so we decided to have a couple of drinks before driving home.

Encore "interesting." This one involved a young boy walking up to the bar with a handful of change, hoping to buy some ice cream. Unfortunately, it was at the same time Carolyn was walking up to the bar to buy some drinks. He paid the price after being "gently" pushed aside. I believe the quote was "Get out of the way, kid. I need a beer." We all remember the sound of a bunch of coins hitting the floor.

Yes, it was time to go. We made it home safe and, for some reason, decided to do it again. We are all so, so precious.

'95 Montreal

The '95 hockey season was the last year for the historic Montreal Forum. Saturday, October 28, was the last time the Blackhawks would play there, so I rented a motor home, with seven of us arriving Friday afternoon. Jim and Judy flew there.

Before the start of every game, Montreal would honor a former Canadien player and a former star from the visiting team. The two players picked for the ceremonial puck drop that night were Henri Richard, one of the best Canadiens ever, and Doug Wilson, one of the best Blackhawks.

Montreal won the game 5-3. When it was over Maria, Kirk, Julie, and I waited until the stadium was almost empty, then walked down to the first row. That's when Kirk offered an usher $50 so we could walk out to center ice. Of course, the answer was no.

I didn't realize what was going on in Quebec while putting the trip together, but it was an interesting time to be there. On Monday, the day we were leaving, the people of the province were voting on whether or not to secede from Canada.

On Friday night, about 100,000 people rallied in downtown Montréal to stay in Canada. During the day on Saturday and Sunday, there would be a parade/rally down Sainte Catherine Street in favor of secession, followed an hour or so later by a parade/rally against it. This went on a few times each day, all peacefully. We were able to take a lot of this in because our home bar for the weekend was on that very street. We must have made a good impression because the bartender personally ran across the street during one of the parades to get us some snack foods. And later, he let all of us join him behind the bar for a group picture. We've developed a knack for this over the years. A couple of us have even guest-tended at bars in other cities.

On Sunday evening, Big Don decided to go off on his own. He returned to our home, talking about a guy he met who kept opening his mouth and asking Don to look in. The man was very proud of his fourteen teeth and insisted Don count them. In Montreal?

The highlight of the trip was a picture of Maria proudly wearing her Hawks jersey while leaning back on the hood of a Montréal police car, clutching her half-filled beer mug. Our guess was they had more important things to worry about that weekend.

We left early Monday morning, probably about the same time the polls opened. At home, we were amazed at the results. Almost 95 percent of registered voters came out, and it was incredibly close, with 51 percent voting to stay in Canada.

'95 DC

The Blackhawks were playing the Capitals on November 11, so it was time to return to Washington DC. Again, Southwest was our mode of transportation, with everybody flying there, including me. And this time, there was no 8:00 a.m. White House tour.

As we neared BWI (Baltimore Airport), an attendant asked a few of us sitting in the rear of the plane if we wanted another drink. We said yes, but thought she was messing with us because our flight was scheduled to land soon. She wasn't. I love SWA.

Returning to the Dupont Plaza Hotel meant returning to the fruit loop and returning, en masse, to Childe Harolde's. Remember, it's the bar we adopted as our home in early '94, and sure enough, Roland was working.

As our group walked in, he came to a stop, trying to remember why we looked familiar. Seconds later, he blurted out, "My boys from Chicago are back!" We make an impression wherever we go. On the subway the next day, Maria, my good friend and travel partner, took a hit. She was sitting next to Kirk, another bartender from McMahon's, who is about ten years younger than her. The people sitting across from them thought it was nice that a mother and son could go on vacation together.

During our stay at the Dupont Plaza the previous year, we had the honor of signing and dating the lobby ceiling. This time, our request was denied, basically because we didn't rate. That's when I walked the manager over and pointed to our spot. Then, magically, we did rate, and we were able to sign it again. Late Saturday, after the game, which the Blackhawks won 4-1, some of us ended up back at Childe Harolde's, hoping to grab some healthy fried food, but their kitchen had closed for the night. No problem, they sent us to another bar two blocks down the street that still served a limited menu. We knocked down our one drink, thanked the bartender, and headed out.

Walking into the new place, we realized their bartender had been tipped off because he was already putting our drinks on the bar. It was awesome, but we never got a chance to order our healthy snacks. That was because some delicious fried food magically appeared in front of us before we even asked for a menu.

We scarfed down our "dinner" helped along with a couple of drinks and thought we should end the night back at our home bar. It happened again. Walking into Childe Harolde's, we saw our freshly made drinks waiting on the bar. A guy could get used to this.

While writing this, I discovered the Dupont Plaza Hotel had been sold and the interior had been redone. I think it's safe to assume our special spot on the lobby ceiling is gone forever. And Childe Harolde's closed in 2008.

'96 BELGIUM

Maria and I arrived in Brussels, Belgium, on Sunday morning, March 17; at least that's what my airline ticket said. I had a window seat, but still couldn't see the end of the wing because of the fog. I knew we were getting close to the ground, then all of a sudden, we were on the ground. For the next two days, we would wake up, look out the window, and wonder where Belgium was.

That afternoon, we hung out for a while at the Grand Place, Brussels' beautiful main square. Then, a five-minute walk got us to a two-foot statue of a little guy taking a leak. It's called the Manneken Pis, true story. You'll probably have to look this one up. There's actually a museum in the city that holds all his outfits, many of them donated by people from all over the world. In '96, there were over four hundred. By 2016, there were over nine hundred—really.

The next day, we took a one-hour train ride through the fog, to the town of Bruges, which is known as the Venice of the North. We toured the Church of Our Lady, which houses Michelangelo's "Madonna and Child" sculpture. It's noteworthy because it's his only major work that wasn't in Italy during his lifetime.

We also saw a relic said to be Christ's blood on a piece of cloth, located in the Basilica of the Holy Blood. Then, it was 366 steps up to the top of the bell tower for a great view, followed by a cool boat tour through the city, followed by dinner. While researching our trip, we learned when in Belgium, one had to try the mussels, so I did.

I woke up sick Tuesday morning, pretty sure it was from the famous mussels, so Maria left me all by myself and took a day trip to the city of Ghent. Feeling better that evening and confident I could hold some food down, I went for a good Italian dinner. It had to be Italian; it was St. Joseph's Day.

It's Wednesday morning, and something wasn't right. Holy shit, the sun was out. It was the first time we saw it since leaving home.

We took a three-hour train ride to Luxembourg City, a beautiful place with a thousand-year-old fortress. There are also some great old bridges and something called the Bock Casements, which were built out of the rock that overlooks the city. It's a huge complex of tunnels and stairways that seem to connect everything in the area. It also holds gun turrets and a bomb shelter used during both world wars.

And of course, the tradition of me getting a picture of Maria straddling a cannon continued. With all the war history in Europe, you don't have to go far to find one.

We liked the area and decided to stay the night. It didn't take long to find a hotel, and it didn't take long to figure out why. We were in the red-light district. It had been a long day, so neither one of us cared.

On the 21st, a train took us to Trier, Germany. As the Holy Roman Empire expanded through Western Europe, it became Rome's main city and Germany's oldest city. We saw some great ruins, plus an amphitheater, some Roman baths, and the city's cathedral, which claims to have a piece of Christ's robe as a relic. We ended the day with some apple schnapps.

On Friday, we were back on a train, this time to Libramont, followed by a bus to Bastogne, a famous sight from WWII's Battle of the Bulge. We saw a lot of war relics and two cemeteries: one for German soldiers, the other for the Allied Forces. Remember, my dad was a Purple Heart veteran who fought in the Battle of the Bulge.

Brussels is a great place to base your vacation. Besides the city itself, there are plenty of good day trips to choose from. Our next trip was to Waterloo, only ten miles from the city. In 1815, this is where Napoleon was beaten by the Duke of Wellington and the Prussian Army.

The city's museum has a great panorama of the battlefield, but the thing to do is take a short walk to a hill called the Lion's Mound. After hiking up 226 steps, you're rewarded with a great view and a description of what took place on the battlefield. And yes, another picture of Maria on a cannon. Then, it was back to Brussels.

Sunday was our last full day in Belgium, and Antwerp was our last day trip. It was another short train ride, where we toured the Cathedral of

Our Lady, which holds three of Rubens' masterpieces and should not to be confused with the Church of our Lady in Bruges.

After a quick look at a medieval fortress known as the Steen, it was time for a bar crawl. For its size, Belgium had to be the beer capital of the world, with over three hundred choices, some with alcohol content around 15 percent. Remember, this was 1996, years before the craft beer craze hit the United States.

Since we were leaving the next day, it was finally time to try some Belgian waffles. They were awesome. Had we tried them on day one, I would have put on ten pounds, with a diabetic coma a distinct possibility.

Time to fly home, this time without fog.

BOAT-2 SUMMER OF '96

What time is it? Boat time, whuh!

A year later and we're back at Starved Rock Marina. The routine was the same: We board the boat on Thursday evening but don't leave the dock until Friday morning. That meant a short walk into town for another mini-bar crawl.

And like the year before, it was dinner and a few drinks at Duffy's, this time followed by Ed & Joy's, where Kathy blurted out her first "fuck you" of the night. You probably don't know her, but even one was a surprise.

Our next to last stop was the Blind Pig Pub. I had T-shirts made up in honor of our stop there the previous year, with a picture of a houseboat on the front of the shirt and the words "'til we quiver" just below it.

And sure enough, Randy, the biker dude, was sitting at the bar; at least, I thought it was him. We took a poll and everyone agreed it was the same guy, so I went over to refresh his memory about how we met the year before, and about his penmanship at the bar that night. He laughed, then acknowledged that yes, he was the one.

That's when I showed him the T-shirt I was wearing. He reacted as if he had just won the lottery. A few seconds later, he traded his Harley-Davidson shirt with Brenda right at the bar. Not exactly, she was suddenly shy and changed in the women's bathroom.

He thought he should accompany her and knocked on the door a couple of times, but she said no. For a second, we thought Brenda had a new old man (Randy), which meant his girlfriend would become my new old lady. Didn't happen.

With drinking time running out, we headed to Cousin Junior's, leaving us about ten minutes before they closed—déjà vu all over again, almost to the minute.

It was an uneventful walk back to the boat; at least I thought it was. There was something written in the log we kept about a few of us almost drowning. The only thing anyone remembers is it had something to do with the lack of railings overlooking the river, but there is one thing nobody has forgotten. It was Mo trying her best to imitate Mary Lou Retton at the intersection of Church St. and Mill St. as we headed past Duffy's. Not one perfect score.

With Boat School completed, we spent a relaxing day on the Illinois River, then found a sandy patch of land and beached the boat. Once we got the bonfire going, everyone got naked. Not really, this year it was just me.

A notable quotable from Friday: JD, those aren't pillows, and that's not the zipper to the tent.

This year, we started a tradition that would continue every time we rented a houseboat, then every year after that, when we started renting a beach house. There would be a party theme. Toga party was the first.

After another quiet day on the river, it was time to park and get the toga party started. The first problem we ran into was Carolyn's Jell-O shots. The question to her was if she had put any Jell-O in them. She assured us the Jell-O was in there but admitted she might have forgotten to include some water with the vodka.

Before it got dark, we got the bonfire going. Everyone donned their togas so we could get a group picture, but while trying to get organized, somebody was asked to squat down. Not you, Kathy; she was the one taking the picture.

Then it was time for music from the *Animal House* soundtrack and for our neighbors to run for cover. A couple of us were assigned to be Toga police so we could enforce the "no bare ass" rule, but we didn't do a very good job.

Remember, we were on the Illinois River, which handles a lot of barge traffic. Late that night, while still dancing around the bonfire, we spotted one coming toward us. The boat's spotlight was trained on the shoreline to give the pilot an idea where he was, but that's when it moved a little bit inland to see what was going on. After a couple of seconds, it started to move back toward the water but, a couple of seconds later, jerked back toward the fire. Our guess was the crew thought they were witnessing some pagan ritual.

The next morning, when we finally started moving and cleaned up our area, we heard our neighbors chanting "Toga, toga, toga." Luckily, they had a sense of humor.

We made it back to the dock without sinking, then went directly to the marina's bar and grill, where we raised a few eyebrows. Why, you ask? We were still wearing our togas.

A couple of drinks, then home safe.

We are all so precious.

'96 ATLANTA

Atlanta hosted the Summer Olympics in 1996. I made it to Montréal for the 1976 Summer Games and Lake Placid for the Winter Games in 1980. I couldn't skip Atlanta; it was on the same continent.

On July 30, I hopped into my 1989 Eagle Premier and started driving south. That night, my car doubled as a hotel room, with a truck stop doubling as my hotel parking lot, getting to the Atlanta area the next morning.

The plan was to stay a couple of nights with the daughter of an old friend of mine. I remember her as a kid playing Pac-Man at the bar while her dad had a "couple of beers." Now, she was all grown-up and pregnant.

I got to her place on the morning of the 31st, but she wasn't there, which created a dilemma. Not knowing when she would return put the rest of the day in jeopardy. The alternative was trying to find a room, which wouldn't be easy. With only three days in Atlanta, it was time to start searching.

Route 285 circles the city, so my plan was to jump off at every exit with a hotel sign. Surprisingly, it didn't take too long, finding a place that had one room because of a cancelation, but only for one night. It was a Jacuzzi suite. That was the good news. Then the desk clerk gave me the bad news. The rate was $250 a night.

My reaction was a big laugh because it wasn't exactly in my price range. He understood, and lowered it to $200. That's when I whipped out my travel agent business card and asked for an industry discount. The next big laugh came from the clerk as he lowered the price again, this time to $160—not bad, in a city hosting the Summer Olympics.

With a real bed to sleep in, I then drove into the city. The plan for the day was I had no plan. My first event was a women's basketball game between Australia and the United States, buying a ticket from somebody outside the arena. Location wasn't a priority, and it didn't take long to figure out why it was so cheap. It was in the middle of the Aussie cheering section. Didn't matter, I had a blast.

Later, I found my way to Centennial Park. It was an emotional time, because it was the day the park reopened after the bombing. Santana played that night and helped everybody take their minds off what had happened. When it was over, it was time for me to take full advantage of my Jacuzzi suite. Well, maybe not full advantage, I was alone.

Day 2 was pretty much the same as day 1. In the afternoon, it was a baseball game between Cuba and Nicaragua, followed by some boxing in the evening. That night was the only time I paid over face value for a ticket, probably because it was the quarterfinals.

After boxing and a couple of drinks, it was time to return to my hotel, even without a reservation. It was the one place in Atlanta I was familiar with, so after I found a comfortable-looking parking space, my car became my hotel room again. The next morning, a quick dip in the pool followed by a little deodorant qualified as an awesome shower. Refreshed, it was last call for the Summer Olympics.

I only saw one event, but it was track and field, which took up a good portion of the day. After that, it was time to start my drive home, heading north on Route 75 for a while. Far enough from the city, where security wouldn't be so tight, I stopped at a Holidome. With a book and a towel in hand, I headed for the indoor pool, found a table, and made myself at home. A little downtime followed by a little swim and it was time to get back in my car.

Chattanooga, Tennessee, was my last stop for the day, and like the trip down, I found a truck stop. The parking lot was huge and almost full. It looked like a lot of people were doing the same thing I was, because it wasn't all trucks. Time wasn't an issue, so my drive home started when I woke up.

It turned out to be a cheap vacation, with gas being my only major expense. I paid up for one event, with the rest of them below face value. And if you divide my hotel bill by the four nights I was gone, it came out to $40 a night.

God bless America.

'96 New Orleans

The Bears were heading south to play the Saints on October 13, so I put a large, very handsome group together and invaded New Orleans for the weekend. Our flight was on Delta Airlines, which meant the mandatory stop in Atlanta.

The approach to Hartsfield Airport seemed pretty routine. After flying a few times, you can sense when the plane is about to touch down. That's where we were when it abruptly lifted up, slamming everyone back in their seats. And here's a quote from our captain: "The runway was a little congested, so we're just gonna saunter back around." That translates to "We almost crashed into another plane."

On this trip, we stayed at the Day's Inn on Canal Street, where Bourbon Street heads into the French Quarter. The hotel was going through some renovation work, but I hadn't been informed, so there were a lot of unhappy people.

Like any normal group, we headed to Bourbon Street, returning to the Tropical Isle and their famous Hand Grenades. Returning to the hotel the first night, we found our buddy Finn and his date, asleep (passed out) on the floor outside their room. They were so close.

The last night, a few of us closed the Tropical Isle, stayed a while longer, then we were sent down the street to another bar that opened early. Not sure, but I think I was the last one to return to our hotel. How did I know? Because most of our group was standing outside, waiting for cabs. I had just enough time to go up to my room, grab my bag, and head for the airport.

Oh yeah, the game—we lost, 27-24.

'97 London

Mo, Tracey, and I worked together at McMahon's and decided to take a vacation together. On Monday, February 17, our plane touched down at London's Heathrow Airport. After buying our travel cards, we hopped on the Tube (subway) and headed into town. It would be seven days in a small loft we rented, just south of Kensington Park and a short walk from the Gloucester Road tube stop.

We quickly settled in, then took the Hop-On/Hop-Off bus to get a feel for the city. The weather was cold, windy, and rainy, and it would stay that way most of the week. We hopped on anyway, ending up on the open top deck, and didn't hop off.

With that done, we took a walk through the neighborhood, in search of a pub we could call home. It's a great plan because it gives you the chance to meet some of the locals. After playing tourist during the day, you have a home away from home to hang out at every night and being in the same business always helps. It didn't take long.

Day 2 started at Westminster Abbey, taking the free one-hour tour of the Tower of London and skipping the Changing of the Guards. After lunch, we finished up at the London Dungeon, getting a great picture of me and Tracey beheading Mo.

While walking back from our adopted home that night, we took a wrong turn and got a little lost. It actually helped, because we discovered a twenty-four-hour grocery store, which thrilled Tracey. She made a beeline to the snacks section in search of Bugles and, with bag in hand, joined Mo and me, who were dancing in the aisle to some Motown music playing on the store's sound system.

The next morning, the 19th, was a short trip to Wimbledon. Mo's a big tennis fan, so we took the thirty-minute ride to the Southfield Tube Stop, followed by a mile walk to the tennis grounds. We toured its awesome museum and got to take a walk onto Centre Court. No, it wasn't during the tournament.

Back in London, it was time for some culture, maybe a play or a musical, so we headed to Leicester Square and its half-price ticket booth. After standing in line in the rain for a few minutes, one of the girls spotted a pub's neon sign on the second or third floor of a building across the square. So much for culture, because that sign was a sign. We found the pub and settled in.

We also learned about the late-night buses because the Tube had shut down by the time we left the place. They didn't run often, but they ran late, so we made it home.

It's day 4, and the plan was to take a trip to the town of Canterbury, about an hour and a half ride from London. First, here's a Tracey story about our walk to the subway.

Every time we left our place, the routine was the same. It was a left turn out the front door, followed by a one-block walk, then a right turn. One more block got us to Gloucester Road and its subway stop. Not brain surgery but today, Tracey was in the lead, so at the right turn, she went left. Mo and I stopped to see how far she would go before realizing her mistake and, while watching and waiting, noticed another problem. It was her purse. She had it slung over her shoulder, completely open. After she lost her subway pass the day before, this wasn't good. And the day before we left, she lost her replacement pass. That's Tracey.

We made it to Canterbury and took our own walking tour seeing, among other things, the Cathedral, Westgate Gardens, and the ruins of St. Augustine's Abbey. Yes, we finished the night at our pub.

It's Friday morning, the 21st, and a half-hour ride took us to Windsor for a tour of the castle and the local area. When we got back, I took a walk along the Thames River, and I was able to take a tour of the new Globe Theater. It was built as a duplicate of Shakespeare's original theater and was scheduled to open two weeks after we left.

Day 6, and it was time for a free day, which meant the girls and I went off in different directions. I went in search of something a little off the beaten path, ending up on the north side of the city, where I found a huge flea market called Camden Market. A little while later, I found Camden

Locks, part of a local canal system that reminded me of a similar area in Milan, also a little off the beaten path.

Next on my list was the Imperial War Museum, but before getting there, I took a detour to the St. John's Wood Tube Station. Why? Because a short walk would get me to Abbey Road Studios and my Beatles fix.

I had heard stories about people having to wait in line to take their walk across Abbey Road. I waited too, but it was because there was nobody else around. When a woman showed up, I asked if she could take a picture of me crossing the road. She missed the shot with my arms fully extended, but I'm not complaining.

Now, the War Museum. It turned out to be a great stop, especially because of the exhibit that told the story of the Nazi bombing of London.

A man dressed in a wartime uniform explained to our group what the people had to go through. Thousands would go down into the subway every night, hoping to survive and hoping they still had a place to live when they walked up the stairs the next morning.

Twelve of us were sitting on a few benches in a replica of the subway, listening to our guide and listening to the simulated dull thuds of bombs going off above us. Then a really loud fake bomb went off and shook the place. There were a few screams, plus the woman sitting next to me grabbed my leg. It was that real, but that was the only grabbing.

My free day ended with dinner at an Indian restaurant, and here's a quick story about what the girls did on their free day.

A little over two hours after boarding an early morning train at Waterloo Station, they got off at Paris' Gare du Nord Station. The Chunnel had opened three years earlier, and with all we had heard about the cold/rude Parisians, they came back raving about the ones they met.

The best story took place in a subway station, when a woman noticed them trying to figure out the subway map. She could tell they were clueless, so she walked over, gave them the right directions, then gave them her map. Then it was back to London, where we met at our home.

And here are a couple of pub stories:

1. I mentioned earlier how we found our home away from home. In a lot of the bars, the regulars have special privileges at last call. They're able to order a couple extra drinks, settle in, and when the last of the non-regulars leave the place, the doors are locked.

Yes, being in the bar business helped. After a few days, we started to get comfortable with the regulars and the corner they hung out in. Because of that, we got locked in twice, on days 5 and 6. It was pretty cool and we were very honored.

2. On the last night in London and the last night in our pub, we noticed a couple walking from table to table. We also noticed the strange reactions from the people sitting at them. There were a lot of weird looks on their faces and a lot of "no thank yous." After striking out at almost every one, they finally got a guy to leave with them. Our little group watched as he got into a van parked across the street. The antici . . . pation.

Seconds later, the guy jumped out and ran back to the pub, shaking his head. Turns out, he had volunteered to help in the making of a very low-budget porno film.

That would be it because we were leaving the next day and it was time to say our goodbyes at our home away from home. Then home.

'97 Toronto

Big Don and I took a trip to Toronto for a Maple Leafs hockey game on March 12. So did the Chicago Blackhawks.

Just days before we arrived, a smoking ban had begun that would affect the bars there. At our first stop, the place was completely smoke free, well almost. We heard people talking about the $50 fine for any violation, but when a customer lit up a smoke, he was given a saucer to use as an ashtray, so maybe not every violation.

The next bar was way different, with cigarette smoke being the first thing we noticed. Minutes later, I saw a big smile on Don's face as he lit up his cigar.

I don't remember much, but we did make it to the Hockey Hall of Fame, which, at the time, was located in an office complex/shopping mall. We did the tour, and we were almost out the door when one of us remembered the Stanley Cup. Shit, we almost missed it.

After a quick U-turn, we found the room where it was on display. It was a short walk up a short ramp, but there was a short wait because one of the famous white-gloved security guards was telling a short story about it.

In 1979, after winning the cup at home, Montreal Canadien Guy Lafleur got to take it home for the night but got a flat tire just a few blocks from the Forum. To get to the jack and the spare tire, he took everything out of his trunk, including the Stanley Cup, but forgot to put everything back in before pulling away. And yes, the Stanley Cup was one of the things he left behind. At home, something clicked, and he made a beeline back to the city, where he found the cup right where he left it, with a handful of people standing guard—only in Montreal.

When the story ended, I asked if it was possible to touch the cup. The guard solemnly nodded yes, so I stuck one finger out and got my fix. The story wasn't that big a deal until the Blackhawks won the cup in 2010. Then, all I heard was "You touched the cup—that's awesome!" Yeah, about thirteen years ago.

Don also had to remind me how I tried to pay for a hooker. It wasn't for me; it was so he could get laid in his second foreign country. Mexico was first, just after high school, but he's still holding at one.

The Hawks won 3-2, and we got home safe.

Movie Extra '96 and '97

In August '96, it was one day of work on a show called *Early Edition*. No, it wasn't the news program; it was about a guy who got his newspaper delivered a day early, and what he did with the information.

The episode was about a lottery scam in the city, and I was one of a group of reporters camped out on the steps of City Hall, trying to question the mayor about the ongoing investigation. I made it on camera for about three seconds.

In June '97, it was one day of work on the movie *Simon*. You won't recognize the name because it was changed to *Mercury Rising*. It was a hot day for June, and I was dressed in a suit and tie. People that knew me were shocked because I'm a T-shirt and jeans/shorts guy. I had to be hired as an actor to put that stuff on.

The scene began with Bruce Willis and another actor walking out the front entrance of the Tribune Tower and across the Chicago River on the Michigan Avenue Bridge. During the first part of the day, my starting point was next to a little ice cream cart manned by a young woman. I would walk across the bridge, maybe twenty feet behind the two actors, then return to the cart every time they had to reshoot the scene.

After a few takes, Bruce Willis walked up and asked the girl if there really was ice cream in her cart. She started to answer before looking up, explaining, "Yes, but only for . . ." That's when she came to a complete stop, realizing whom she was talking to. We all had a good laugh. Bruce consoled her, then gave her a hug. She was never quite the same the rest of the shoot. Oh, and Bruce did get his ice cream.

Later in the afternoon, I got moved near the front entrance of the Tribune Tower. Between takes, the guy next to me pointed to a good-looking woman walking toward us with a couple of young children in tow. I said it looked like Demi Moore. I was right.

She decided to bring their kids down to the set, hoping they could see Dad at work, and patiently waited at one of the barriers. Bruce was walking back to his starting point after a take, when the kids let out a big yell. He then ran over and gave them a big hug. It was nice, because he really looked surprised.

A couple more takes, and my career as a movie extra came to an end. We'll see.

BOAT~3 SUMMER OF '97

It was time for another houseboat trip, but after two years on the Illinois River, it was time for a change of scenery. We got tired of the barge traffic, the river currents, and the full holding tanks, so in March, Mo, JD, and I took a drive south to check out Lake Shelbyville and Lithia Springs Marina about forty miles west of Charleston, Illinois. We liked what we saw, and booked a houseboat for the weekend following July 4th. The new location meant a new routine. This time, we would meet on Thursday at a hotel on the west side of Charleston. Depending on their schedules, people would arrive there at all different times but would always end up at Stix, a college bar near Eastern Illinois University. And it might only be the third year, but the tradition of boarding the boat hungover on Friday morning was already in its third year.

In my notes for this trip, "Hawaiian" is listed as the party theme. A couple of the guys remember a couple of the girls doing a hula dance and singing, "We bring you more beer" while drinking a beer, but that's pretty much it. There's no log and no pictures. See you next year.

We are all so precious.

'97 Madrid

In the fall, I returned to Madrid with my friends Maureen, Pat, and Denise and got to visit a few places from '72. The year '91 didn't count because I was only there for thirty-six hours. It may have been twenty-five years, but not much had changed.

We saw the Royal Palace, hung out in Retiro Park, and drank in the *mezones* (bars) that surround the Plaza Mayor. While walking up and down Atocha Street, I found the building that was home during my semester and the bar where I was arrested for not having my passport. Remember the story? I was the smart-ass.

When you live in Madrid, the evening begins with a tapas (small appetizers) crawl. Dinner starts after 9:00 p.m. Walk into a restaurant at six or seven o'clock, and it will be empty. If it's not, the customers are tourists. I love the lifestyle. If or when I retire or win the lottery, I'll be spending a few months there every year.

In the old town area, it was a quick walk between stops. After one or maybe two short drinks and a couple of tapas, it was on to the next bar. We lost track of time one night, not realizing we missed dinner until about one o'clock in the morning.

Anyway, we kept going. Our final stop was a bar somewhere near the Royal Palace, somewhere around four o'clock in the morning. Walking in, we noticed the music playing on its sound system. It was opera, but we didn't really give it a thought, assuming it was the jukebox, or maybe a local radio station.

I was the first one to go in search of a bathroom and discovered the adjoining restaurant down a short hallway. It was empty except for one small group. There were six or seven people sitting at a table and one sitting at a piano. They were the ones we were listening to. One played the music, while the others took turns singing arias from different operas. They were really good, so I sat down in a booth.

A few minutes later, a young guy came over and asked if he could join me because he was also intrigued with the whole scene. He was from Peru and would speak to me in English, trying to improve his language skills, then I would try to answer him in my best high school Spanish. This was going on while listening to opera sung in Italian, oh yeah, while we were in Spain. This is why you travel.

When we finally left the bar, the sun was up, so we went to El Rastro, Madrid's famous flea market. When you're there, churros con chocolate is a must. Look it up.

There are some great day trips you can do from Madrid. Our first one was Toledo, an hour ride south. The city was built on a hilltop overlooking the Tajo River and is listed as a national monument and a UNESCO World Heritage site. The highlights are an impressive cathedral, a 1,000-year-old Moorish fort called El Alcazar, the El Greco Museum, and a slow walk through the old city.

Back in Madrid, Pat and Denise decided to catch a flight home the next day. Mo and I stayed the course, with two more cities on our list. Segovia, another UNESCO site, was next, this time an hour north. It's a medieval town whose main attraction is a huge aqueduct that runs through the center of the city, built by the Romans in the first century.

Another highlight is the view looking down into the valley where the Church of Vera Cruz sits. It's famous throughout Spain for the relic kept there: a piece of the true Crucifix. And like Toledo, just walking through the city is worth the trip.

That left us with one more day trip. It was the town of Cuenca, another UNESCO site located in the La Mancha region, about a hundred-mile train ride from Madrid. I don't remember who told me about it, but thank you.

Cuenca can be a tough walking city. The old town is built on a few hills that are almost completely surrounded by deep gorges. It's famous for its *casas colgadas* (hanging houses), which are built on the edge or side of some of the cliffs. Mo and I did our best but, at one point, stopped for a break.

Seeing us standing there with a map, an old man walked over, guessing we needed the help of a local citizen. Actually, we were too embarrassed to tell him the real reason we stopped. It was because we couldn't catch our breath. He didn't seem to have a problem getting around, but we sure did.

There's a narrow footbridge at one end of town that extends across a gorge, but most people only walk about halfway, then turn around and take some great pictures of the houses. This is also where I discovered Mo was afraid of heights. She walked out maybe ten feet, looked down, then scampered back to safety.

We got back to Madrid that night and flew home the next day.

'98 TRACEY

In February 1997, Tracey went to London with Mo and me. On Valentine's Day 1998, Tracey got married. The next afternoon, she and her husband, Dan, were scheduled to leave on their honeymoon. They were going to Europe, with Munich, Germany, their first stop. For a small fee, I helped them put the trip together, booking their hotels, and giving them some good information.

Because of a little too much partying at the wedding reception, they overslept and missed their flight. So what did they do? They went to the airport the next day as if nothing happened. And what did the airline do? It honored their tickets.

It gets better. The hotel reservation in Munich was for three nights, but remember, they got there a day late. The logical thing would be to stay one less day at their first stop, putting them back on the original schedule. They didn't, they just continued their vacation through Europe as if nothing happened.

Amazingly, every hotel honored their reservation, even though they were off by one day. And once again, even though the date on the tickets to fly home didn't match the day they walked into the airport, the airline honored them.

Only Tracey.

'98 GREECE

It's May, and my flight to Athens was uneventful. I don't like checking luggage, so my carry-on bag and I were the first to arrive at the gate for my flight to the island of Rhodes. The employees were sitting around, having a smoke, and didn't seem too interested when they finally noticed me. After a quick look, I was waved through. In certain instances, that was customs before 9/11.

Rhodes is the farthest Greek island southeast of the mainland. The city of Rodos (Rhodes Town) sits at its northern tip. On a good day, looking east, you might see the coast of Turkey.

I met up with Mo and Maria, who flew there a day earlier. Their flight was also uneventful, except for one thing. The people sitting next to them thought it was nice a mother and daughter could get on a plane and vacation together. Sound familiar? In '95, it was Maria and her "son" (Kirk). The thought was nice, but Maria wasn't thrilled. Just like in '95, the age difference was only about ten years.

We may have landed in Rhodes on different days, but we still had the same experience. Its airport was inundated with cats. They would actually wait by a door until a human would enter or exit, then use the open door so they could enter or exit. Nobody seemed to mind.

Rhodes probably wouldn't have been on our list, except for the connection I had with a bar there. The owner grew up in the southwest suburbs of Chicago and his best friend's father owned the golf course where I used to work. It was also the golf course where I hosted over twenty golf outings.

He had traveled to Greece to seek out his roots and, once there, decided to stay and opened a bar. When we met, he told us how he split his year between two homes, spending about six months in Rhodes and six months in Amsterdam. Poor guy.

We had a hotel for three nights in the Old Town area near the spot where the Colossus, one of the Seven Wonders of the Ancient World, was supposed to have stood. On our first full day, we rented a car and toured the southern and eastern portions of the island. One of the stops was Lindos, a small town of whitewashed buildings, narrow cobblestoned streets and a large acropolis (fort) that overlooks the city. It's where we got our view of the Turkish coast.

Touring the area, we were treated to something we weren't expecting. It was the road signs. All of them were in Greek, of course, but also in English, so navigating the island was a breeze. If you're a traveler and only speak English, I hope you realize how spoiled you are.

After being a tourist during the day, nights were spent at Down Under, our new home. Because of the name, you would think the majority of its customers came from Australia, but most of them came from Scandinavia. It was a fun place where women, mostly blondes wearing short skirts, were encouraged to dance on the bar.

On our last night, Mo and I were offered bartending jobs with a cheap place to stay just a block or so from the bar. I needed a trip home to figure out what to do with my apartment, and the extra, expensive airfare took me out of the running.

Mo wanted to stay. She actually called her other part-time job and requested a leave of absence but, because of the short notice, was turned down. When we took off on our flight home, I detected a couple of tears. I think she might have stayed.

While working on the book, we talked about the opportunity and how our lives would have changed had we stayed. The big question was, would we have gotten married or killed each other? Mo's answer was quick and to the point. We would have killed each other.

Our next island was Santorini. Instead of the cheaper, relaxing, but much longer ferryboat ride, we opted for the short flight in a very small plane. Fira, its main city, is amazing, with a large portion of it sitting on the side of a cliff overlooking the caldera left by an ancient volcano. The view was fantastic, especially as the sun went down. Our hotel faced west.

First was a short boat cruise, where we got to go swimming, then hike up onto an active volcano. To get down to the boat from our hotel, there were 588, mostly very wide stairs. After the cruise, the girls decided a donkey ride would be a much easier way to get back up. I decided to walk, and I made it.

For sunset on the island, people traditionally flock to Oia. It's a charming little town located on its northern tip, also with whitewashed buildings, which we learned were the norm on most of the islands. We also learned making the short trek wasn't worth it. The sun sets over open water. Yawn. The sun setting through the caldera in Fira was so much better. Actually, Michigan City, Indiana, is better. For a good part of the year, the sun drops down through Chicago's skyline.

The next day we toured Akrotiri, an ancient city buried by a volcanic eruption around 1500 BC. It's a well-preserved area, which some historians believe is the site of the city of Atlantis. In Athens, at the end of our trip, we were lucky enough to see some of the colorful frescoes that had been moved from the island to the National Museum.

After Rhodes and Santorini, it was time for a couple of days of doing nothing. We heard some good things from other tourists about the island of Naxos, so it was time to hop on a ferry for a leisurely five-hour ride to its port city of Chora (Naxos Town).

If time isn't critical, ferryboats are the way to travel around the islands. They're cheap and usually populated with friendly tourists doing the same thing. That means eating, drinking, and relaxing, either in or out of the sun.

When you get off the boat in the port cities, there are two ways to find a room. The first one is to deal with a swarm of people shoving pictures in your face of the hotels they're trying to sell. The other, safer choice is the hotel/info office. You'll find them in every town where the ferryboats dock.

We opted for the office. After a couple of minutes and a couple of questions about what we were looking for, they directed us to the Hotel Proteas, just a short cab ride to Agios Prokopios, a small beach town with one main street and a handful of hotels scattered around it.

From our room, it was a short walk to the beach, but before getting there, it was time to make a big decision, especially if you're a conservative American. Go left, back toward the town? More clothing. Go right? A lot less clothing. The girls would go left. I would go right.

On the first day, I learned one of the basic rules of nude sunbathing. Obviously, a guy needs to put sunscreen on every part of his body, but he needs to do it in the privacy of his own room. There just isn't a polite way to do it in public. I'll stop there.

On the second day, I was walking down the beach only wearing a baseball cap. That night, Mo and Maria were talking, and Maria mentioned she had wandered down into the naked territory and was checking out some guy walking along the beach only wearing a baseball cap. Mo then broke the news to her about who she had been looking at—just a little throw-up in her mouth.

With our batteries recharged, we took another ferryboat ride, this one to Mykonos, just two hours away. It's a beautiful island, but we thought it was way overpriced. It also had a large gay community and a large gay beach. No, I'm not getting naked there.

While walking through the old section of the port town, we kept listening to a bunch of gay guys behind us, talking about some TV commercial. They kept saying "Grrreat!" but couldn't come up with the character. I finally had to stop, turn around, and tell them, "It's Tony the Tiger!" I could've had my pick.

Actually, the main reason we were in Mykonos was to tour Delos, a small island that is the center of the Greek Cyclades Islands and, in ancient times, the center of Greek civilization. It's an amazing archeological site, but we missed it.

Then, one more ferry boat ride. This one took a little over six hours, dropping us off in Piraeus, the port of Athens. From there, we took a cab into the city and got lucky, finding a hotel in the Plaka (old town), near the base of the Acropolis. It was a great spot with a great view, especially at night, when the whole area was lit up.

The next day, we went our separate ways. I hiked up Mt. Lycabettus, a small mountain literally in the middle of the city, for a great panoramic view. Later, we met up and saw the original Olympic Stadium, which hosted the first modern Games in 1896.

Athens had been awarded the 1996 Summer Games to celebrate the one-hundred-year anniversary but lost them because construction was so far behind schedule. It was 1998, and they still weren't ready. They hosted the 2004 Games.

That evening, the three of us were sitting outside at a restaurant in the Plaka. Thinking we were European, our waiter started venting to us about a group of Americans he was waiting on. He couldn't believe how impatient they were, needing everything now.

He was embarrassed when one of us told him we were from the United States, but he felt a lot better when Mo and I told him what we did for a living. How could anyone be in a hurry sitting in an outdoor restaurant in Athens on a beautiful night, a stone's throw from the Acropolis? We sure weren't. A good part of our last day was spent at the National Museum, finally making it up to the Acropolis, where we have a picture of Maria and another woman comparing their fish watches. Don't ask. I have no idea.

Then home. (Another story)

'98 Greece—Flight Home

We flew home together on British Air. With a six-hour layover in London, Maria met up with a Spanish cousin who happened to be in the city at the same time. Mo and I had been there the year before with Tracey and had a good feel for the city, so we hopped on the Tube and headed into town.

Mo needed her fix, so our destination was the pub we hung out at in '97. The reason was mashed potatoes—no lie. It wasn't some kind of alcoholic drink; it was mashed potatoes. Evidently, peas and sour cream were the magic ingredients.

Settling in, we told the bartender how we hung out there for six or seven nights the year before, and wanted to say hello to the woman who waited on us most of our time there. Problem was, we couldn't remember her name, plus the bartender was relatively new and wasn't sure she could help. And finally, we were there during the day, so no nighttime regulars were around.

The one thing we did remember was the guys talking about what a nice bum (ass) she had. With no hesitation, the bartender answered, "That would be Natalie." With no hesitation, I asked if she was from Ontario, Canada. After a surprised look, she answered yes. That's when I knew we had the right one.

It was a quick stop, and with Mo satisfied, we headed back to Heathrow to meet up with Maria. Sitting at a table having a drink, I noticed the T-shirt on a guy walking by. The name printed on it was a softball team sponsored by a bar in Mt. Greenwood, a neighborhood on the far southwest side of Chicago. From '90 to '95, I lived seven houses down the street from the same bar. We traded a couple of stories but didn't know each other.

After a second call for our flight, we got up and started a quick walk to our gate, getting in a very long line leading to the checkpoint. A man in front of us mentioned how he traveled through Heathrow a lot, but he had never seen anything like this. Now in jeopardy of missing our flight, we asked the nearest person in uniform for some help. He took a look at our tickets, then told us to walk up to the front of the line where the metal detectors were located and plead our case.

When we got there, Mo decided stopping wasn't an option. She calmly pushed aside the red "Do Not Enter" gate/sign and the three of us calmly walked through the checkpoint. Amazingly, nobody noticed, or nobody cared. Today, the airport would shut down, and I'm pretty sure we would be thrown in jail. I think people on our flight assumed we were the reason for the delay because we got a lot of dirty looks while finding our seats. I wish they could have seen us going through the security checkpoint.

Maybe two hours into the flight, people in the middle of the plane started waving for a flight attendant because a woman lit up a cigarette. When one showed up, the smoker lady kept complaining, then disgustedly threw her cigarette on the floor and ground it into the carpet.

On my flights to and from Europe, I always spend some time in the back of the plane because I'm a bartender used to standing, not sitting. During one of my upright breaks, I met the woman and we struck up a conversation. I was a little surprised because she was interesting and intelligent, but the severity of the problem she caused hadn't really sunk in. I told her there was a good chance she would be arrested when we landed in Chicago, but she didn't believe me.

We stood there and talked for a while, even discussing the Chicago Symphony Orchestra and Sir Georg Solti. I don't know how we got to that point and don't know how I lasted that long, but the flight attendants loved me. Later, the girls told me keeping the woman occupied kept her from thinking about her next cigarette.

Back in my seat, they told me about the impact I had on the rest of the passengers. As long as I stood there and talked to the smoker lady, the rest of the plane was out of Bacardi rum. Mo tried to order a couple of little bottles so I would have something to drink when I sat down, but got the same answer. Once she explained who was sitting in the open seat next to them, little bottles magically appeared.

Landing in Chicago, the police were waiting for the woman. Not positive, but I don't think she was arrested. Our guess was after a little lecture, they let her go.

As the three of us walked down a long hallway to US Customs, two flight attendants came running up to thank me again. They then handed me a bouquet of flowers and a bottle of wine. Mo and Maria looked at each other, shook their heads, and continued walking.

Home safe.

Boat-4 Summer of '98

Our first trip to Lake Shelbyville was a success, so we came back the next summer, the perfect time for a "Christmas in July" party theme.

Like the year before, the hotel pool in Charleston was our starting point on Thursday afternoon. A few early arrivals actually walked to the bars, knowing they would be well over the legal limit to drive back. It's about a mile, assuming you walk in a straight line.

Puddin (George) was one of the late arrivals. Walking into Stix and needing to catch up, he ordered a beer, a vodka on the rocks, and a Jameson. This would happen more often than you think. Our first surprise was when they were about to give him three drinks at the same time. The next surprise was when the bartender hesitated, then asked if he wanted the vodka and Jameson in the same glass.

Another tradition at Stix was Carolyn ordering a fruity, slushy drink. It would start with a big sip, followed by a nasty look on her face. After that, she would put it down and order something else. A year later, it was the same routine. A year later? You guessed it.

The first notable quotable: I'm not an alcoholic. Alcoholics have to go to class.

While talking to a couple of college guys, I learned they had a few friends at the TKE fraternity house just a block away. I'm a Teke, so we walked over and they introduced me to a couple of brothers. After giving them the password and the secret handshake, I was welcomed in. A few drinks and a few stories and it was time to catch up with my friends for the serpentine walk to the hotel.

On Friday, as usual, we boarded the boat hungover. Out on the lake, it was time to decorate. Somebody came up with the idea that we didn't need any Scotch tape to hang the Christmas lights, just run them through and around the cabinet door handles. Sounded great, until someone tried to open a cabinet door, then not so great.

Before leaving the dock, we were warned not to go past the bridge. We did. Actually I did, I was the pilot. The boat ran aground in the shallow water and jammed the prop. At that point, we thought jumping off the back of the boat and giving it a good push would get us off the sandbar, also thinking we would land in three or four feet of water. The first two guys came to an abrupt stop because it was barely a foot deep. Oh, that's why we got stuck.

Instead, it was time to break down and call the marina to tell them what we did. It was too late to come out and help us, so that's where we spent the night. The problem would cost about $1,000.

Saturday was our Christmas grab bag with the Water People, some friends who were staying in a nearby hotel and had rented a couple of small boats. "Bryce" also made an appearance that day. He would show up on one more trip.

The best photo from the trip was of drunken Carolyn dancing on the edge of the back deck, wearing a Christmas present as a hat. Luckily, somebody was paying attention. Even though the next picture in the sequence also shows her dancing on the edge of the back deck, this time she's wearing a life jacket.

On every boat trip, there was a place called the No-Mo Zone. That would be the kitchen. When Mo was single, the area near the stove was like a foreign country. She was very proud of the fact she would usually be able to boil water. "Little baby bubbles" were the words she used. We also had to explain to her pouring cereal in a bowl does not qualify as cooking. She's come a long way since then. Almost forgot, stomach and screen door.

Notable Quotables:
Who put my pajamas on me?
Dickie, can you wear something other than fishnet?
Hey, Water People, soda is for mix only.
EEEEEE. coli!
Seven twats a-twitching.
I pull a hat out of my trick every once in a while.

We are all so precious.

Boat-5 Fall of '98

Since we had been having fun and nobody had drowned, we decided to do a boat trip in September. The weather in downstate Illinois would still be OK and the lake water would still be warm, so we went for it. The theme for the weekend was "Harvest Moon," with a semiformal dance taking place Saturday night on the top deck.

An early notable quotable came from Mo. While the girls were grocery shopping Friday morning, she got in line at the store's deli. When her number was called, she ordered some turkey. Not a big deal, until the person behind the counter asked her what kind she would like. Her answer: "Huh, there's different kinds?"

When the shoppers returned, we left the dock, and I didn't dare go past the bridge. The only problem was Bryce, but that was solved when we found him hanging on the front deck (inside joke). And sometime during that first afternoon, Mo continued her two boat traditions.

Before leaving home, I got a big box of used golf balls from my friends at Hickory Hills Golf Course, so each day, after beaching the boat, a few of us would get in some practice time.

It's Saturday night and time for our semiformal dance, but a couple of problems arose during the festivities. One was serious, one not so much.

Let's start with the not-so-serious one. The premise of the dance was semiformal, so the guys were told they had to wear a shirt and tie, sport coat optional. What the girls forgot to mention was we were also supposed to wear pants. Oops.

Now, the serious one: We came real close to having our first fatality when Carolyn, decked out in a big, long taffeta dress, decided to go down the waterslide. When the dress got wet, it got heavy and she started to sink. Two of the guys dove in and dragged her to safety.

Finally, on Saturday afternoon, Spice was grounded for being too active. He apologized, saying it would never happen again. It would.

We are all so precious.

'99 Europe

On Thursday, March 11, I flew out of O'Hare Airport with my good friends Mo and Maria, landing in Milan, Italy, on Friday morning. We didn't stay, but would finish our trip there.

About a four-hour train ride got us to Locarno, spending the afternoon on the north shore of Lake Maggiore. We got lucky and found a hotel near the water. It's where Maria decided to take a nap: in our hotel room, not on the shore.

It was similar to the stop Vic and I made in '83 because with Maria awake, we rented a couple of pedalos and pedaled around the lake. Maria and I shared one while Mo went solo. After a short ride, it was time for a few drinks. A floating bar was the start of a nice, leisurely bar walk. There were only a few places to choose from, but it was still pretty good.

We had some time on Saturday, so similar continued when I brought the girls up to the Madonna del Sasso Church that overlooks the city. The first time, Vic and I did the thirty-minute uphill walk. This time, the three of us took the three-minute funicular (cable car).

A train back to Italy was next, stopping for a couple of hours in Lugano, Switzerland, where we took a walk around town. It was followed by a quick lunch break where I flipped off Swiss Tommy, our waiter. Sorry, another inside joke.

Now it's Sunday, and we were in Milan, excitedly waiting for the arrival of JD. When he got there, we grabbed the next train to Florence because Maria had access to a place from a doctor she worked with. It was a villa in the Oltrarno district, a good walk from the train station, with the second half mostly uphill after crossing the Arno River.

Walking in the front door, we immediately headed to the back door and the villa's back deck. It was huge, bigger than a two-bedroom apartment, but that wasn't the best part. The view looking down at the city of Florence was spectacular. After dinner at a local restaurant and a few drinks on our deck, we were done.

On Monday, our first full day in Florence, we got up early and went shopping. It wasn't for souvenirs, it was for stuff to stock our kitchen, and luckily, somebody brought along an Italian-English dictionary. "Whoa, that's goat cheese? No thanks." It was two o'clock before we were ready to start playing tourist. Unfortunately, most of it was spent in a light rain, but we did see the Duomo, the baptistery, and after walking up around 400 stairs to the top of the Campanile (bell tower), another great view of the city. Then it was shopping for the women and drinking for the men. It was Maria's birthday, but she didn't even party at her own party.

Tuesday was a no shopping day, with only tourist stuff allowed. The Pitti Palace was our first stop, but a couple of wrong turns got us lost. It's hard to do in Florence because the Old City isn't that big, but we found a way. Our bad luck continued when we got to the Accademia to see Michelangelo's "David." The line was around the block, so we decided lunch was the better option.

Now it's three o'clock, and the only thing we saw was the Boboli Gardens, which happened to be next to the Pitti Palace. That's right, the palace we couldn't find. We tried the Accademia again and got lucky, this time getting in after only a few minutes. After that, the guys and the girls went their separate ways, with the only question being what time the midnight buffet would start. It took place after midnight and started to remind us of the boat trips.

Wednesday was a day trip to Siena, about a forty-mile bus ride from Florence. Somehow, we were out the door by 8:30 a.m. We walked around the small city center, hung out in the main square, then got to climb the Torre del Mangia, another famous bell tower. It was almost as good as being at the top of Pisa's Leaning Tower with Vic in '83—not really.

We were back in Florence by 6:00 p.m., with our bar walk beginning at 6:01 p.m., eventually followed by . . . the midnight buffet. Yes, it was just like the boat trips.

The next morning, JD decided to take a vacation day and headed off by himself. The three of us took another early morning bus to another Tuscan town, this time, Lucca, an old medieval city encircled by a three-mile wall.

It was a pretty quick stop, so Mo and Maria went to Pisa. Having been there a few times, I took a pass and returned to Florence.

Later, with the four of us together, we went out to dinner, found a local restaurant, and we were given our own room. It held exactly four people. We never did find out if we should have been honored or embarrassed.

Another day meant another early start and another bus, this one taking us to the town of San Gimignano. It's known by some as the Manhattan of Italy because of the old medieval towers. I don't know how many were built, but fourteen of them were still around in 1999.

That night, we had an awesome dinner, which included a wild boar appetizer—true story. Then it was time to walk off our big meal, stopping, of course, at a few drinking establishments. Mom (Maria) headed home early again. She just didn't want to set a bad example for her daughter (Mo). (Remember the flight to Greece the previous year.) And this time, the midnight buffet started around 2:00 a.m. Tomorrow was gonna suck.

It's day 10, and yes, it sucked. We left our beautiful villa that morning and took an afternoon train to Venice. After hearing the story of my arrival in 1972, Mo was hoping the guy with the guitar who sang "Guantanamera" would be sitting on the steps when she walked out of the Santa Lucia train station. I think he called in sick.

It was a long search for a hotel, which only left us time for a late dinner and a few drinks. After that, it was *buona notte*.

On Sunday, the four of us did the typical tourist stuff, with Mo posing as a tour guide. She did a great job leading us through Venice's maze of streets. We're guessing the large arrows on each sign at each intersection probably helped.

After a great dinner and a mini-bar walk, we split up. Mo and I headed off together and met a couple from Istanbul at one of the stops. After telling them Turkey was on our list of places to see, they offered their help and traded email info. Five months later, northwest Turkey was hit by a strong earthquake. We wrote them and got a reply saying they were OK.

Then it was back to Milan for two nights and two dinners, in two different restaurants, both spent with relatives from my mom's side of the family. The first night, we met at a cousin's condo and took a short walk down the street. A left turn got us to a small local restaurant, where my Uncle Salvatore picked up the tab for everyone, around twelve to fourteen people.

The next night, after playing tourist during the day, the plan was the same, this time taking a right turn. The four of us agreed we should buy dinner, using my credit card and later dividing it up. During dessert, I called the waiter over and told him, "Io pago por tutti," hoping to say I would pay for everything. He understood me, gave my uncle a quick look, then turned back and told me no while giving me a wave of the finger. That's family.

Home the next day.

'99 Steph

In June, my daughter graduated from St. Francis, a Catholic grammar school in South County, St. Louis. I drove down for the graduation dinner, arriving in the early afternoon.

With plenty of time, I was "fortunate" enough to hang out with Steph and a couple of her friends while they got their hair done at a local salon. Denise, her uncle's wife, worked there and did the honors. I'm willing to bet I was the only dad who spent his afternoon that way.

At the dinner that night, Vic and I decided it would be a good idea to smuggle in some Bacardi rum. We quickly became the most popular couple there, probably because we were the only degenerates who thought to bring alcohol to a grammar school graduation.

It was a fun night, but there was one sobering moment. It happened when my daughter and six or seven of her girlfriends got together for some photos. Almost in unison, the dads groaned and shook their heads. With the girls all dressed up, it looked as if they were graduating from high school, not grammar school. If you have a daughter, you know what I'm talking about, or you will soon.

Boat-6 Summer of '99

It's July and we're back at Lake Shelbyville. The party theme this year is "the '60s," so the boat was infested with hippies and a couple of go-go dancers.

You know the routine. The early arrivals hit the bars on Thursday after spending some time at the hotel pool; the late arrivals meet up and try to catch up. A few of us decided to try a place called Ike's, around the corner from our home bar and loved their drink special. It was mixed drinks made in beer pitchers and it was cheap.

Now it's Friday morning, and we slowly left the marina. Wait till Bryce sees us—he loves us. Oh wait, we found Bryce hanging on the front deck on the fall '98 trip. By the way, Bryce is a scarecrow.

Notable Quotables:

The first one came from Brenda: "I like my fries soft and my men hard." The other girls quietly nodded in agreement.

Blow me, Mr. Spice. This was while he was getting his hair dyed on the front deck.

Do we have a can opener? No, but we have a bottle opener. Not a clue.

Reprimands were given to some of the crew because there was too much activity. They didn't learn anything from Spice on the 9/98 boat.

JD was our grill master both days and made sure the "peace sign" cheese slices were properly placed on the hamburgers as they came off the grill. He was also Saturday night's DJ, surprising everyone on the top deck when he hit the dance floor with two go-go dancers (Mo and Carolyn).

That was surprising enough, but the pictures of him clad only in Union Jack underwear were a stunner. God save the king.

And finally, we set off the smoke alarm. The weather was hot, so we ran the A/C, then did some smoking in the enclosed boat. Remember, it was the '60s. In hindsight, we should have stayed with the brownies.

We are all so precious.

BOAT-7 FALL OF '99

We decided to do another September boat trip, this time traveling to Lake Monroe, just south of Bloomington, Indiana. It's similar to Lake Shelbyville because it also came into existence with the help of the Army Corps of Engineers, but there's a difference. Monroe is a large lake with sailboats on it.

Shelbyville reminded us of a wide meandering river. The theme was *M*A*S*H*.

The first thing we noticed was our boat and its size. Yes, it does matter. I believe it came in at seventy-two feet, much bigger than what we were used to, plus its reaction time was much slower than what we were used to.

Turn the wheel, wait, then turn it a little more. When the boat finally reacted, it was too late, and the turn would be much too wide. Our reaction was to turn it hard in the other direction, so if you were sitting on the back deck, its wake looked like a big giant S. It reminded us of our walks back from the college bars in Charleston.

Here are a couple other odd things about our trip to Lake Monroe:

1. Alcohol. Drinking while boating was frowned upon, so before leaving the dock, we were lectured about being discreet. It was important to keep any beer or liquor bottles away from the front deck and off the kitchen counter because there was a good chance the water police would stop by.

2. The bathroom. For some strange reason, toilet paper wasn't allowed to be flushed down the toilet, so the used sheets had to

233

be placed in a plastic bag strategically located next to the toilet. It wasn't pretty.

Now, back to the party theme. The main decorations started with a large white sheet with a red cross painted on it, hung in our largest window, plus some cool camouflage netting draped across most of the exterior of the boat. We were hoping the water police wouldn't see us.

The cast, in costume, of course:
Hawkeye: Me
Trapper: JD
Winchester: Puddin
Lt. Dish: Mo
Frank and Hot Lips: Benny and Joon
Klinger: Spice
Spearchucker Jones: Mac

I think I've been slaked.
And now a few awards, given out by JD:

1. Bravery. For anyone who sat down in the bathroom.
2. Suds. To the idiot who put Ajax on the waterslide.
3. When do we eat? To whoever gave Mo the can opener.
4. Cold lake water. It's never this small. (me)
5. Different drinks at one time. Three (Puddin).
6. Different drinks in the same glass at the same time. Three (Puddin).
7. *E. coli.* Puddin's bloody chicken breasts at the midnight buffet.
8. Lack of personality. Anyone who worked at the Lake Monroe Marina.
9. MVS (most valuable scumbag). Easily, Puddin.

Yes, we were slaked, and yes, we are all so precious.

'99 Tiger Stadium

The 1999 baseball season was the last one for Old Tiger Stadium in Detroit. As a kid, I vaguely remember it being called Briggs Stadium. I had never been there, so on September 21, I got in my van and drove up for a game between the Tigers and the Cleveland Indians.

It was the last week for this famous old park, and I was surprised at the size of the crowd. Attendance was announced at just over 24,000 people, but that had to be tickets sold. My guess was about six or seven thousand fans.

It worked out great, because it gave me the chance to walk around and take a seat in a different spot. It reminded me of Wrigley Field, only bigger. When the game was over, I hopped on the interstate, which happened to be right next to the park, and drove home—a quick and easy road trip.

While writing this, I learned the stadium was eventually torn down in 2009, but as of 2016, the actual playing field was still there. It had been preserved and maintained by a group made up of Tiger fans and local residents from Detroit's Corktown neighborhood.

00's

2000 GREECE

Mo and I returned to Greece in May, this time with her boyfriend Nick and our friends Carolyn and Mac. The itinerary was the same as '98, starting with our flight to Athens, where we encountered a short delay while waiting for our flight to Rhodes.

When someone asked an airline employee when our flight would be arriving, this was the answer: "When it gets here." Very official. Landing in Rhodes, it was the same welcoming committee. Yes, it was the airport cats.

We found a cheap hotel in the old town area and a cheap bar whose special was "Buy one, get two free." With dusk approaching, Mac and I put the bar on hold and took a walk along the northwest edge of the city, which is also the northwest edge of the island. The plan was to get something to eat before hitting the bars that night.

After grabbing a couple of seats at an outdoor café and ordering a couple of drinks, we sat there looking at the menu, not able to make a decision. At that point, the owner sent us a platter with small portions of just about everything he had and was very gentle when it came to the bill. We both sat there, as the sun set down into the water, thinking how great this would have been if the other guy was a girl.

Later on, Mo and I brought the rookies to Down Under, the bar we almost worked at. It was just how we left it, with cute blond girls dancing on the bar, but this time there was something new. It was three men leaning back and resting their heads on the bar, trying to get a look at the girls in the short skirts. Yes, the guys were from Chicago and yes, I was one of them and yes, we are one classy group.

For our three days there, we played tourist early then partied late at

Down Under. This time, our favorite bartender was a young guy with spiked hair. His name was Tuesday, but we were never there on a Tuesday, so it was a little confusing.

Before leaving Rhodes, a funny thing happened while walking through the ancient city. Mac got a call from a client who needed some computer help, but obviously had to refuse the request. The last thing we heard was "Sorry, I'm in Greece. No really, I'm in Greece." Our guess was he lost that client.

Santorini was next, again flying, not sailing, again making our way to Oia for its "famous" sunset. Being there a second time just reinforced my opinion that it's way overrated.

We took a cruise similar to the one two years before and, with the help of a few other tourists, drank the small boat out of beer. We also took the tour of Akrotiri again. It wasn't that we were in a rut; it was because Mo and I wanted everyone else to experience what we did. We give and we give.

Naxos was next. We took the slow, relaxing ferryboat and headed to the same hotel in the town of Agios Prokopios. While walking down its small main street the first day, Carolyn got the urge to be a kid again and climbed into a police wagon. It wasn't real, it was a ride, and it was pretty funny. It got a lot funnier when the adult realized she was stuck in a ride built for a child.

The walk to the beach was the same. When you got to the sand and went left, people wore clothes. When you got to the sand and went right, people didn't.

It wasn't totally rest and relaxation like our first trip. This time, we rented a car for a day to explore the rest of the island. We tried to scale Mt. Zeus, but Nick was the only one who made the 3,200-foot hike to the cave where Zeus was born. The rest of us made it to an elevation of about 2,000 feet.

And after all our time in Greece, Mo and I encountered our first language problem. Between the two trips, it was almost thirty days, but at a restaurant off the beaten path on Naxos, which is also a little off the beaten path, it finally happened.

The problem was omelets. That's right, omelets. We stopped at a small, local restaurant, and after looking at the menu, everyone agreed they sounded good, so we all ordered one. Our waitress asked more than once, mainly in Greek, if each of us really wanted our own. Yes.

The extra questions and strange looks made sense when the first two plates were set down in front of us. The omelets were made with six eggs and meant to be eaten by two or maybe three people. Luckily, they had to make them in shifts because there were only three large frying pans in the place, and luckily, they were nice enough to cancel the other half of the order. Isn't travel great?

One more thing before leaving Naxos: Did you hear the one about the guy who walks into a bar with a horse? No joke this time. A guy with a horse did walk into the bar we were at and didn't raise any eyebrows, except ours. Yes, both of them were regulars.

On to Mykonos. For the second time, we decided to skip Super Paradise Beach. We were there to go to the small island of Delos, which Mo and I missed in '98. It's one of the great archeological sites in the Mediterranean and only accessible by boat. It's also day trips only. Don't tell anyone, but I did take a small rock from the island.

One more relaxing ferryboat ride got us to the port city of Piraeus, followed by a short cab ride to Athens. We spent two days there, again seeing a lot of the things Mo and I saw two years before. This time, after playing tourist, we were able to end each day on our hotel's roof, relaxing by the pool.

Home safe.

BOAT-8 JULY 2000

It's Thursday, July 6, and we were back in Illinois, doing the preliminary drinking at our hotel in Charleston. Sound familiar? When should we start walking to the college bars? When we're over the limit to drive.

It was around 10:00 p.m. at Stix when Spice declared he was trashed. The bar's special that night was Budweiser "bottles as big as your head" (60 oz.), so we'll go with that. Buff's official time of death was 10:35. At 10:36, Drunis was born. Who the hell is Drunis? You'll hear more about him later.

I was sitting at the end of the bar when I mentioned to the young guy next to me how difficult it was to get a drink. His reply? "How do you think I feel? The bartender is my roommate." It was time to go to Ike's. We were looking forward to the special they ran the previous summer. It was the mixed drinks served in beer pitchers. Fortunately, or unfortunately, they didn't exist anymore, so we ended the night at Marty's, then took the long, serpentine walk back to the hotel.

While on the boat, we had two rules: (1) Never go to bed hungry. (2) Never go to bed sober. The rule also applied to Thursday nights at the hotel.

It's Friday morning, and we made it to the marina on time, then spent a very quiet day on the lake. Once we dropped anchor, it was a long walk up to the top deck. I'm pretty sure there was a party theme, but nobody seems to remember and nobody has found any pictures. That was pretty much it.

On Saturday, the water people arrived and turned two of our crew. Activities other than eating and drinking were frowned upon, so when Spice and Drunis went waterskiing, they were sent to the hole for insubordination. They needed to think about what they did. What they

242

did was cross the line to the dark side. May they rest in peace with the others that came before them: Sean, Kirk, Dan, Trish, Brenda, Cathy, Mac, Julie, Tim, and Big Don.

Notable Quotables:

Monopoly, monogamy, mahogany. Huh?

Let your mind go and your ass will follow.

Bernie, that's not your husband. That's Puddin.

Mo: I'm sitting in a wet spot.

Now it's late Saturday night, which means *A Fish Called Wanda*, followed by the midnight buffet, closely followed by John Valby when we woke up. Remember, he's our annual hangover cure on the morning ride back to the marina. We are all so precious.

2000 Titanic

In 1995, five years after our divorce, Vic and Steph moved to St. Louis. Fourth grade was Steph's first year there, completing grammar school and four years of high school before attending Loyola University in Chicago for her freshman and sophomore years. A year and a half later, she graduated from the U of Missouri.

In July, after her first year of high school, she came up to Chicago to hang out with me for the weekend. For her sanity, she got the OK to bring her friend and classmate Megan along for the ride. The girls were fifteen years old.

They did their research before leaving home and decided the place to go was the Museum of Science and Industry to see the *Titanic* exhibit. Not my first choice, but I wasn't going to argue with two teenage girls.

We drove there in my van, which the girls immediately named the pimpmobile. Wait a minute, how old are you?

As it turned out, the exhibit was worth the trip. As each person entered, they were given a boarding pass with the name of an actual passenger. Looking at our tickets, Megan and I discovered we were husband and wife. I quickly explained it was only at the museum, not in real life.

At the end of the tour, there was one more thing. A wall leading to the exit listed every passenger that had sailed on the *Titanic* and what happened to them. There were two categories. You either Lived or Died. My pretend wife made sure I saw where my name was. She lived. I wasn't so lucky.

2000 Ixtapa

It's November, and we had a seven-day trip from McMahon's to an all-inclusive in Ixtapa, on the west coast of Mexico. Leading up to it, Roger and Ron, who organized it, made a bet to see who could lose the most weight. I don't remember what the stakes were, but I do remember it being a wake-up call.

I didn't join their contest, but it was time to lose some weight. After I searched the Internet, a no-carb diet jumped out. A couple of people told me picking the Atkins diet was a good move. It was. Over the next couple of months, I lost about twenty-five pounds and have kept it off to this day.

My Friday night shift at the bar ended early Saturday morning and we were leaving Saturday morning, so sleep wasn't on the schedule. I lived two blocks from the bar, so my friends Mo and JD came over and waited while I grabbed a quick shower. A rumor had been going around about my plan to wear a thong at the resort, so not surprisingly, my "friends" started searching for it. Remember, I said a quick shower; they didn't have enough time.

We checked into our resort, and the partying began. Even without sleep, I made it through most of the night until my roommate found me passed out, face down on my bed—not in my bed, on my bed.

The next day, we went down to the front desk and complained about our room. I don't remember what the problem was, but they quickly gave us keys to another room. Funny thing was they never asked for the keys to the original room. That meant two single guys had access to two rooms. No, it didn't help as much as we thought.

By the second night, people had begun calling our place the Compound because we had to present an ID at the guardhouse to reenter the grounds.

There wasn't much to do except lie around and eat and drink, which is fine if you're there for the weekend, but not for seven days.

Early on, I remember a small group of friends sitting on the beach one night. We had been playing tourist in Europe for a few years, and we weren't used to doing nothing. That's when somebody came up with a great idea: Why don't we meet back here tomorrow and do nothing? OK.

Instead, I rented a bike and hit some of the trails in the area, vowing to do it a couple of more times. It didn't happen. There were always two excuses available: I was drinking, or I was hungover.

That night, my friend Diane and I left the compound. Walking by the restaurant next to us, we noticed a mariachi band playing in a large beer garden in the front of the building. We walked in and grabbed a small table, just in time for last call. There were maybe twenty people left, so the staff moved everybody to a couple of big tables and started cleaning the rest of the beer garden. The band then played another thirty minutes just for us. Our stroll turned into a great time, so we decided to come back the next night, earlier and with a bigger group.

Diane and I put the word out, and about twenty-five people showed up. The band loved us and played to our tables for a good portion of the night. I have two pictures in my possession from that night, both involving a tambourine: (1) Carolyn playing one while leading a conga line, (2) me playing one on the singer's head. He must have liked it, because he's laughing his ass off in the photo.

Carolyn and her boyfriend had come down separate from our group. Since their room had a balcony the size of a small apartment, we thought it would be a good idea to have the mariachi band play there. I returned to the restaurant, and in my best high school Spanish, I was able to work out a deal. Yes, they spoke some English.

Their plan was to take a long break and walk over to the Compound. When it was time, I went next door and accompanied them back. When they walked up to the entrance, the security guards did a double take, first looking at them, then at me. That's when one of the members of the band spoke up and, in his best English, explained they were "doctors on emergency." The guards shook their heads, everyone had a good laugh, and we were waved in.

There were about twenty people on the balcony and a lot more hanging out at ground level. Remember the thong? That's right; it made its debut, on me, on the balcony. The reaction was a lot of groans and a few screams, but I did get my ass pinched—only once. She'll remain nameless.

The band played for about twenty minutes, then a few of us sat down and tried to figure out a way to smuggle them back to the United States so they could play in McMahon's beer garden. Unfortunately, we had to leave them in Ixtapa.

Home hungover.

2001 ROME

In March, twelve of us went to Rome for a week, including Steph, who got to go with me for her sixteenth birthday. That meant my daughter got to hang out with eleven immature adults. I booked three apartments just outside Vatican City.

Working online before we left, I discovered Wednesday, our first full day there, was the day to see the pope in St. Peter's Square. I ordered our tickets through the Church of Santa Susanna, a couple miles from the Vatican, picking them up that morning.

Once a week, the square would turn into a giant rally, with big cheers going up as each group or parish was announced. A few of us grabbed a spot off to the side near a barrier and got lucky. When Pope John Paul II took a short tour around the square in his popemobile, he was not more than ten feet from us.

One night we decided to hang out in our building—actually, on our building. With a couple of drinks in hand, we camped out on the roof. Remember, we were just outside the Vatican, so sitting there and looking at everything lit up, including the Dome of St. Peter's, was pretty cool.

The next day, a few of us toured the Sistine Chapel. This trip was even more amazing then '83 with Vic because the paintings had been cleaned slowly and painstakingly. What I saw was a vibrant mix of colors that had been hidden for hundreds of years.

After that, some of us returned to St. Peter's Square, where a couple of interesting things happened.

1. Mike and Greg walked into St. Peter's Basilica. After a couple of steps and a quick look at the interior, one of them blurted out,

"Holy fuck!" It wasn't loud, but the man standing next to them happened to be a Catholic priest. His reaction: "I've never heard it described in quite that manner." They apologized a couple of times, and the three of them shared a laugh. The priest then made the sign of the cross and quickly walked away—amazingly, no lightning.

2. Steph and I started talking to a priest near the entrance to the basilica. She was hoping to find someone that could direct her to the Cor Jesu Convent. Cor Jesu is the name of the girls' Catholic high school she attended, and the plan was to make a lot of brownie points back home by visiting the convent in Rome. Unfortunately, there were a few convents with that name, or something similar to it, and the priest didn't know which one was affiliated with her school.

I was able to add this to my list of "small world" stories because the priest was from Belleville, Illinois, maybe twenty-five miles from South County, St. Louis. He laughed when Steph told him where she went to school because he had actually been there a few times.

Dinner that night was at a neighborhood restaurant, with all of us at one long table. After reading one of the drink menus, somebody mentioned Malibu rum was on the list. Immediately, my daughter spoke up, explaining Parrot Bay rum tasted better. Eyebrows raised and everyone turned to look at the source. Then they turned the opposite way to look at me. My response: "She lives with her mother."

Soon after taking our order, the waitress returned. Someone had ordered a Long Island iced tea, and she had a question about the ingredients. Again, my daughter came to the rescue. She called her over, talked for a minute, then accompanied her back to the bar to make sure they got it right—yes, my sixteen-year-old.

Steph spent her first two years of college at Loyola University in Chicago, and I remember talking to her about the dangers of binge drinking. She told me not to worry. As a teenager at home, Mom would let her have a drink or two at family parties and never made a big deal of it. And remember, I have a picture of her drinking a glass of wine at dinner with relatives in Milan, Italy, when she was nine.

I've traveled a lot in Europe and have come to the conclusion Americans are wound way too tight when it comes to alcohol and to nudity. I went through the nudity thing in 1998, and again in 2000. I would tell people how I hung out (literally) on nude beaches on two separate trips to the Greek Islands. Americans freak out. Europeans yawn. And when you see an obnoxious drunk in Europe, chances are it's an American.

One of the stops on this trip was off the beaten path. It was to the Church of Santa Maria della Concezione dei Cappuccini, which translates to the Church of Our Lady of the Conception of the Capuchin. Did you get all that?

There's an immense crypt underneath the church that holds the bones of almost four thousand friars who were buried there from around 1500 to 1800 AD. Their bones and their skulls were used to decorate the walls and ceilings, with some of the skeletons dressed in their own robes. It's hard to describe how elaborate the crypt is, and hard to imagine the devotion it took to place the thousands of bones into such intricate designs. Seeing is believing.

When exiting the crypt, you can't miss a plaque on the wall. It reads, "What you are now, we once were, and what we are now, you shall be." Kinda creepy?

That same day, JD got hit on by some Gypsies. No, they weren't after him; they were after his wallet. He ended up leaning against a car, with his hands guarding his pockets, so they gave up and ran away.

When you travel in Europe, especially in the south, be aware of your surroundings. Distraction is the key. If somebody drops a baby in front of you, let it fall. The odds it's a real child are about one in a million. Sometimes it's tough, because our first instinct is to help, but that's when it happens. With all the commotion and people in close quarters worrying about the "baby," somebody is going to bump into you and go for your wallet.

With our vacation coming to an end, Steph, my sister Nancy, and I took a train out to Ostia Antica for the afternoon. I did the same day trip with Vic in '83, this time skipping the topless beach and focusing on the Roman ruins. The photo op of the day is Steph posing as some Roman goddess on the top of an ancient pillar.

And finally, for last call, the guys did a bar crawl. Pretty uneventful, but we did run into Jesse's twin. At one of the stops, I got a picture of a guy who could have been the twin brother of my Lake Placid travel partner. He denied everything.

Wait, one more thing. There was a man outside the Colosseum dressed as a Roman gladiator, so everyone grabbed their camera for this photo op. Seconds later, everyone stopped when our gladiator sat down and started talking on his cell phone.

Then home.

Boat-9 2001

This year, the boat became a '50s diner, but not before our traditional Thursday night in Charleston. At Stix, Puddin got his usual three drinks, and yes, Carolyn ordered her annual slushy and didn't drink it. We had three new recruits on this trip: Tracey, Trixie and Lisa. I don't remember where the inspiration came from, but on Saturday evening, Tracey and Lisa tried to do the sixty shots of beer in sixty minutes. Trixie took a pass. Both woke up to see another day.

Here are some Notable Quotables:
Vodka is our friend.
Lisa: Stevie Nicks? He's still alive?
I only smoke when I drink a lot. So, what's that, three packs a day?
They let us have this boat by ourselves?
What time is the midnight buffet?
Carolyn: "George, what were you thinking?" George: "I wasn't."

Sunday: Puddin-Slept   Stu-Slept   Mimi-Drank   Carolyn-Drank
   Spice-Cuddled JD-Drank   Stu-Drank   Bernie-Drank
Trixie-(See Spice)   Me-Drank and Drove   Tracey/Lisa-Coma

From JD: What's wrong with us?
A-Alcohol/Assholes
B-Booze/Betty Ford
C-Cocktails/Chicken
D-Drinks/Derelicts
E-Excess

F-Food/Fuck you
G-Grill/Grey Goose
H-Hangovers/Hang-ups
I-Insanity
J-Jameson
K-Ketel One
L-Liquor/Lick me
M-Meat
N-Nuts
O-Obscene
P-Passed out
Q-Queezy/Queeny
R-Rum
S-Stix
T-'Til we quiver
U-Unique
V-Valby
W-Water/Waves
X-X-rated
Z-Zzzzz . . .

1-Brain between us
2-Bottles of red wine
3-Days of . . .
4-Bottles of Boone's Farm
5-Whole chickens
6-1/2 gallons of vodka
7- Different meats
8-Hours of grilling
9-Funny movies
10-Coolers
11-Passengers
12-Nasty hangovers

We are all so precious.

2001 COLUMBUS PRE-50

It's early November, so JD and I drove to Columbus, Ohio, on a scouting mission. In two weeks, a group of friends would be taking a motor home there for a Blackhawks game against the Blue Jackets and my fiftieth birthday celebration. Saturday's schedule was college football in the afternoon, with Purdue in town to play Ohio State, followed by Bob Dylan that night at Nationwide Arena.

It was a casual two-mile stroll to the football game up High Street, where a lot of drinking establishments were located. The street was definitely given the right name.

We saw quite a few signs advertising a special I had never seen before. They read, "Kegs and Eggs." On game days, the bars would open at 7:00 a.m. for breakfast, so a good percentage of the student body was pretty juiced by game time.

After the Buckeyes beat Purdue 35-7, it was time for our fact-finding mission. On our walk to the hotel, it was one drink at every bar that was on our way or in our way, and it mattered. The goal was to take diligent notes so we could find a good place for my fiftieth birthday party.

And here are the (diligent?) notes I remembered to write down:

Cornerstone—piano man

Skully's—finally some food

Panini—giant beers

Downtown Connection—Cabana Boy rum (yuck)

Spirits—cans of Busch

Basement Bar—real cheap, but only one

And finally, Elevator's, just around the corner from our hotel, which would become our home base in two weeks.

We almost missed one bar because it didn't have a sign, but a quick glance in the window made us slam on the brakes and walk in. It was Mike's, a local tavern with a good feel to it. We quickly decided it would be the final stop in two weeks. We even allowed ourselves a second drink.

After a quick stop at the room, it was time for the concert. On the walk over, Tapatios, a Mexican restaurant, got in our way. I drink Bacardi and Diet Coke with a lime. I gotta have a lime, but when the bartender came back with my drink, he told me they were out of them. Unacceptable, and what are the chances of it happening in a Mexican restaurant?

He then explained there were limes, but he had been busy and didn't have a chance to cut them. I stayed calm, then asked for a knife and a cutting board. All he had to do was cut one so I knew how they liked them and I would do the rest. After filling a big container, our drinks were free until we left for the concert.

When it was over, we headed a couple of miles south of downtown to German Village, an ethnic neighborhood listed on the National Register of Historic Places. It was a short cab ride.

Our driver dropped us off at a place called Max and Erma's. It seemed like a good spot to change the menu and have a couple of German beers, but it didn't happen. Not one in the place, so it was a quick stop. On our walk through the neighborhood to the next bar, we ran into a bachelorette party. The bride-to-be was wearing a dress with pieces of candy that needed to be bitten off, and we were just the guys for the job.

Later, on our way back to the hotel, this time on foot, we met up with who we thought was the same bachelorette party. I went up to the bride, gave her a kiss on the cheek, then started looking for more candy to bite off. Oops, wrong girl. Luckily, she had a sense of humor once I explained what I was doing.

After that, we made one more stop while trying to find our hotel. It was at a Buffalo Wild Wings, probably because it was one of those "it's in our way" places. It did have a familiar ring to it: no limes.

We made it safely to our room, then safely home the next day.

2001 COLUMBUS, MY FIFTIETH

Two weeks after the scouting mission with JD, I rented an RV, and our group invaded Columbus. The hockey game was on Friday, November 23. I turned fifty the next day.

The six-hour drive was highlighted by a pyramid made of Absolut bottles. Good job, Puddin (George). While waiting to check in at our hotel, the pyramid king couldn't get to his room fast enough and took a piss in a hallway around the corner from the main desk. After getting to our rooms, we immediately left them and took a long walk, in a light snow, around the corner to Elevator's.

Puddin was already speaking in tongues from his Absolut attack, so the warning from the waiter about his steak being served on a hot plate went on deaf ears. Ouch! A few minutes later, he went on a rant about two short people sitting near us. He didn't understand why they should be allowed in public because they were small and hard to understand. This is what happens when you mix beer, vodka, and Jameson.

Finishing his food and his rant, he decided to take the short walk back to the hotel. The flurries had turned into a heavy snow, which must have confused him. We left about thirty minutes later, and everybody made it back before he did. Then everybody, including Puddin, made it to the game and saw the Hawks and Columbus play to a 2-2 tie. A couple of drinks in a local establishment and we were done.

Yes, Friday was a long day, but Saturday was a free day, so we rallied early. A Saturday afternoon in autumn means college football. A Saturday afternoon in late November means Ohio State vs. Michigan. We found a spot in a big bar and grill and picked up where we left off the previous night, except for Tina, my new girlfriend, who slept in.

When the game ended, it was time for her to catch up and start playing catch-up. The short walk to the bar was uneventful, except for a homeless guy who decided to be her chaperone for a couple of blocks and, hopefully, a couple of bucks. Sorry, no tip for you.

Ohio State won 26-20, upsetting the eleventh-ranked team in the country. "North 'til you smell it, West 'til you step in it."

The vast majority of customers were Ohio State students, and the most popular cheer of the day was "Set them free!" The guys should be able to figure that one out. It was then I decided my daughter wasn't going away to college—just kidding.

After a couple of quick stops, it was time for Mike's, the tavern I picked for my party. The place had a long bar, so we moved to the back and hooked up with a bunch of college kids still celebrating the Buckeyes' victory. The regulars quickly migrated to the front.

George and I made friends with a couple of coeds, I'm guessing because we were all drunk. While dancing with his new friend, whom I think was of Korean descent, George told her, "Me so horny, we make love long, long time." Everybody waited for the punch, or at least the slap, but a miracle took place. Her response? "Oh, you're so cute." It was followed by a big hug, but that was it.

A few minutes later, it was time for me and my coed to consummate our relationship. We ended up in the missionary position on top of one of those old bowling machines, and I wasn't slapped either. Hey, at least it was my birthday.

After that, we hooked up with Frank, the bartender, who bonded with Puddin so they could do some shots of Jameson. Soon after that, Frank started hugging, kissing, and dancing with any girl in reach. Since he was away from the bar, George and I decided to begin our Columbus bartending careers.

Maybe a minute later, a young guy walked up and asked for a Coke. Coke? You must mean rum and Coke. No? Oh, Jack and Coke? No? Sorry, can't help you. The guy walked away shaking his head.

Maureen, a good friend and travel partner, wasn't able to make the trip, so seeing her walking into Mike's that night was awesome. At the last minute, she was able to fly out late Saturday afternoon and spend the night: with us, not with me.

Watching me and Puddin in action, the girls decided it was time for them to give it a shot. They spotted a cute guy from the same college group, but there was a problem. It was his ensemble. He was wearing a pair of bright pink pants, so they took a pass.

She sat there like a spider waiting to pounce. As soon as Pookie (JD) was alone, she made her move and slid over next to him. Pookie, being a one-woman man, couldn't forget he had just professed his undying love to his sweetheart, who will remain nameless. He sent the beautiful blonde back to her seat and gave his true love a big kiss. He then ordered a double because, in reality, his sweetheart didn't exist. The beautiful blonde? She wasn't very beautiful and was in desperate need of some dental work.

Near the end of the night, we learned Frank, the bartender, had been on the wagon for over a year. Everyone felt bad, hoping we weren't the reason he fell off. A couple of regulars came over and told us not to worry, explaining it was because of some other issues in his life. Even so, it was a kind of a bittersweet end to an otherwise hysterical trip.

We left Columbus the next day and the ride home through Ohio was slow because of the snow. While driving the RV, I turned to JD, who was in the passenger seat, and asked if my memory was playing tricks on me. Did I really hump a young girl on the bowling machine the previous night?

He gave me a funny look, nodded yes, then looked down at Tina, who was sitting on the floor between the seats. She looked up at me and nodded in agreement. A dirty look was also included. A few minutes later, I reminded my girlfriend I saw her fall off a bar stool at Mike's. It was a draw.

Home safe.

2002 JD's Fiftieth

Two months after my fiftieth, it was JD's turn, but the party's location was a little different. In January, eight of us (JD, Mo, Carolyn, Stu and Bernie, Margie, Denise, and I) went to Las Vegas.

At my birthday bash in November, a cute college boy caught the eye of the girls in our group because he was wearing pink pants. As a tribute to him, Mo and Carolyn got dressed up one night in their own version of pink pants so JD wouldn't feel slighted.

The Rat Pack Tribute Show was on our schedule one night, and everyone went, except me. Earth, Wind & Fire was playing at the Paris Hotel, and I had to see them.

My walk took me past the Aladdin, where the TV show *Alias* was filming an episode. I found a production assistant and asked if they needed any help. I thought working on a show in Las Vegas would be a cool addition to my library of work as an extra. He did a quick check, then told me everyone had shown up. Oh, well.

I walked into the Paris Hotel, bought a ticket, and had a few drinks. My seat was twelfth row center, and the rum got me ready to dance with some hot black women, but there was a problem. The crowd was basically made up of middle-aged white folk. The guy sitting next to me could have been me. I didn't get my wish, but did enjoy the concert.

The next day, our group went to the Bonnie Springs Ranch and Ghost Town, a family-oriented tourist spot where I got some good pictures. One is of the Evil One (Mo) sitting in a wooden casket. This is the same woman who requested 6-6-6 for her PIN number at her job. I do have a picture of her on a Donald Duck ride, so there's hope.

And once again, we have a picture of Carolyn on a kid's ride. On the plus side, she didn't get stuck like she did in the kid's car in Naxos, Greece, in 2000.

We also took a three-hour tour on Lake Mead, which included Hoover Dam. Not positive, but I think there was a bar on the boat.

Then home.

2002 Boston-Harrisburg

In March, I went online and bought two tickets to a Red Sox game. It was time for my pilgrimage to Fenway Park. I met a woman from Connecticut a few months earlier and our plan was to meet in Boston for the game. Yeah, she canceled, but it turned out to be a good thing.

I slept in my van on the drive east, arriving in Boston early on April 29 and got a spot at a youth hostel two miles from the park. It was $27 for a bunk bed and a locker. Not bad, but it cost me $30 to park the van overnight, so basically, I paid $27 for a shower.

With two tickets, I used the first one for batting practice. The place was empty, so I was able to walk around and get a good feel for the park. While standing in the lower boxes down the third base line, I asked an usher if he could snap a photo of me with the Green Monster in the background. He took a great picture.

After that, I took a little tour of the area, using the second ticket to reenter the park for the game. My seat was in the centerfield bleachers; first row, section thirty-seven, looking down at the bullpen. Baltimore beat the Sox, 5-3.

The next day, I played tourist for a few hours, then drove about seven hours to Harrisburg, Pennsylvania, found a truck stop just outside the city, and slept in my van.

On May 1, I went to see the Harrisburg Senators play the Reading Phillies at Riverside Stadium in a minor-league baseball game. Why? Because Matt, my ex-wife's little brother, played for the Senators, the Double-A affiliate of the Montreal Expos. They come from a big family, with Vicky being the oldest and Matt the youngest, separated by twenty-two years.

During batting practice, I got the attention of one of his teammates, who was able to get Matt's attention, which gave us some time to hang out.

When the game ended, he took a bat, signed it, and passed it around to whoever was left in the dugout. I still have the bat and the program, but I never really checked the names until I started working on this book.

It's tough to read someone's signature on a round bat, but most of the players that signed it also wrote their uniform number. After cross-checking the names and numbers with the program, I was pleasantly surprised to find the names of Brandon Phillips and Cliff Lee.

It was another cheap trip. After paying $57 for a bed and a parking spot, it was only $20 for the two tickets in Boston because it was half-price Monday. My ticket in Harrisburg cost $7. Gas was my biggest expense, with alcohol coming in a distant second.

2002 STEPH

In late April, during my daughter's junior year at Cor Jesu High School, their class trip was . . . you guessed it: Chicago. There were five or six buses of Catholic schoolgirls, some moms, and a few nuns. I met them at Sears Tower and joined the tour for the rest of the day.

Chicago's Art Institute was next. On the way there, I broke out some pictures of Steph when she lived in Chicago. She freaked out and tried to hide, which is hard to do on a school bus. Anyway, I went easy on her. The pictures were cute, not embarrassing.

At the Art Institute, I became a tour guide, but not in the museum. Some of the moms and some of the girls needed to get their shopping fix, so we snuck out a side door and headed to Michigan Avenue. Nobody missed us.

Our last stop was dinner at the Rain Forest Café. The girls were moving around, taking pictures with different friends, and just before a group photo in which I was included, one of the girls ran over and sat on my lap. I tapped her on the shoulder and asked how old she was. Her response: "Seventeen." My response: "Get off." She knew exactly what I meant.

The next day, I met them again, this time at Chicago's Shedd Aquarium. After that, they headed home.

BOAT-10 SUMMER OF 2002

We're back at Lake Shelbyville, but we decided to change it up a bit and rented some cabins near the marina. That meant we did our drinking on Thursday in the town of Shelbyville, not Charleston. Drinking on the lake would start, as usual, on Friday, not long after leaving the dock.

Thursday night started at the Spigot, where our first round of nine drinks cost $15. Not surprisingly, after a couple of stops, including one for dinner, we finished the night there. We made it safely to our cabins, but nobody seemed to remember the mud we trudged through until looking at our shoes the next morning.

On Friday, while boarding the boat, a big thank you went out to Bernie for helping the two hungover women (Mo/Brenda) responsible for the grocery shopping. There was also a reprimand directed at me for keeping Mike and Mo awake late into the night. "Tina, hold on to the chair." I was told that was a quote. Sorry, guys.

We left the dock around 11:00 a.m., and Brenda redeemed herself with something called strata, an awesome breakfast casserole of eggs, sausage, and cheese, plus a French-toast casserole, which set us up for a long day of drinking. Then it was time to decorate while we were still sober.

The theme was "Mexican fiesta," with Stu, our Polish chef, providing us with a great mango salsa, followed by some queso fungus provided by Tina. I remember the salsa, but have no clue what the queso fungus was.

On Saturday, Mike unveiled one of his toys. It was a very small boat, steered by remote control, so Mo opened a shot delivery service. No alcohol was harmed during the day.

Here are some Notable Quotables:

I thought you were coming through the ceiling.

Stu, thanks for helping me with my pants.

Brenda, I have always wanted to play with your maracas.

Remember the noise Sean's body made when he used the slide without wetting it down?

What do you do on the boat all day?

Now, it's Sunday, and time for our annual hangover cure. Yes, John Valby came to the rescue. Had we been hydrating properly, we might not have needed him, but at the end of the trip, our inventory consisted of one bottle of beer and one case of Gatorade.

Special thanks go out to

Mo—for not making Mike stay up to watch *A Fish Called Wanda*.

Brenda—for her awesome breakfast.

Brian—for bringing the Box of Fun, a giant box of snacks.

Tina—for the sombreros, and maybe the queso fungus.

Me—for the festive decorations.

Puddin—for his meat. Steaks and chops, not that meat.

Stu—for his mango salsa.

Bernie—for helping two drunks do the grocery shopping.

Mike—for the generous use of his boat.

Carolyn and Tracey—for gracing the JD Hilton, his tent on the top deck.

We are all so precious.

2002 MATT—WRIGLEY/ MILWAUKEE

On July 22, Matt was called up to the majors by the Montreal Expos, and they were coming to Chicago on September 9 for three games. On Tuesday the 10th, most of his family made the trip from St. Louis to see him play at Wrigley Field. I went too.

The park is equipped with some private rooms under the grandstand. It's an area where players can meet up with family and friends after the game, so we all went down to one of the rooms to hang out with Matt.

My ex-mother-in-law, now the proud mother of a Major League ballplayer, was a riot. She kept putting programs, baseballs, and anything else that wasn't nailed down, in front of him so he could autograph them. The funny thing was a good portion of them were meant for me. We tried to stop her, or at least slow her down, but she was out of control, in a good way.

The next day, I was back at Wrigley for another afternoon game. I made a point of getting there early with the hope of seeing Matt again, so once inside the park, I headed for the Expos' dugout. Seconds later, so did an usher.

After showing him my ticket, which didn't exactly match the area I was standing in, I got lucky. Before asking me to move along, I got to tell him how my ex-wife's little brother had just been called up to the Major Leagues and, at that very moment, was out in right field shagging fly balls.

He only hesitated for a second or two, then gave me the OK to stay, figuring the chances of me making up a story like that were pretty slim. A couple of minutes later, it was Matt's turn in the batting cage, so as he

266

came in from the outfield, I gave him a yell. He looked over, spotted me, then said to stay right where I was because he would be able to spend a few minutes after he got done hitting.

By coincidence, my brother and his two sons had tickets to the same game. At the time, the younger of the two was announcing baseball games at his high school, so he was the one who got to come down, meet Matt, and get his autograph.

Three weeks later on Saturday, August 10, I went to Milwaukee with my girlfriend, Tina. We spent the night drinking at a few places on Water Street and along the River Walk, then went to a Brewers game on Sunday afternoon. The reason was to see Matt again.

Before the game, we walked down to the Expos' dugout, got a player's attention, and asked if he could find the rookie. Seconds later, Matt popped up, and he was able to hang out for a couple of minutes. He didn't play that day, but five days later, hit his first major league home run against the San Diego Padres. After the game, it was a short drive back to Chicago, checking into the Cass Hotel. Its location was great because we were across the street from Pizzeria Uno, a famous Chicago pizza place that opened in 1943. We were also across the street from a bus stop for the free shuttle that runs to Navy Pier. We hopped on, got to the pier, and took a cruise on Lake Michigan.

Everybody on the boat talked about what a beautiful city it was, especially looking back from the water, and everybody on the boat was from somewhere else. That meant Tina and I became the unofficial tour guides—still waiting for our paychecks.

On Monday, after a little shopping and a couple of museums, it was time for a night game at Wrigley against the Houston Astros.

When it was over, it was time for a few drinks. I had a friend at a local bar who always took care of me, so that was our first stop. It wasn't often, but when I was there, drinks were free. Luckily for my liver, I wasn't a season ticket holder.

The bar had a couple of batting cages on the second floor, so Tina said bring 'em on. Surprisingly, she didn't embarrass herself. That would happen later in the women's bathroom. While sitting, she leaned forward to pick up something, she dropped, but hit her head on the jagged edge of the toilet paper dispenser when she sat up. It drew blood. Who knew toilet paper dispensers could be so dangerous?

A couple more stops and it was time to get on the el for our ride to the hotel. Tina tried to talk me out of it, but we got off the train one stop early, leaving us about a half-mile walk. It was still hot out, so I took my shirt off, then convinced her to do the same.

We left for home the next morning, and that's when she remembered her shirtless walk.

Boat-11 Summer of 2003

Mardi Gras was the theme this July, but it was time for a change of venue, so we headed to the Mississippi River near La Crosse, Wisconsin. It would be the weirdest boat trip, starting on the drive up, when we witnessed a huge car fire near Hampshire, Illinois. It would also be the last boat trip.

The marina's schedule was different from what we were used to. On the previous trips, we would leave the dock in the morning and have hours before even thinking about beaching the boat for the night. This time, we left the dock around 7:00 p.m.

The "fun" began as we got out into the middle of the river. We weren't ready for the Mississippi. The only time we experienced a current was on the Illinois River for Boat 1 and Boat 2, and it was pretty slow. Two minutes into this trip, with people waving at us from the dock, we got our first call from the marina, wanting to know if we knew what we were doing.

We got our act together, found a place we liked, then tried to beach the boat. After scraping the side of the boat next to us, we headed back out on the river. A few minutes later, the current came into play again. This time, with no other boats near us, we ended up sideways under a bunch of low overhanging trees. That's when we got our second call from the marina—not a good start.

We got out from under the trees to a spot we hoped wouldn't draw any attention, but we were still parked sideways. At this point, it didn't matter because it was time for dinner, which consisted mainly of "dancing chickens" on the grill, which was a puppet show put on by Stu, followed by the same "drunk chickens," now cooked in cans. Don't ask me. It's what I was told.

Then it was time to move to the rooftop deck. It was awesome, with a big bar and a big hot tub. Brian was the first to get naked, which was odd; usually it's me.

We were awakened early Saturday morning by the marina, this time, in person. Evidently, someone noticed our sideways park job and called it in using the phone number posted on the side of the boat. It was reprimand #3 in just over twelve hours—amazing, since a good portion of our time was spent asleep.

It's also when we discovered our near-empty hot tub. Because of the current and our sideways park job, the boat had been jostled around, and quite a bit of the water had splashed out. To refill it, Mike and Brian ran a hose down to the river and, somehow, got water up to the top deck and into the tub. It didn't take long before someone named it the the Petri Dish.

So after a late start, we eventually cruised about twenty-five miles up and down the Mississippi. No boats were damaged that day. We even docked the boat correctly, which meant we didn't get a call from the marina.

One very cool event did take place on the top deck just before dinner. Mike had thrown a fishing line down into the water, then a few minutes later, asked Mo to reel it in. After pulling it up, she discovered an engagement ring attached to the hook. Luckily, none of the fish in the area found it attractive.

Easily, the oddest thing that happened on the trip was what didn't happen—no Valby! The other scheduling difference came on Sunday, returning to the marina much later than we were used to, which meant a late dinner and a late drive home. When asked what we ate, all Tina remembers is wearing a bib. I don't even remember stopping.

Yes, this would be our last boat trip, and yes, we are all so precious.

2003 STL

When the hockey schedule came out, I put together a trip from McMahon's to St. Louis for a Hawks/Blues game on Saturday, November 1. Amtrak was our mode of transportation, and the Drury Inn was our hotel, a couple of blocks from Union Station, arriving that afternoon. I didn't know it at the time, but it was the last trip I would ever run from there.

With a few hours before the game, we did a little bar crawl in Soulard, a predominantly black neighborhood just south of downtown. You go there for a couple of reasons. The first one is the music. There are plenty of bars and restaurants, many of them serving up some great live blues and jazz. Since the mid-nineties, the Mardi Gras there has developed into one of the best around. The other reason? If it's not Mardi Gras, there aren't any tourists.

At each stop, I would try to talk to an employee with some authority and tell them about Hurricane Gumbo, a zydeco band from Chicago's southwest suburbs. I worked with Kenny, one of the band members, and he was hoping they could get hired to play there during Mardi Gras. He gave me a handful of their CDs and their business cards, which I would leave at every establishment.

As it got closer to game time, everyone started finishing up and heading to the arena—well, almost everyone. There were more CDs to pass out, so I continued my quest and, before I knew it, missed the entire game.

Finally running out of bars and CDs, it seemed like a good idea to walk, a little drunk, back to my hotel. I didn't get very far before a St. Louis police officer pulled his car over to ask me where the hell I was going. I pointed toward the Drury Inn and told him it was my final destination. It was over a mile away, plus I still had to get out of the neighborhood, walk under a couple of interstate highways, and walk over some railroad tracks.

He told me to get in the car, but I hesitated and asked why. When he assured me I wasn't being arrested, I got in, and he drove me to the hotel's front door.

By the time I got there, people from our group had already returned from the game and were heading back out for a few more drinks. On Sunday, during the ride home, a couple of friends were telling me about the conversation we had as I was walking in. Don't remember; they must have been lying.

The Hawks beat the Blues 3-2.

OK, I was back to work on Monday evening. One of the guys at the bar who was dating a waitress at the bar knew what was about to happen and told a couple of regulars to stick around.

That's when Roger sat me down at a table next to the bar and fired me. I left there not really knowing why. I worked there for thirteen years, and my brother was one of the three original owners. It all made sense when I learned the guy dating Roger's daughter got my hours.

Michigan City 2004

After the debacle on the Mississippi River the previous year, we decided to try something different. Instead of a houseboat for a weekend, we went with a beach house for a week. It was a big, five-bedroom place in Michigan City, Indiana. Take a right out the door, walk past four houses and over a small sand dune, and you're at the beach on Lake Michigan.

Friends would come and go during the week, depending on their schedules, but it was important to keep alive the traditions of a party theme weekend and the midnight buffet. For our first beach house, it was a two-day pajama party.

The rental started on a Sunday at the end of July, with a few of us arriving late that afternoon and a couple more on Monday. Sunday's highlight was JD winning $1,000 at the Blue Chip Casino, conveniently located about a mile from our place. The girls loved our location, because there was also an outlet mall nearby. That meant just a few minutes from the house, you could gamble, shop, or lie on the beach—not bad.

Wednesday was Mexican night with dinner cooked by our Polish chef (Stu). Ole! Ole! Polska! Polska! Yes, Thursday was spent gambling, shopping, or lying on the beach. It was a quiet day because Friday was the start of the pajama party. Stu and JD hit a local golf course in the morning, then it was time to get dressed, or undressed. The talk focused on Stu. The words "pretty in pink" came to mind because he was wearing short pink pajama bottoms and a pink top that a young, in-shape woman would wear. And no, Stu was not in shape.

There's more. He was wearing the most darling pair of Eeyore slippers and had the most darling big cigar in his mouth. Almost forgot, pigtails too.

Around eight o'clock, we heard an ice cream truck coming down our street. It was time for dessert, so we all ran out still dressed in our pajamas. A bunch of kids from a couple of rental homes across from us came running out too.

It took a while for them to process what they were seeing. The looks on their faces were priceless. Stu got most of the attention, so he offered to buy everyone a treat, but one of the moms said no, then told the kids to stay away from the weird people. We weren't offended, but we did hear the ice cream truck driver went into therapy the next day.

Saturday was more of the same with a memorable game of Twister taking place that night. A few minutes in, Carolyn stopped the game. She thought the hardwood floor was dangerous for us drunks, so we dragged the king-sized mattress down from my room. A few minutes later, she stopped the game again. This time, she declared it would not continue until I put underwear on under my old-man nightshirt. There was no rebuttal.

Seconds later, after she gave the OK for the game to proceed, JD's head ended up between her legs. She looked down and proclaimed, "Oh, look everyone, I'm having a JD." Amazingly, they weren't the winners. The honor went to Mike and Mo.

Next, was a game of Chutes and Ladders. In reality, it was "Shots and Ladders," and it wasn't pretty. Brian ended up asleep (passed out) on the mattress, wearing only a leopard skin thong. That was bad enough, but him spooning a passed-out JD was wrong on so many levels. I found another bed and put my mattress on the disabled list for the rest of the week.

Recovering from that night was slow for most of us. I'm guessing it was even slower for our neighbors.

Some Notable Quotables:
1. Stu: I like long walks on the beach.
2. Brian: I like fat men in pink pajamas.
3. I need a poker. No, you need a pokee.
4. Is the Little Dipper to the left of the Big Dipper? It depends on where you're standing.
5. When's the midnight buffet?

We are all so precious.

Fox's 2004–Gator's 2005

In the late summer of 2004, still looking for a job, I got an interview at Fox's, a local family restaurant known for its pizza. It wasn't exactly what I was looking for, but it could help pay my rent while continuing my search for a place that was a better fit.

I didn't get the job, but got a call back a week later because they thought I would be a better fit at the bar they had purchased two storefronts away. It was an old tavern that had been around since the '50s, and when they finished renovating the place, I had a job.

When the person who was hired at Fox's instead of me didn't work out, they called me back. Come and work there until the new bar was ready. That way they could see how I worked and I could see how they operated. The renovation took a little longer than expected, so I ended up working at Fox's for about four months.

On my first night, a couple of friends came to see me, including Tina, who had recently stopped dating me. At my last job, at McMahon's, I wore shorts or jeans with a T-shirt, so when they saw me wearing a white shirt with a tie and vest, we all had a good laugh.

It's a good place to work with a great reputation, but it wasn't what I was used to. There were some nights I might have been the youngest person in the bar. My bosses sensed it and later told me they thought I would quit before the new place opened.

While working there, I struck up a friendship with a waitress named Jessica. At the time, there were three women with that name. Her name tag read "Jess S." After work, we would hang out for a few drinks. Just friends, I was a few years older than her—actually, almost thirty.

She didn't live far from me, so one night I got a call, inviting me to stop in. She had some friends coming over for a few drinks, and I was welcome to join them. I've worked as a bartender in Oak Lawn from '77 to '82 and since 1990 and have lived most of my life here, so whenever I leave the house, there's always a chance, good or bad, somebody will recognize me.

Walking up to the apartment building, I kept trying to think of her last name. All I could remember was the S on her name tag, and it wasn't helping. I got to the entrance, scanned the list of names, then spotted one that looked familiar and started with an S. I rang the bell, got buzzed it, and walked up to the door of the first-floor unit. When it opened, the guy inside took one look at me, then said, "Dick, what the fuck are you doing here?"

It was a county police officer who had been a customer at McMahon's. We had a good laugh, then with some help from his wife, I was sent up to a second-floor apartment.

After knocking on the door of the unit they directed me to, I was immediately welcomed in and offered a drink. I stood there for a second, looked around, then asked, "Where's Jess?"

"Who?" Again, wrong place. I could see a guy sitting on a couch, pointing up. He was pretty sure the girl in question lived upstairs. He was right. When I was welcomed into the third-floor apartment, I found Jess and gave her a hug to confirm it.

So in conclusion, I walked into two apartments by mistake, and people in both places knew me. I even got invited in and offered a drink at the second one.

Now it's early 2005, and the new bar was ready, but the owners threw me a curve a week before the opening. With some outside help, they decided the staff would be made up of only women. Instead of quitting on the spot, I worked my scheduled shift at Fox's that night. The next day they changed their minds, and on February 15, 2005, Tailgator's opened for business. I think it's worked out for both of us. My advice: never burn any bridges.

Eight months later, on October 26, the White Sox won the World Series. For a Cub fan working in a bar on the southwest side, it wasn't a lot of fun. It wasn't my night to work, but because of the crowds, I worked the door, which meant I didn't make much money either.

I did congratulate some of our patrons, saying they were lucky because they got to see a championship in their lifetime. It doesn't happen very often here. The Cubs had won two World Series and now the Sox had three. What a great city for baseball.

2005 MILWAUKEE/MATT

In July, I made the ninety-minute drive from Oak Lawn to Milwaukee for a baseball game between the Brewers and the Nationals. The reason was another chance to see Matt, who had recently been called back up from Triple-A, this time with Washington.

The game was on Thursday, July 14, the first game day after the All-Star break. I had read somewhere the Nationals had acquired outfielder Preston Wilson during the break, so it was a good bet Matt would be the one sent down to make room for him. I went anyway, hoping my theory was wrong.

While I stood in a short line at Miller Park's ticket office, a guy walked by, asking if anyone needed a ticket. I caught his attention and told him I needed one, so he handed me one.

My plan was to go cheap, so I asked how much he wanted. Nothing, it was free. I took one more look at him, then said, "In good conscience, I can't take this from a guy wearing a Green Bay Packers jersey." He let out a laugh and replied, "You gotta be from Chicago!" Then, it was my turn to laugh. We shook hands, and I went into the park, where my theory was confirmed. Matt was the one sent down.

Fast-forward a year because it was time to return to Wisconsin. Amy, one of the girls I worked with, had seen Crosby, Stills, Nash, and Young at an outdoor venue in Tinley Park, a Chicago suburb on its far southwest side, and raved about how good they were. I wasn't surprised they sounded good, just a little surprised because the review came from a twenty-three-year-old.

After listening to her, I checked CSNY's tour schedule and discovered they were playing a Thursday night at Milwaukee's summer fest outdoor venue. I don't work Thursdays, so I headed north. At the box office, I learned there were a few single seats down near the stage that cost $100. It was out of my price range, so I hung out for a while to see if anyone had a single ticket to sell. A spot on the lawn was fine with me.

Spotting a guy holding up a ticket, I walked over, hoping it wasn't a $100 one. And just like the year before, a good citizen of Milwaukee handed me a free ticket. I tried, briefly, to pay for it but he refused to take any money. At least he wasn't wearing a Green Bay Packers jersey.

And Amy was right. CSNY was definitely worth the trip.

MICHIGAN CITY 2005

It's late August, and we were back in Michigan City, and yes, we gambled, shopped, and laid on the beach.

The theme this year was "Arabian Nights," with the house becoming a desert oasis. The front deck was covered by a large tent with pillows scattered everywhere. It quickly became a conversation piece on our small street, especially with Karen's hookah pipe and all of us in costume.

There was one other conversation piece. It's called the Clapping Monkey, which to the girls, was the cutest thing in the house—to the guys, not so much. Luckily, the clapping wasn't too loud so it didn't bother our neighbors.

Leading up to the trip, Brenda and I were shopping for some party stuff at a local thrift store, where I found a cool large caftan robe in the women's section. I also ran into my cousin in the same section, so I got a strange look from her. She shopped there a lot, buying retro clothes and selling them on eBay and was interested in the caftan robe. When I got back from the house, I gave it to her, no charge.

The main party was on the weekend with a couple of highlights. The first one was the food, which included hummus, couscous, baklava, and Brenda's shish-kabobs. After she slaved in the kitchen for a long time, her food got rave reviews.

The other one took place outside. Carolyn had hired a belly dancer for early Saturday evening. When it was time for our lesson, the two of them headed to the middle of the street dressed like Barbara Eden from the TV show *I Dream of Jeannie*. The rest our group reluctantly followed behind. With the music playing, it didn't take long to draw the attention of our neighbors. Minutes later, there were about a dozen new recruits that decided to go to belly-dancing school. And that's how we ended our week.

We are all so precious.

2006 Nashville #1

The Blackhawks were in Nashville on February 4, so I headed south with my friend Sue and my old roommate Jim. None of us had been there before, so we booked a hotel downtown and found the area to be small, safe, and very walkable.

Our first stop was the Market Street Ale House. We liked the bar, and the employees made us feel at home, so home it was for the weekend. We would start our day there and end our day there.

If you like live music, Nashville is the place to go. It didn't take long for us to discover Lower Broadway, a street full of bars and restaurants that runs for almost a mile from the Cumberland River to the hockey arena. And what we discovered was almost every place offered live music from the time they opened until the time they closed, with the bonus being no cover charge. Band members would pass the hat (beer pitcher), and most people would chip in. There was one more bonus for us Northerners. It's not all country music.

If you're there for a few days and frequent the bars like we did, you'll begin to notice changes in some of the bands: maybe a different drummer one night, or a different guitar player. Or you might notice the same musician playing with two or three different groups. Everyone there is hoping to get discovered.

Anyway, we had a great time. It's a great city with friendly folk, so we'll be back. Oh yeah, the Hawks got their asses kicked 6-0.

2006 Gumbo

In February, Hurricane Gumbo was playing at a bar in Libertyville, a far northern suburb of Chicago. A mini road trip seemed like a good idea, or maybe just a good excuse to go and party in a different bar, in a different suburb where nobody would know us.

My plan was to go with Laura, a friend and coworker at Tailgator's. We even booked a masseuse to come to our hotel room. It was gonna be a spa day followed by a drink night, but at the last minute, she had to cancel.

I toughed it out and went north because I knew a couple of women who were also making the trip, although without massages. At least, I had a couple of friends to hang out with.

Hurricane Gumbo is a zydeco band, so it's Mardi Gras whenever they play. There are two things you need to know when you go to see them: (1) they're gonna be a lot of fun, (2) they have a lot of beads to pass out. Over the years, I decided #2 was the real reason I went to see them. Not true. Well . . .

I hung out with their manager for a while, and it turned out to be a good move. He had an amazing collection of beads and was on a mission to give all of them away. At one point, a very healthy young lady came up and asked about the coolest set of beads he had and how she could acquire them. He hesitated for a few seconds, took another look at her, then gave his answer: "Ten seconds."

She looked back at her girlfriend while deciding what to do, then calmly lifted up her shirt, oh yeah, and her bra. That meant it was time to start counting to ten. One, two, three, three, three, three, three . . . After four or five threes, she finally caught on. Her reaction: "Aw, c'mon." When he finally made it to ten, she grabbed the beads and walked away. That's when I applied for his job.

After the bar closed, I went back to the hotel and met up with the two women I knew, which made us a threesome. Laura, sorry you missed it. A foursome? No, I'm not that good.

A couple of months later and it was time for more Gumbo. This time, it was a Saturday night in Rock Island, Illinois, for the city's summer fest. Rock Island is one of the Quad Cities located on the Mississippi River about 175 miles from home, so a few of us decided to drive out there.

The fest takes place downtown, in an area known as the District. The main street is shut down, and all the bars and restaurants open up their floor-to-ceiling windows; weather permitting. It's a great venue, but the windows didn't stay open very long. I didn't think it was possible, but we had a wind chill alert in June. Thank God for alcohol.

The weather might have sucked, but seeing the band was fun as usual.

2006 Dad

In late February, my dad was diagnosed with colon cancer. It was pretty widespread, so the prognosis wasn't good. He was eighty-two years old, and his doctor gave him maybe six to eight months to live.

On Sunday, April 2, after visiting my dad at the hospital, I went to work at the bar. My shift started at 7:00 p.m. My brother called at 8:00 p.m. Dad was already gone. It wasn't six months; it wasn't even six weeks. I asked Amy, my waitress, to watch the bar while I took a short walk around the neighborhood. I needed some alone time to clear my head, then came back and finished my shift.

By coincidence, Mike T, one of my oldest friends, had stopped in the bar that Saturday, wondering if I was around. He was in the funeral business and happened to be doing a luncheon at Fox's Restaurant. Luckily, he left his business card.

I called him Monday, and he was happy to hear I got his message, until I told him the real reason for my call. He told me not to worry; he would take care of everything. He picked up my dad's body from the hospital and brought it to a local funeral home where he made all the arrangements. He was awesome. I'll never forget it.

Now, it gets interesting, but in a good way. In 1957, our family moved into St. Catherine's Parish in Oak Lawn, actually moving in before the school was ready to open.

My dad lived there for almost fifty years, so at the funeral mass, the priest talked a little bit about him, mentioning how he had still been active in the Senior Pinochle League and that he had also been . . . That was when he started to struggle for words. Uh, uh, and he was . . . an active golfer. My brother, sister, and I exchanged weird looks, then turned back to listen to the rest of his talk.

After mass, while standing in front of the church waiting for the casket, my good friend Maureen walked up and grabbed my arm. "We have to know. Did your dad ever golf?" My answer: "Never, was it that obvious?"

"Oh God, yeah!"

Then, the cemetery. As the people walked from their cars and filled in the space around the gravesite, a bagpiper began playing "Amazing Grace." He had been hired by guys from my college fraternity, which was pretty cool since I graduated in 1974.

My dad was a Purple Heart veteran from World War II, so when the bagpiper finished, an honor guard presented a US flag to my sister. Then, somewhere off in the distance, a soldier played taps. I never did see where he was.

There's more. When it ended, my friend Mike thanked everyone for coming, then told them about the luncheon that would follow. After saying a few words about my dad and about us growing up together, he started to get emotional.

Remember, he does this for a living. This isn't supposed to happen. He tried to laugh it off while explaining his connection to me and my family, then looked down at the ground while trying to compose himself. When he thought he was ready, he looked up, unfortunately, right at me. I was doing OK until that point, but when our eyes met, we both lost it.

Obviously, it was a sad time, but if you had to pick a way for things to play out, I couldn't have asked for anything more. My sister wasn't so sure. She was upset about what transpired at mass, because it was apparent the priest hadn't done his homework. My brother and I were actually thankful for that little bit of comic relief.

One more thing: Remember the priest at the funeral mass mentioning my dad being a golfer? On the Sunday my dad died, the *Chicago Tribune Magazine* ran its spring golf special. I still have it.

2006 STEPH

On March 5, my daughter turned twenty-one. For her birthday, I rented a small motor home, and six of us drove to Fulton, Missouri, for the festivities. The town is about twenty-five miles from the University of Missouri campus, where she was a student.

Remember, she attended Loyola-Chicago her first two years, then transferred to Mizzou to finish her college education. Her mom and I were thrilled. The two years at Loyola were expensive, even with her scholarship money. At Mizzou, she became an in-state student, so the cost of her education, which the two of us split, dropped dramatically.

Jaime, my roommate on the trip, was a new friend who was going through a rough time in her life. She found out her best friend had been "involved" with her boyfriend so she dumped both of them.

I was taken aside by my friends, Mo and Brenda, who lectured me on how to behave. I needed to give Jaime some space and not act like a normal guy (in female speak, that means "asshole"). It was going to be tough, because I had reserved a Jacuzzi suite.

It turned out the girls were right. We may have ended the night naked in the hot tub and naked in the same bed, but I was a gentleman. It was hard. Sorry, bad choice of words, but it did solidify our friendship. Anyway, we spent the night celebrating Steph's birthday at a couple of bars in downtown Fulton, a quaint little area with cobblestone streets.

One of the bars had a pool table, and Jaime is a pool player. The fact that she's pretty, blond, and about 6'1" drove the young boys crazy. They would get in line to play her, then get their asses kicked. I'm guessing concentration was a problem.

The highlight of the night was when Steph walked up and heard Jaime and me talking about doing a couple of one-hitters once in a while. Her reaction: "Oh my God, my dad does weed!"

Now twenty-one years old, she was officially old enough to start hearing some of my stories. Story number one was from spring break in Fort Lauderdale, Florida, during my junior year in college. The look on her face told me she hadn't given much thought to what she was getting into, especially when I told her my nickname on the trip. It was Dr. Bong. Her reaction was simple and quiet. She rolled her eyes and walked away.

Happy twenty-first, honey.

2006 Cubs with Brenda

On April 26, I went to a Cub game at Wrigley Field with Brenda, a friend who worked in the office at Fox's Restaurant. The daytime regulars at the restaurant's bar knew we were Cub fans, so when one of the guys had a couple of extra tickets, they immediately thought of us. It was the first time we would go to a game together, but not the last. It was an afternoon game against the Florida Marlins.

Remember, we work in Oak Lawn, just a few miles south of Midway Airport, so we drove there, parked the car, and took public transportation. It was the Orange Line el train east to the near south side of the city, transferring to the Red Line north through downtown. Exiting the train at the Addison stop, it's a one-block walk to Wrigley Field.

I'm not a beer drinker, so when I go to ballgames or concerts, I'll usually hide a water bottle filled with rum somewhere on my body. We walked up, got our tickets scanned, and entered the park. No problem, that is until a Cub employee came over and asked what I had in the side pocket of my shorts.

I said it was a bottle of water, so I pulled it out and showed her. Looking back, what saved me was grabbing the bottle very naturally and grabbing it by its top, which meant she couldn't see if the seal was broken. After a long look, I got the OK to enter the park. Phew!

Now the game: Our seats were in the fourth row, directly behind home plate. You've seen the guy that sits there with the radar gun, right? He was sitting behind me. Yeah, the seats were pretty good.

After an inning or so, I headed to a concession stand and ordered the biggest diet pop (cola) they had. While we waited for the foam to settle,

I told the employee not to worry because I needed the extra room for my rum.

Either he didn't hear me or didn't care, because he took my money and turned around to the cash register without saying a word. This is the point where I whipped out the "water" bottle and poured myself a drink while standing at the counter. I couldn't help it; I'm a bartender. Nobody noticed.

Back in my seat, I told Brenda the story. She shook her head and told me I was crazy, but also had a story for me. In those few minutes, she got a call from her son who lived in Florida. Remember, the Cubs were playing the Florida Marlins, and he was watching the game on WGN.

He felt compelled to call his mother and express his sympathies for the guy (me) sitting next to her. Brenda is a talker and he explained we were on camera a lot because of the location of our seats, and every time he saw her, she was talking to me and not paying attention to the game.

His call didn't make much of an impact until her phone rang a couple of innings later. This time it was the regulars at Fox's who also felt sorry for me. She quickly came up with a solution to the problem.

"We're never sitting in these seats again."

Our first stop after the game was a bar across the street from the park. Remember, a friend worked there and always took care of me when I dropped in. After our free drinks, we stopped at a bar on Clark Street where Brenda had connections. A couple more stops heading south got us to Belmont Avenue.

This was the point where we would turn east, walk about a block, then stagger up the stairs to the el train, but there was a problem. Is that a bar? We had stopped at almost every place on our little stroll, so God forbid we would walk past this one.

The name of the place was the Berlin Club. Our first impression was we had walked into a black gay bar. It wasn't just black, but it was definitely gay. Leaving that night, we decided to make it our last stop every time we went to a game. Brenda also decided there would be a competition to see who would get the most phone numbers. I usually won, but I was strong enough to walk away.

One more thing; it was how we got home. It didn't matter if it was a day game or a night game; the important thing was to make it back for last call. Difficult? Yes, because we had a habit of getting on the wrong el train. Here are some of our attempts:

1. Leaving Wrigleyville, we got on a Red Line train going north instead of south.
2. Leaving Wrigleyville, this time going south, we failed to transfer from the Red Line to the Orange Line and kept going south.
3. Leaving Wrigleyville, we remembered to transfer, but got on a Green Line train instead of an Orange Line train.

There were a couple of interesting nights where we missed last call because we ended up in a couple of interesting neighborhoods.

Always home safe.

MICHIGAN CITY 2006

The rental started on Saturday afternoon, July 29, ending the following Saturday morning. This year we turned the beach house into a *M*A*S*H* unit, with half of the medical staff reporting in that day.

Dinner the first night was at Ryan's, a restaurant in the city. The area had been struggling through a very hot stretch, and the restaurant's air conditioning system was going through a struggle of its own. It wasn't much fun eating dinner in a sauna.

Sunday, day 2, and the temperature topped out at 105 degrees, which is amazing for northwest Indiana. Fortunately, the air conditioning at the house was working, because it was too hot to lie on the beach. That night, a few of us made the long, one-block walk to Lake Michigan to kill some time before the midnight buffet. We took a dip, cooled off, and for some reason, kept our clothes on, a rarity for me.

While sitting on the beach, Brenda decided she was going to give up grocery shopping. She then clarified her statement, saying she would continue shopping at home for her daughter, but was putting a stop to drunk shopping at the house. The final straw was finding Hot Lips potato chips at a local grocery store, which freaked her out, since *M*A*S*H* was the party theme.

It cooled off on Monday, with the high only reaching 99 degrees. Some of the group headed to the casino, about a mile from the house. The rest of us went to the Shoreline Brewery, about a mile in the other direction, where we got to return to our childhood days. Yes, we were in a bar, but each of us was given an Etch-A-Sketch to play with. Some of you might have to look it up.

Another local bar was next, but two problems arose: (1) no rum, actually no hard liquor, just beer and wine; (2) no air conditioning.

The guy behind the bar that day had an interesting ensemble, which we hoped wasn't mandatory for the rest of the employees. He was wearing shorts, slippers, a White Sox T-shirt, and some cheap hair dye that, because of the heat and humidity, had begun to decorate both sides of his face. It was a quick stop.

For dinner that night, Stu, whose name ends in -ski, treated us to a great Italian meal while we watched *Lady and the Tramp*. It was a lovely *bella notte*. Can this group party?

A cold front came through, and the temperature dropped dramatically—well, not exactly. It dropped below ninety degrees, but not until twelve o'clock. We watched *A Fish Called Wanda* so Mo could get her yearly fix then, amazingly, skipped the midnight buffet.

Tuesday, day 4, and it was 100 degrees again. The other guys hit a local golf course around 7:00 a.m. I took a pass on the golf and skipped my bike ride. On Monday, the route I picked, combined with the heat and humidity, almost killed me. Let's try the beach.

It was me, Brenda, and Jaime, who is about 6'1" and was wearing a thong bikini. Remember, this is the Midwest, so she quickly got the attention of almost every person on the beach. We even got a visit from the Michigan City Beach Police, who checked to see if she was properly covered.

That night, we returned to Shoreline but were disappointed because the Etch-A-Sketches were gone. We finished the night lounging on the second floor open deck at Matey's, another bar and grill near the house. Wednesday was hot and humid again. I think the beach came in third after the casino and the outlet mall. A couple of the guys had friends with a house a few miles north of us, but still close to the lake, so the plan was to invade their place for dinner and drinks.

Dinner was great, plus we got to watch an awesome light show over the lake. It wasn't fireworks; it was lightning from a storm that had rolled into our area. It continued through the night and, on the plus side, knocked down the temperature. On the minus side, it knocked out the power, which luckily came back on around noon just as it started to heat up again.

Because we had to be out of the house early on Saturday, the *M*A*S*H* party officially began early Thursday, ending Friday night when the last medic passed out. The decorations looked great, with camouflage netting covering a good portion of the front of the house and a big red cross painted on a white sheet hanging in the front window. It was grape Nehi for everyone.

Just before Friday's dinner, Jaime left on an undercover mission, decked out in her camouflage shorts and T-shirt. While creeping through the brush, following some teenage girls walking over the sand dune on their way to the beach, she lit a pack of firecrackers and threw it into the weeds next to them. When they went off, the girls screamed like . . . teenage girls.

Then it was time to eat. Our mess hall put out a great spread consisting of Spam, Spam, Spam, beans, beef stew, creamed corn, corned beef hash, and . . . some Spam, all served on metal trays I bought at an army surplus store. The beverage of choice was Red-Headed Sluts served, for the effect, from a few IV bottles. Suicide is painless.

Finally, on the last night of our third year in Michigan City, we walked to the beach to watch the sun go down. What we discovered was a retired army veteran and his sunset ritual. He lived in a third- or fourth-floor condo that faced the water, and he would come out on his balcony every day to play taps. It was really cool and being in uniform (costumes) made it even better.

We are all so precious.

2006 JAIME

It's early August, and a small group of friends were out on a Saturday night for dinner and a few drinks—fun, but pretty uneventful.

The next morning, Jaime, who was part of the group, got a call from her mother-in-law. When Jaime and her husband separated, he kept custody of their two young girls and moved in with his mom. She lived in rural Pennsylvania, between Pittsburgh and Interstate 80, and the reason for her call made the news through a good portion of the country, including the Chicago area.

Steven, Jaime's brother-in-law, was riding his motorcycle on a two-lane state road near his home when he lost control on a turn, crashed into a signpost, and died. When he was late coming home, Jeremy, Jaime's husband, went out on his bike, thinking he could track him down at one of their regular stops.

No luck, but on his way back, he came around a bend on the same road and had to swerve out of the way because of some traffic tie-up. He lost control of his bike, crashed into one of the stopped cars, and died. The reason for the tie-up was his brother's accident. About two hours and one hundred yards separated the two.

Jaime flew out the next day, but she was going there alone. It was going to be tough, especially when she learned her mother-in-law was planning to file an injunction to keep the girls in Pennsylvania. This would give her time to try proving Jaime was an unfit mother.

We talked on the phone, and she updated me on what was going on. That's when I decided to drive to Pennsylvania and give her some support. I figured having a friend there would make a big difference. My van was getting old and I didn't feel comfortable taking it on a long drive, so I borrowed my sister's Chevy Cavalier.

I got there and found a hotel near Route 80 and called Jaime to tell her my location. I then called a friend who was an attorney and gave him the short version of what was going on. He wasn't familiar with Pennsylvania law, but he couldn't imagine it being much different from Illinois. Basically, they were her kids.

We met up and went out for dinner and a couple of drinks at a local bar and grill. Halfway through our first drink, after ordering some food, she asked me if we could do a shot in her husband's memory.

It was time to be careful because I was driving in an unfamiliar area with out-of-state plates. I agreed to one, and we were both surprised when the bartender told us the shots were on the house. He saw our reaction, then explained to Jaime he knew who she was and why she was there. A little unsettling, but that's small-town America.

The next day, knowing her mother-in-law had hired an attorney, we got out the Yellow Pages. Butler, PA, was the nearest city, so I randomly pointed to an attorney's phone number with that address, called it, and handed Jaime the phone.

Just seconds into the conversation, the attorney she was talking to stopped her in midsentence. "Am I speaking to Jaime?" I saw the reaction on her face and knew something wasn't right. The attorney said she already knew the story and gave her some free advice. This is a quote: "Get out of Dodge now. They're your kids. Just go."

That afternoon, we sat down with the family. When Jaime's mother-in-law learned we had talked to an attorney, she immediately got up and called her attorney. The call was short. She then walked back and calmly told us we were free to go, now knowing she didn't have a case.

We packed my sister's Cavalier with me, Jaime, her two girls, and as much of the kids' stuff that would fit. Randy, the remaining brother, sympathized with Jaime and helped us load the car. We left as fast as we could, heading north to Route 80, then west toward Ohio.

A few miles from the Ohio/Pennsylvania state line, flashing lights appeared in my rearview mirror. I didn't say a word, just held my breath. As the police car passed us, Jaime turned and looked at me, then breathed a big sigh of relief. About a minute later, we left Pennsylvania.

Maybe an hour later, we found a hotel with an indoor pool, where we all got to blow off some steam. I got a suite and slept on the couch, giving Jaime and the girls the bedroom.

Home the next day.

2006 NASHVILLE #2

On December 2, ten months after my first trip to Nashville, the Blackhawks were back and so were Jim and I. It may have been the same calendar year, but it was a different hockey season.

With a one-day head start, I used part of it to tour the Country Music Hall of Fame. The highlight was how the hall sets aside a large room every month to showcase a different artist. I was lucky enough to see the exhibit for Ray Charles. I'm not a huge country fan, but I do like some of the old guard like Waylon and Willie and Ray.

I waited until Jim arrived before returning to the Market Street Ale House. Walking in, we were immediately recognized by the same girls that served us in February. Way to make two guys from Chicago feel welcome. And of course, we fell right back into our routine of the two stop minimum each day.

The night before we left, it was late and we were heading back to our hotel, but we decided to try getting one more drink at our spot. The bar looked empty from the outside, but I tried the door. It wasn't locked, so we walked in. After a few steps, a waitress stopped us and explained they had been really slow toward the end of the night and closed a little early.

Not the end of the world, so we turned around and started to walk out. That's when one of our friends behind the bar spotted us and yelled to her coworker to let us stay. Evidently, we were special.

By the time we walked up to the bar, the girls were done making our drinks. They said not to worry because the drinks were on the house and they would join us in a couple of minutes. We hung out with them for one more drink, then said our goodbyes. Spoiled? Yes.

And this time, we won 4-3 in overtime.

2006 My Ribs

On December 23, I got a call from Tina, an old girlfriend, who was wondering if I wanted to come over and hang out for a while. I agreed, with one stipulation, she had to have Bacardi rum. She did, so I did.

Around nine o'clock that night, she let her dog out for a pee break. Back inside, she asked me to remind her about the dog, just in case the alcohol and the —— made her forget. I laughed and told her she couldn't be serious. I really didn't care for the dog when we were dating, so there was a good chance I wouldn't remember it now.

Hours later, after more booze and more ——, she looked nice and comfy curled up on the couch, so I threw a blanket over her. After doing a little cleaning, I headed out, knowing there was still time for a couple of drinks at a neighborhood bar.

I walked out the side door, closed it behind me, then realized the lock wasn't set. If it was, I would have walked down the driveway and been gone, but during those few extra seconds it took to set the lock, I heard whimpering coming from the backyard. That's right; the dog was still out there. I told her I wouldn't remember.

The weather was good news/bad news. It was an unseasonably warm night for December in Chicago, so the dog didn't freeze. The problem was it had been raining most of the night, so he was soaking wet.

I started to walk away, then decided to do a good deed and reached over, unlocked the gate, and walked into the backyard. Amazingly, I think the dog was happy to see me. I went up on the back deck and opened the door that went into the house through her son's bedroom. It wasn't locked because the dog was only supposed to be out there for fifteen minutes.

Now, after four hours and fifteen minutes, the dog spotted the open door and did his best imitation of a cartwheel on his way inside. Knowing my new buddy was safe, I closed the door, made sure it was locked, and headed down the deck stairs.

That's when it happened. They were slippery and I was a little drunk, so it was probably a combination of both when I fell and landed on my side. Ouch.

Even after the drinks and the other stuff, it hurt bad. That should give you a clue as to how serious it was, but it didn't matter. It was last call. I made it in time for a couple of drinks, but the bartender knew me and knew something wasn't right.

After hearing my story, she told me to go to the emergency room. I didn't have health insurance at the time, so my plan was to go to a local care station the next morning. I did, and the X-rays showed two cracked ribs.

Back at home, I called Tina to tell her what happened, and that's when she remembered her dog. I did remind her like she asked. The only problem was the timing. It was about fifteen hours later, not fifteen minutes.

Her reaction was very sympathetic: "I know you're in a lot of pain, but the fact this happened helping my dog is actually kind of funny." Ha ha. Almost as funny was the upper-body wrap I was told to wear. A nurse at the care station explained the only reason to wear it was to remind me to do things more slowly because nothing really helps heal cracked ribs.

At work that night, I quickly learned how much bending, stretching, and reaching I did without thinking. Slowing down helped a little bit, but laughing definitely didn't. On a good note, my man-bra was a big hit with the customers.

2007 STL

On Thursday, January 4, I hit the road early (for me) and drove to St. Louis. The Blackhawks were in town, so I met Steph and her boyfriend for the game. No motor home, no Amtrak, just the three of us. After the game, we ended up at a bar called Nadine's on the west end of Soulard, just south of downtown. The bar was pretty quiet, so while my daughter shot some pool, the bartender and I traded stories. The usual: "Where are you from, what do you do and how did you end up here?"

Learning I worked as a bartender in Oak Lawn, he needed to know where. When I told him Tailgator's, he laughed and told me about a customer of his who talked about the bar I worked at. The guy was divorced, and when he came down to see his kids, would always try to stop at his favorite St. Louis bar, Nadine's.

The bartender felt like he knew my place of employment just from listening to his customer. He described the guy to me, but I figured he was a daytime drinker and I worked nights, so there was a good chance we had never met. As it turned out, I did know him, but rarely saw him.

My daughter's boyfriend sat there listening to the whole conversation and couldn't believe the connection. "Oh my God, that's amazing!" Steph just laughed and told him to relax. "It's not a big deal. My dad runs into people in other countries that recognize him."

We lost 2-0.

2008 PA-NY

After my shift at the bar on Tuesday, May 6, I hit the road, driving to Pittsburgh to catch a baseball game. It was my first trip to PNC Park, so after a quick nap in the van in a truck stop somewhere in Ohio, I got to the ballpark and walked up to the ticket window. For $9, I got an upper-deck box seat in the first row just past third base. There were two people in my section.

By coincidence, an old college friend happened to be in Pittsburgh for a couple of days of sales meetings and his company happened to have a skybox for the same game. I knew this because we met the previous weekend at a wake for the Mom of a mutual friend.

He tried to get me into the skybox, but the extra tickets were given to a couple of local employees. That meant he had to lower himself and join me, oh, and the other two people in my section. We hung out for a couple of innings, then he came to his senses and headed back to the suite. Can't say I blame him. After the game, I headed east again. It had been a long day, so after two hours of driving, most of it through a heavy rain, it was time for bed. I found another truck stop and called it a night. They're safe places to stay. You can grab a meal and a shower, plus the parking lot is considerably cheaper than the average hotel. Sometimes I sleep better in my van than I do in my bed.

I woke up refreshed and continued my drive, heading to New York City and Yankee Stadium. The year 2008 was the last for the old park and my last chance to see a game there. The plan was to find a cheap ticket, go to the game, then start driving home when it was over.

When I pulled into a parking spot, the people next to me seemed to notice the Illinois license plate. I knew exactly what they were thinking when I noticed their Ohio license plate. The Yankees were playing Cleveland and they were now in jeopardy of being stuck next to a White Sox fan. I'm guessing it wasn't their idea of a good time.

A couple of steps out of the van, I heard, "Please tell us you're not a Sox fan." My answer: "I'm a Cub fan, and I'm here to root for the Indians." Their response: "Then get your ass over here and join us." It was two brothers, maybe in their early forties, traveling with their mom. Dad wasn't feeling well, so they left him at home.

We hung out for a few minutes, then it was time to go, telling them I needed to find a ticket. After a couple of steps, I was ordered to stop. Since Dad didn't make the trip, they had an extra ticket. My goal was to do this trip as cheaply as possible. Seat location wasn't a priority, so I hesitated. It's New York, so I assumed just paying face value would be expensive.

They told me the ticket was free, but with a small stipulation: buy a round of drinks in the park. I agreed, but with my stipulation: I wouldn't be joining them. I was living in my van for a couple of days, and just to be safe, I cut out the alcohol—no problem.

We sat nineteen rows behind the Yankee dugout, face value $120. Turns out the one brother worked for Rawlings Sporting Goods and got his tickets through Major League Baseball. I never did buy a round.

After settling in, it didn't take long to notice the big, loud Yankee fan in front of us and just like the brothers from Cleveland, he was there with an older woman. While getting acquainted, we learned it was his mother-in-law, so the brothers had to give him some shit. They were dying to know what he did wrong. It must have been pretty serious when the punishment was going to a baseball game with your wife's mother.

The Yankee fan explained his wife was eight months pregnant and needed to stay in or be close to a bed. They hated to give up the tickets, so Mom decided her daughter would be fine at home for the day. Then someone asked if they knew the sex of the baby. It was a boy.

Hearing that, the Rawlings Sporting Goods brother pulled out his business card and handed it to the future dad. He said to send him an email with the name and birthday of his new son and remind him where they met. With that, he would send the family a Rawlings Major League Baseball bat with the boy's name, birthday, and Yankees logo etched into it. The guy sat there with a blank look on his face, asking why. The answer was quick and to the point: "Because I can."

Leaving the park after the game, I started thinking about all the good people I met in Pittsburgh and New York, but needed to find one more to help me get across the river into New Jersey and start my drive home.

Standing at my van looking at all the different levels of roads and ramps made me think I might be in New York for a while. I had this vision of driving up, down, and around for hours and then a light bulb went on.

I spotted a car with New Jersey plates, and when the family that belonged to it showed up, I went over and asked if they could help me get out of the city and on to Route 80. The dad laughed and told me it wasn't as bad as it looked. All I had to do was follow him out of the parking lot, up the nearest ramp, and I would be across the river in no time. He was right.

I drove across New Jersey and all of Pennsylvania, finally pulling into another truck stop in eastern Ohio, where I had another good night's sleep. I might sell my bed.

And yes, it turned out to be a cheap trip. First of all, I didn't drink—not lying. Counting the stop in Ohio on the way home, I spent three nights in the van, leaving me a hotel bill of $0. Game tickets totaled $9, so basically, I did this great little road trip for the cost of gas and a few meals.

God bless America.

2008 JORDAN

On October 8, I flew out of Chicago with my good friend Maria and her good friend Kathy. The next morning, we landed in Amman, Jordan, where we met our contact and paid for the one-week trip Maria set up. The package included hotels, entrance fees to all the historical sites and our own tour guide at each one. It also included a car and driver. Our driver's name was Abdun and he was great. He even knew where to buy alcohol.

First on our list was the Dead Sea, the lowest inhabited area on the planet. We were booked at the Movenpick, a beautiful five-star resort located at its southeast corner. It was way out of our league but was included in the package, which was pretty reasonable, costing about $975/person. The hotel also passed my first test; its bar carried Bacardi rum.

The Dead Sea has a very high salt content, so sinking under the water wasn't an option. Our only concern was breaking an ankle walking on the extremely rocky bottom. The other popular thing to do was take a mud bath, so Maria joined a group of people who were scooping up mud just a few steps into the water and rubbing it all over their bodies. It's supposed to be good for your skin. Kathy and I took a pass.

When we were done floating, it was time to get the salt off our bodies. The resort had a few showers by the beach for that reason, but the combination of salt and mud was much worse. It took Maria a lot longer before she declared herself clean.

The next morning, after an awesome buffet breakfast, it was a four-hour drive to the city of Jerash. The area was an old trade route between Europe, Asia, and Africa, which meant the city had a lot of Greek and Roman ruins and it is considered the best-preserved Roman city outside Italy.

A couple of hours later, we made a pit stop, and to nobody's surprise, it involved a souvenir store. It was a large, two-story building that must have been put there to handle the tour bus crowds.

Before leaving home, we read about Jordan and what to expect when we got there. We learned it was a safe destination, and the worst thing that would happen was not being able to honor all the requests from locals to join them for tea. It was true; the people were incredible.

The store we stopped at was no exception. The owner welcomed us in, looked at how we were dressed, and correctly assumed we were Americans. He was interested to know where we were from, so when one of us said Chicago, the next words out of his mouth were "North side or South side?" You have to know something about our city to ask that question.

When we told him south, he thought for a second, then asked if we lived near Ford City Mall, a shopping center in the southwest corner of the city. It's about a mile south of Midway Airport, and about three miles north of my condo. Maria and I have traveled a lot together, so this didn't surprise us. It gets better.

She has spent her career as a nurse in a local hospital, and amazingly, the store owner's best friend worked in the same hospital and, amazingly, in the same department. Not only were we in Jordan, but we were pretty much in the middle of nowhere in Jordan. We made sure to get a picture of Maria with the owner.

Now, Jerash. One cool highlight during our two-hour walking tour was the Temple of Artemis and its moving columns. Most of the structures were built to withstand high winds and some minor earthquakes, so at one of the columns, our tour guide took a spoon and placed it into a crack at its base. With a couple of people pushing against the column, you can see the spoon move. That's when the tour guide asked if anybody wanted to replace the spoon with their finger. Everyone was sober, so there were no volunteers. Included in the ruins was a 15,000-seat hippodrome where chariot races were held and two smaller theaters, both with amazing acoustics. And finally, there was an ancient Roman amphitheater where we saw Jordanians in traditional dress, playing drums and bagpipes. That's right—bagpipes. You can look it up.

Next was Madaba, a city known for its mosaics. Kathy and I weren't sure when it happened, but Maria was now being called "Princess" or "Your Highness" by Abdun. We don't get it, but it seems to occur wherever we go.

It was a quick stop, maybe two hours. We saw the School of Mosaics, and after asking a woman for permission, I got a picture of her working on a tile project. We also toured the Church of St. George, home of the oldest map of the Mideast, which was done on the floor of the church, with local tiles. It was estimated around two million were used to make the original. About half of them still exist.

Late that afternoon, we arrived in Amman, which has been called the oldest inhabited city in the world. It reminded me of Rome because it was originally built on seven hills, but the landscape in Amman was more dramatic.

While driving down an average-looking street, Abdun pulled the car over and told us to get out, cross the street, and check out the view. We did as we were told, all the time looking up, wondering what he was talking about. We didn't get it until we looked down. Below us was a huge Roman amphitheater that seated almost ten thousand people.

Now, it was time to check into the Amman Meridien, another five-star hotel. To enter, we went through something similar to an airport checkpoint, with us and our luggage given a quick scan. It was a little disconcerting the first time, but after that, you realize it's done for your safety. From then on, I never had a problem walking in or out of our hotel.

It had been a long day, so the girls were ready to crash. I was ready for a couple of drinks and went to the hotel bar. While closing my tab, I asked my waitress if she would consider coming back to Chicago with me. She loved the idea, but figured her husband and two children wouldn't, so she took a pass. Oh, well.

On day 3, before leaving Amman, Abdun took us to a liquor store. He was great, but the prices weren't. Jack Daniels was $65/bottle. That was bad enough, but the worst news was they didn't carry Bacardi. The only rum in the store was made in France, and it was only $30 for two bottles. Sound too good to be true? You're right. Don't ever buy rum made in France.

An hour drive got us to Mount Nebo, known as the spot where Moses died and was buried. Its church had some great mosaics, similar to what we saw in Madaba, plus a great view of the Dead Sea. On a clear day, you can see the city of Jerusalem. It wasn't clear.

Abdun then took us to Al-Karak, a large fortress important in ancient times, but now overlooks pretty much nothing. On the way there, we stopped for a photo op on a bluff looking down across the desert, and that's where Abdun ran into a friend, just like Maria and I do when we travel.

Out of gas, he handed his keys to Princess Maria, who finished the drive to the fort.

The tour in and around Al-Karak was great, but we never did learn why it had been built in the first place. One tradition did continue. It was me taking a picture of Maria straddling a cannon. It never gets old. After Al-Karak, we checked into another Movenpick Hotel and, yes, another five-star hotel. The room they gave us had two beds, not three like we requested, so we went back to the front desk to see what they could do. What they did was move us to a suite, which sounded great until we saw the room. This time, there was only one bed and one cot. Not hard to guess who got what.

The next morning, Abdun picked us up and drove to Petra, another part of the crisscrossing trade route between Europe, Asia, and Africa. The word *petra* means rock in Greek, and when you see pictures of the place, you'll understand. It's where we met Mudji, our personal guide for the day.

Entering Petra, a ride on horseback got us to the opening of a long narrow gorge called the Siq. The ride was the first of many firsts for me on this vacation, then it was time to dismount and head through it on foot. Twenty minutes later, nearing the end of our walk, we got a glimpse of a huge, ten-story structure built out of the rock. One more bend in the road got us to the Treasury Building, which was made famous in the movie *Indiana Jones and the Last Crusade*. Yes, it's real.

After that, it was around 800 big, wide stairs up a narrow gorge to Ad-Deir, also known as the Monastery. Maria took the easy route on the back of a donkey. Kathy and I did it on foot. Another hike, not nearly as long, got us to the High Altar of Sacrifice, where Maria got a cool picture of me at the edge of the cliff.

It's day 5, and we were back at the entrance to Petra at eight o'clock in the morning. Kathy's knee was giving her some problems, so she took it easy. Maria went her own way and ended up getting a picture taken with Marguerite van Geldermalsen, the author of the book *Married to a Bedouin*, who happened to be doing a book signing.

I decided to do my best impersonation of a mountain goat and hiked up and around the Royal Tomb, which meant another 400 steps. During the walk, I met a young couple basically doing the same thing, so we hung out together. He was German; she was an Aussie.

We eventually made it to the Treasury Building, this time with a completely different perspective than the day before. I remembered feeling pretty small, looking up at the immense structure carved out of the side of a mountain. Today, looking down, I could hardly see the people at ground level. Yeah, it was a good hike.

A little later, I came to an abrupt stop and ordered the couple to do the same. There it was! I had only heard about it in whispered stories from Kathy and Maria. It was the blue lizard, a rarely seen (ugly) creature. I was lucky enough to get a couple of pictures of it, which thrilled the girls. I later learned the lizards turn blue for the breeding season—their breeding season, not mine.

I got one other great picture during the walk. It was looking back across a huge expanse of rocky hills/mountains toward the Monastery that we had hiked up to the previous day. I even impressed myself with what I accomplished on foot those two days.

The three of us eventually met up and found Abdun, who took us to our next hotel, called Taybet Zaman. It was a very small ancient village that, instead of being torn down, had been turned into a beautiful resort, with every small home becoming a large suite. After checking in, a short walk down a couple of narrow winding streets got us to our home; I mean our suite.

This is where I experienced my first and pretty sure, my last Turkish massage. It was thirty dollars for a thirty-minute session where a man soaped me up, then rubbed me down. That's all I have to say.

That night, we were scheduled to return to Petra for a two-hour show starting at 9:00 p.m. The late start gave us time for a few drinks before we left. After my Turkish "massage," it was time to find some rum and find it fast.

We grabbed our drinks and headed to the west side of the resort, joining a handful of other guests to watch the sun set down through the mountains. Thirty minutes later, it was time to move to the other side of the resort, where we were able to watch a full moon rise up in the eastern sky. Then it was time to leave for Petra. The timing was perfect.

The walk through the Siq was lit up with over a thousand large candles and, don't forget, the full moon. The area around the Treasury was also lit up, and we were treated to some live traditional Jordanian music. The only downside was returning to the hotel and finding its bar closed. That left us with the dreaded French rum.

My estimate for the two days and one night in Petra was over twelve hundred official stairs, hundreds of unofficial stairs, ten to twelve miles on foot, and ten to twelve ounces of French rum. Three out of four ain't bad. Now, lights out.

The next morning, Abdun brought us to a much smaller version of Petra called, by coincidence, Little Petra. He showed up in a suit because of an appointment scheduled for later that afternoon, then hung out with us to kill some time. The 100-degree weather didn't seem to bother him. I don't think he even loosened his tie.

The highlight for me was another hike. This time, it was only about fifty stairs, up through a crevice in the rock that gave me a great view of the area. At the top, I met a Bedouin couple who made a living camping there during the day. When I finished taking in the scenery, they invited me to stay and have a cup of tea with them. I accepted. When we were done, I asked if it would be OK to take a picture of them. They accepted. I then thanked them, left a gratuity, and made my way back down.

The following day, shortly after we left our hotel, traffic in the area came to a halt, with an obvious military presence. Abdun told us it wasn't a big deal; it was "just" the caravan of Abdullah, the king of Jordan. It reminded me of Madrid in 1972 when General Franco would enter or exit the city, but with a much bigger show of force.

Kathy and I had a theory. We think the traffic jam might have been because of us. Was the king stalking "Her Highness" once he learned she was in the country? We were never able to confirm it.

After the traffic cleared, we headed to the desert and got in a four-wheel-drive jeep for a tour through a protected area called Wadi Rum, also known as the Valley of the Moon. It's also famous because many of the desert scenes from the movie *Lawrence of Arabia* were filmed there in 1961.

After another awesome sunset, we settled into a tent in a Bedouin camp. It was included in our package, and it had its good and bad points. The cool thing was we spent the night in a small tent in a Bedouin camp in the desert in Jordan. The not-so-cool thing was about one hundred other people did the same thing.

And it wasn't as spartan as it sounds. It turned out to be pretty commercial, with the ability to purchase food and drinks while listening to some annoying music. There was even a dance floor. And the icing on the cake was no Bacardi. Amazingly, the French rum came to the rescue again.

Now it's 7:00 a.m. and time for breakfast, followed by another first. It was me on a camel for an hour ride through the desert with Kathy and Maria. Early on, the camels stopped and munched on some brush growing along our route, so the girls grabbed their cameras and shot five or six pictures of them having lunch. Ten minutes later, they stopped to eat again, and the girls clicked away again. This went on for the whole ride. A conservative estimate was about thirty photos of camels chewing on some weeds.

We also got to see a couple of them go on strike. Maybe thirty to forty yards away, there were four camels being led in the opposite direction, when one of them spotted his buddy, who happened to be transporting Maria. The guide leading our camels explained since they couldn't be with each other, both camels decided to stage a sit-in. It took a few minutes, but once they got their fix, both got up and we finished our ride.

Our last stop was the Egypt Air Office in Amman to confirm our upcoming flights. The first one was to Cairo. The other one would take us back to Cairo from Aswan after our cruise on the Nile River. While the girls were inside, I stood outside waiting for Abdun.

During that short time, an old man walked by, noticed how I was dressed, and asked if I was an American. I said yes, I was from Chicago, so of course, his response was "Where in Chicago? I lived there for ten years."

I said, "Oak Lawn."

He said, "Oak Forest." They're two suburbs about six miles apart. He lived two blocks from my brother.

Seconds later, Abdun pulled up and, while waiting for the girls, told me a story about camel milk. I don't remember how we got on that subject, but he explained how it was good for certain types of cancer and how it would make a man hard as a rock. He then raised his fist, with his arm in an L-shape. Camel milk!

When the girls got back, I told them the story. As a Muslim, it was OK for him to tell me the story, but not OK for me to tell the girls in front of him, so he was a little embarrassed. Sorry, Abdun.

It's our last night in Jordan, so after dinner in a local diner, it was time for a couple of drinks. As I sat down at the bar, a waitress immediately pointed to me. Yes, I was the one who wanted to take the other waitress back to Chicago with me.

I was a big celebrity for a few minutes, that is, until I had to pay for my drinks, so maybe not so big. What confirmed it was when I was told the bar was out of Bacardi. A couple of beers and it was time to go to bed as a mere mortal.

Egypt in the morning.

2008 Egypt

On Thursday, the 16th, we had our buffet breakfast at the Amman Hilton and checked out around noon. It was time to fly to Cairo, but our ride to the airport wasn't until 4:00 p.m., so we got to work off our meal by lying around the lobby. The girls did some work on a couple of hotel computers while I read a book. My celebrity status was completely gone.

Our flight was scheduled to depart at 7:00 p.m., and that's when we learned about Egypt time. It left two hours late. We made it to Cairo, leaving the airport around 11:00 p.m. Holy shit! The population was in the neighborhood of fifteen million, with about the same number of vehicles, so the ride to our hotel was a real eye-opener. Our driver told us traffic was crazy twenty-four hours a day. The icing on the cake was the three of us and our bags jammed into a little baby cab that was constantly surrounded by much bigger cars. Size mattered that night.

One more thing: In the few minutes waiting for our cab, we experienced something that would happen over and over again. There was always someone with their hand out, asking for change.

Without a package deal like in Jordan, we were on our own. Location was the thing, so we got a room at the Nile Ritz-Carlton, another five-star hotel. The only thing separating us from the Nile River was five lanes of one-way traffic, but I quickly learned how far away it was. The markings on the street didn't make much of an impact because there were usually at least six vehicles across the five lanes.

The Egyptian National Museum was five minutes away, which meant we could get there without getting in a car. Half of our first day was spent there, touring the Royal Hall of Mummies, with the highlight being King Tut and a lot of his stuff. One room over, we saw another mummy whom we swore was Whoopi Goldberg. We were later informed Whoopi was still alive.

Now, not even twenty-four hours into our stay, Maria had a new admirer (stalker?). It was Amir, a bellhop at our hotel, who immediately began referring to her as "Queen Maria." Nice guy, but Kathy and I wondered about his taste in women.

For a moment, let me backtrack to talk about the traffic. I actually asked Amir for a few tips on how to cross the street. I know it's hard to imagine it being that big of a deal, but if you were in Cairo with me, you would understand. He was happy to help, probably because I was a friend of "the queen."

Yes, the traffic was crazy, and one other thing stood out. It was the lack of traffic signals. There were plenty of roundabouts, which meant coming to a complete stop didn't happen very often and never happened in front of our hotel.

Now it's time for Amir to explain the trick of getting to the other side of the street. He said to wait until there was a gap in traffic, then start walking, keep the same pace, and don't make eye contact. Just look straight ahead, and God forbid, don't panic and stop in the middle of the street. Seriously?

Here's why. He explained the drivers would adjust to my walk, so stopping would screw everybody up. Getting to the other side of the street would help me get to the other side of the Nile River, so I did as I was told. The first few steps were a little scary, but once I got going, it was a breeze, with the only downside being the adrenalin rush after reaching the other curb.

On vacation, I keep a log of the things that occur each day so I'll remember them later on. My entry that day? "Crossed the street, all by myself."

Later that afternoon, we got to take another cab ride, this one to the airport for our flight to Luxor. During the ride, we booked our driver and his vehicle for a day trip to Giza when we returned after our Nile cruise. He gave us a price of 350 Egyptian pounds, which translated to about sixty dollars for the day. Deal.

We landed in Luxor, found a place called the Oasis Hotel, and got a room with three beds and our own toilet and shower. It also included a Continental breakfast, and all for the price of twenty-seven dollars. And that wasn't per person; it was the total bill.

Once we settled in, Maria and I went out to explore the neighborhood while Kathy stayed in and chilled out. After our walk, we ended up having dinner right next to our hotel. It was a small, open-air rooftop restaurant where everyone sat on cushions next to small tables.

Dinner was cheap, around $7/person, plus we got to hang out with people from Australia, Japan, and England. We also met a young guy from Arizona who had just been discharged from the army and decided to travel until his money ran out. I wonder how he did.

During dinner, one of our new friends mentioned how a short walk would get us to a large park by the Luxor temples. Maria was ready to crash and took a pass, but I wasn't done yet. Walking through the park that night with everything lit up was incredible.

Early on, I heard some live music and stopped to look around, trying to find the source. My guess was it might have been a small concert in the park, but I quickly discovered a wedding party dancing in some kind of conga line.

While taking in the whole scene, four young boys walked up, guessing I spoke English, and asked what my name was. I answered, "Richard." Then one of the boys wanted to know if it was like Richard the Lionhearted. I'd love to know where he came up with that one. Then they asked if I would come and dance in the wedding. I took a pass.

As they walked away, the youngest boy tapped me on the arm and asked if I would buy him a Coca-Cola, but before I had a chance to answer, one of the older boys smacked him. After saying something to him in Arabic, the boy immediately apologized. With all the people approaching me with their hand out, it was refreshing to see how these kids acted.

Right after that, one of the dads came over to see if the boys had been bothering me. I told him they were fine, but they did try to get me to dance with the wedding party. He had a good laugh and told me it probably wasn't a good idea. We agreed on that one.

Back at our room, I was able to grab about four hours sleep—only four hours because the hotel owner was able to book us on a hot-air balloon ride over the Valley of the Kings. We left the ground just after 5:00 a.m. so the sun and the balloon would rise at about the same time—another first.

I was a little nervous as the balloon lifted off, but once we got up in the air, it was so peaceful. The 360-degree view of the area wasn't bad either. There were quite a few balloons up there with us, and we were amazed at the size of some of them. I remember our captain telling us some of the gondolas held as many as twenty people. By comparison, we were one of the smaller guys on the block. It was the three of us, a young guy from Scotland (traveling solo), and Husam, our pilot.

We made it up to about 1,000 feet, and looking down, we could see the Nile River, about a half mile of green crops, then nothing but desert. Wait, did I just hear Husam utter the words "Uh-oh!" This came shortly after he let Maria pull the cord to fire up the balloon and give it some lift. And yes, the captain was another admirer of "Queen Maria." Seeing our reaction, he quickly assured us everything was OK, so that's when we renamed him. He was now Captain Uh-oh.

As the ride was coming to an end and the balloon got close to the ground, it floated over those green crops, which we later learned were alfalfa and sugar cane. After that, it was guided down by a crew on the ground, landing on the back of a flatbed truck. Even with their help, it was still pretty awesome. With our feet on the ground, the four of us were presented with commemorative certificates from Sinbad Balloons, listing our name, the date of the flight, and the name of our pilot. He signed it, "Captain Uh Oh."

Now it was time to get back to our hotel and check out. That's because it was time to check in to the *Sapphire*, a boat that would be our home for the next three days as we cruised the Nile River. And you know what? I got my own room.

Before leaving the dock, we were able to go back on land and tour the Temple of Karnak, the largest temple complex in Egypt, located in the park where I almost danced with a wedding party.

Returning to the boat, we met up with Maria's friends. There was a medical conference going on in Cairo and she knew two couples who had come from the southwest side of Chicago to attend it, so the four of them joined the three of us for the cruise.

It was John/Denise and Mike/Winnie. John, Denise, and Mike are doctors, and my roommates are both nurses, which left Winnie and me. The two of us would hang out on the top deck for a little while, just to get away from all the medical stuff. It didn't always work, but we both were happy the other one was on the boat.

At dinner that night, we met the rest of our group. Together, we numbered fifteen, divided between two tables, and we would take our land tours and all of our meals together. Our new friends were a couple from Oklahoma married fifty-one years, two women from Nova Scotia, and two young couples, one Dutch and the other French/San Diego. We couldn't have picked a nicer group of people and I think everyone else felt the same way.

On Sunday, the 19th, our wake-up call was at 5:00 a.m., and everybody made it on the bus for our 6:00 a.m. departure. We toured the Valley of the Kings, the same area Maria, Kathy, and I viewed from the hot-air balloon and saw the tombs of Ramses VI and Tutankhamen, probably the two most famous men in the history of the country. We also got to see the Colossi of Memnon, two statues sitting all by themselves on the side of a road.

Our last stop was the Temple of Queen Hatshepsut, Egypt's first female pharaoh. She also goes by the name Hot Chicken Soup, which was given to her by the local tour guides. It evolved over time because the average English-speaking tourist couldn't pronounce her real name.

Back on the *Sapphire*, when the boat authorities were sure every morning tour had returned, we set sail for Edfu. It's about seventy miles south of Luxor, but before we got there, the boat had to pass through a set of locks. While waiting in line, a bunch of small rowboats surrounded us, trying to sell all sorts of stuff.

That's when Dr. John stepped up and became the boat's sales rep, doing the bargaining for us and a bunch of other passengers.

We got our shopping done first, grabbed a drink, then kicked back to watch the show. The guys in the boats would throw a few things up, a pretty good toss, considering we were on the top deck, then John would bargain with them. Either he would throw the stuff back or throw some money down in a small container they provided. This went on for about two hours.

In the end, a lot of passengers bought galabiyahs (long Egyptian robes). With the shopping done, it was bedtime for everyone because of the 6:30 a.m. wake-up call—well, almost everyone. There were three people left on the deck. It was John, Mike, and me, so that's when I told them the story. Camel milk! The next morning was a tour at Edfu, but I took a pass because of some stomach problems. It turned out to be a nice break from everything because I got to lie around on the top deck and take a couple of dips in the pool. I was the only one.

When the tour groups returned, we sailed to Kom Ombo and checked out the Temple of Horus, who had the head of a falcon, then checked out the Temple of Sobek, who had the head of a crocodile. Got that? The stop lasted about four hours, then it was time to sail to Aswan.

Once we docked, the ship threw a party and everyone got to dress up, coincidentally, in the stuff purchased from the boat people the previous night. We listened to some traditional Egyptian music for what seemed like hours, so when it finally stopped, you could hear a huge sigh of relief in the room. Seconds later, you could hear laughter because "La Bamba" came on, quickly followed by "YMCA."

Aswan is where the Nile River meets Lake Nasser, which is actually a large reservoir created when a dam was built in the 1960s for the purpose of providing electricity to the area. It also increased crop production by controlling the annual flooding along the Nile. Sorry, a little boring, but kind of interesting.

Anyway, the next morning we toured the dam, saw an unfinished obelisk, went to a papyrus store, and saw another . . . you guessed it, temple.

That afternoon, John/Denise and Mike/Winnie left for Cairo. It was nice to have Winnie to talk to, but it was also important to have two guys to hang out with for a few days. I made sure I thanked the wives for giving me a couple of playmates on the cruise.

On Tuesday the 21st, Maria and Kathy took a felucca ride on the river. I went in search of some Maalox. Of the fifteen people in our group, about half of us had stomach problems, probably from the food sitting out on the buffet tables every day. My dinner that night consisted of bread, soup with rice, and a banana. Exciting?

We checked out of the boat the next morning, with Maria and Kathy taking a day trip to Abu Simbel. I started my day around 10 am, grabbing a cab to the Nile Hotel, our next stop. My driver then proceeded to take me to the Neel Hotel. After conveniently getting it wrong, he expected me to pay for his mistake. He got an extra dollar.

Our room wasn't ready, so I took a leisurely stroll through Aswan and chilled out in a park overlooking the Nile. Another short walk got me to the Nubian Museum, which contains thousands of artifacts salvaged before the Aswan Dam was completed. It's rated one of the best museums in Egypt.

On Wednesday, we had an evening flight back to Cairo. Arriving at the airport, my stomach still wasn't right, so it was time to find the nearest bathroom. Walking in, I saw a bunch of empty stalls, but after a closer look, realized none of them had toilet paper.

Then, as if on cue, a little old man appeared with a small roll, ready to sell me a few sheets. Over the years, I've gotten into a habit of carrying my own travel roll, so I told him to get fucked. He knew exactly what that meant because he turned around and scurried out.

After the adjustment for Egypt time, our flight left just before midnight, getting us to our hotel around 2:00 a.m. Thursday. My first thought was welcome back to Cairo. There was smog, traffic, car horns, and people with their hand out. It was just like we left it.

At 7:00 a.m., the girls had a wake-up call. Their stay in Egypt was a little longer than mine, so they grabbed a cab for a ride to a bus station to get a couple of tickets to Sharm el Sheikh, a resort area on the Red Sea. After that, they used their driver for a little sight-seeing of their own.

They were late getting back, so it delayed the start of our trip organized by Dr. John, who picked us up in a mini-van. It's where we met Miena, our driver for the day, whom we quickly renamed Meanie. He wasn't; he was a great guy. Along for the ride were Denise, Mike, Winnie, and a cooler of beer. Beer wasn't my first choice, but it was a lot better than the French rum.

Our first stop was Giza, where the pyramids are located, about ten miles southwest of our hotel. Unfortunately, the city's massive sprawl has crept nearer and nearer over the years. We were standing by the Sphinx, looking back toward the city, when someone pointed out the signs of a Taco Bell and a KFC. That's just not right.

We were hoping to stick around after learning about a spectacular light show that took place every night. Unfortunately, it was closed to the public that day, having been booked by a medical conference that was going on in Cairo. Yes, the same conference our doctor friends had attended, but they never got around to getting tickets so they couldn't stay either.

I did get a couple of great pictures at Giza. One is of John and Winnie on camels, with John doing the "camel milk" pose. The other is of our group pretending to be a bunch of cheerleaders making a pyramid. Our tour guide lost it, telling us in his best English, he had been doing these tours for a long time and claimed we were the first group ever to make a pyramid at the pyramids. It was hard to believe we were the first, but it was fun to hear.

Our last stop was Saqqara to see the Step Pyramids. They're the oldest stone pyramids in Egypt and a breath of fresh air. With a lot less tourists, it meant a lot less people selling stuff and a lot less people with their hand out.

That night was last call, so the three of us were able to get a dinner reservation through our driver, at the restaurant the doctors had been to the night before. They really liked it, so we were looking forward to ending our stay on a high note, but somehow, our driver took us to the wrong place. It sounded a lot like my taxi problem in Aswan, so we turned around and walked out. Two minutes later, we found a cool place called La Bodega and had a great meal.

Early the next morning, I left before the girls, got a cab, and as usual, had to negotiate the fare. We agreed on a price, then he proceeded to take me to the wrong terminal. See a trend? Fortunately, making my flight wasn't an issue because we were on Egypt time, so no baksheesh (tip) for him. Get me out of Cairo.

Somehow, I made it to Paris in time to catch my connecting flight home, probably because they were also accustomed to the Egyptian concept of time. Then, sweet home Chicago.

Camel milk!

MOM CALLED

On Christmas Eve 2008, I worked my shift at Tailgator's and, as usual, got to bed around 5:00 a.m. Waking up, I noticed the answering machine's blinking light. Here's the message: "Hello, it's your mother. I know you're probably still sleeping. Call me when you get up." Sound pretty normal? There's a catch.

Anyway, I got up, cleaned up, and drove to my brother's place to spend Christmas with his family, our sister, and some in-laws.

Halfway through dinner, I stopped everyone to apologize. I almost forgot to tell them the news. Mom had called that morning and left a message.

The reaction was a lot of head-turning and a lot of strange looks. And now, the catch: Our mom died in 1991, making the call on my answering machine the perfect wrong number. Once the chills subsided, we all had a good laugh, then gave her a big wave—upward, by the way.

Fast-forward one year, to December 23, 2009. I came home to find this message on my machine: "Hello, this is Dr. Morelli's office calling to confirm your appointment on the 29th." First of all, I didn't have an appointment. Second, I had no idea who Dr. Morelli was. Yes, it was another wrong number, and yes, there was another catch. Morelli is my mom's maiden name. What are the chances?

Two days later, and I was back at my brother's home for Christmas, but didn't wait like the year before. Once inside, I started telling everyone about the new message. It was déjà vu all over again, with more chills and another big wave.

Now it's Christmas Day 2010. The routine was the same, but unfortunately, there was no new message from Mom. When I explained it was probably because I had gotten rid of my landline, my fourteen-year-old niece quickly came up with a solution. "Maybe Grandma will text us." Our guess was no.

About six weeks later, on February 6, 2011, I was at a friend's house to watch the Super Bowl with about a dozen other people. It's when Mom surprised me.

I was standing at the counter that divided the kitchen from the living room and, during halftime, told them the story you just read. The reaction in the room reminded me of 2008 and 2009 at my brother's house, just not as emotional.

As I finished, a little portable light—you know, the kind you can stick underneath a cabinet—fell and almost landed in my drink. That meant it was time for the traditional chills and the wave to my mom. We think this was her way of telling me I had missed her call at Christmas time.

Haven't heard from her since then.

2009 STL

I bought twenty-six tickets for the Hawks/Blues game on Saturday, January 17, so twenty people got on a train that morning with six tickets set aside for my daughter. The routine was to board the train at the Amtrak station in Summit, Illinois, a suburb just southwest of the Chicago city limits, returning Sunday night.

I would also make a stop at the Summit police station to let them know we'll be parking some cars overnight in the suburb's Amtrak lot. They would always thank me for the heads-up, then always take a few extra rides through the parking lot to check on our cars.

The first two weeks of the year had been brutally cold, and Saturday morning was no exception, with the wind chill well below zero. To make it worse, there was a problem with the tracks icing up, so the trains coming out of Union Station in downtown Chicago were running about an hour late. Our train was scheduled to arrive in Summit at 9:45 a.m., but it didn't get there until almost eleven o'clock.

While I boarded the train, a college-aged girl recognized me. She worked at the grocery store just down the alley from my condo and was smart enough to stay away from our group. Good move.

Our friend, whom we call Finn, had fallen down in the bar the night before and split his chin open. He seemed OK that night, but arrived at the station either still drunk or re-drunk.

An hour or so into the ride, when he got up to go to bathroom or maybe the bar, a few people noticed him taking the serpentine route down the aisle. They also witnessed him stumbling into the lap of an elderly woman in a wheelchair. Luckily, she wasn't hurt, and luckily, she had a sense of humor.

While checking into the hotel, an employee at the desk learned I was the one in charge of this interesting group, and felt my pain, so getting a few drink tickets for Steph and her friends and a couple extra tickets for me wasn't a problem. Because of that, some of us missed about half of the first period.

After the game, we skipped the Landing and its tourists and headed to Soulard, just south of downtown, hoping to see some live blues or jazz. So with all this good music in the area, where did we go? An Irish bar. It was only because my daughter had told some friends to meet her there after the game. It wasn't my first choice, or my second.

And as usual, there is always some connection with home. This time, we found out the band playing that night was one of the first ever to play at Fox's Restaurant around forty years earlier.

Later on, I was talking to Angie, one of my daughter's girlfriends, whom I've known since the girls were in fifth or sixth grade and played soccer together. After a minute or two, she started calling out, "Steph, Steph, Steph." When my daughter finally turned around to see what was wrong, Angie blurted out, "Your dad is hitting on me." I didn't think I was, but after a long day of drinking, it was certainly possible. Steph just shook her head and went back to whatever she was doing.

Over the years, after traveling to other cities to see our Chicago sports teams, we know the drill. Bars usually close at 1:00 a.m. As we got to last call, I started saying my goodbyes to her friends, but Steph informed me it wasn't time to go home yet.

I asked what she had in mind, since the bars in St. Louis were shutting down. She said we were going across the river (Mississippi), which had an ominous sound to it. Across the river meant Illinois, and at that time of night, it usually meant strip joints. She then lectured me. I was only in town for twenty-four hours, so I would be staying out until she said it was OK to go to my room.

It was time for a cab, so Steph, a male friend of hers, and Angie, the girl I allegedly hit on, headed to Illinois with me and my friend Brenda. Personally, I'm not a big fan of strip joints. You end up spending a lot of money just so you can go home and take a cold shower, but there was some good news. The cover charge was waived that night when you produced your ticket stub from the hockey game.

We got a table and ordered some drinks. Brenda was shocked when I ordered a beer. I'm a rum drinker, but I figured one bottle of beer would probably last me the rest of the night. It was time to do the mature thing. I even surprised myself.

A few minutes after sitting down, I asked my daughter how often she came to this place. Her reaction was a funny look, wondering where that question came from. It was just a hunch, but a couple of minutes later, a girl they knew came over and joined us. The interesting thing was her outfit. All she was wearing was a G-string.

The best part of the story was when I went back to work. During the next couple of weeks, people would ask how the trip went. My answer was it went great and at the end of the night, my kid dragged me off to a strip club. You have to realize some of the people didn't know me that well, so their response was "We didn't know you had a son." My answer: "I don't." Then I would wait for their reaction.

And we beat the Blues 2-1 in OT.

2009 KENTUCKY DERBY

After my shift at the bar on Friday night, May 1, and a quick stop home to fill a cooler, I jumped back in my van. Destination? My first Kentucky Derby. I snuck in about a three-hour nap somewhere on Route 65, arriving in Louisville in the late morning.

I found a parking lot a mile from the track and grabbed a spot next to the sidewalk that would lead me up the street to Churchill Downs. The sign said $20 to park, but nobody had stopped me when I pulled in. Paying the fee seemed to be the safe thing to do. The alternative was to chance it and hope my van didn't get towed. I took the $20 insurance policy.

It also meant walking back to the entrance to pay the tab instead of heading to the track. Ten steps out of my van and what did I hear? "Hey, Dickie!" Of course, somebody knew me. There were only about 150,000 people in attendance. It was a customer from McMahon's, where I had worked until late 2003. We talked for a minute. I paid my parking fee, then made it to Churchill Downs without anybody else recognizing me.

I bought a ticket to the infield, joining about 75,000 drunks, then a couple of hours later, ran into someone else who knew me. It was a woman I had been with a couple of years back. I think it's called a one-night stand. Ever hear of it? Anyway, we went back so she could introduce me to her friends, and yes, someone else knew me.

It was another female customer from McMahon's who was friends with a guy that was going through a separation with a friend of mine. Staying wasn't a good idea because somebody would probably say something about the breakup I didn't need to hear and that meant I would probably respond.

It was time to move on, but I screwed up and mentioned my plan to drive home after the race. The girls told me no, that was crazy. They had a hotel room for the night and invited me to stay and party with them. Walking away seemed like the right thing to do. Actually, I ran.

The funniest part of the day occurred during my food break. After grabbing something to eat, I found a quiet spot on the grass behind some of the food booths and struck up a conversation with a couple of twenty-something girls sitting to my left.

A few minutes later, the one girl nudged me and pointed to the two girls sitting to my right. A quick look told me they were drunk, and as if on cue, the one next to me started a slow lean to one side. She was a blonde named Brittany, who finally toppled over and rolled down the small slope in front of us. Luckily for her, she was wearing underwear, because her dress ended up around her neck. The quote of the day: "Oh, Brittany, not again!"

As it got closer to post time, I placed my mandatory bet, ordered my mandatory mint julep, and found a spot to stand near the starting gate. Over the years, I heard stories from people who went to the derby, got a comfy spot on the infield, and never even saw a horse. I did not want to be one of those people.

Anyway, I lost the bet when a horse named Mine That Bird, a 50-1 shot who was dead last coming out of the first turn, rallied to win the race. The mint julep was a loser too, but at least I saw some horses as they left the starting gate.

When the derby ends, thousands of people head for the exits. A lot of them come just for the one race, and the rest of them, I'm guessing, are out of money. I stayed for one more race. After the initial rush of people leaving the track combined with a leisurely walk to my van, it was an easy exit out of Louisville.

On the way home, I stopped at a TGI Friday's in Lafayette, Indiana and watched the second half of the Bulls/Celtics playoff game. When it was over, I hit the road again and made it home for last call.

It was a good day.

Michigan City 2009

The theme this year? "Trailer Trash."

I rented the same beach house in Michigan City, Indiana, from Saturday afternoon, September 4, until the next Saturday morning. Again, people would come and go, depending on their schedule, with the main party taking place on Thursday and Friday.

The decor was provided by a few thrift stores, so it didn't cost me much. At the store in Crestwood, Illinois, I found a bathroom sink for a few dollars. As the woman at the counter gave me my change, she said, "I hope it fits." My reply: "No problem, it's going to fit perfectly in my front yard." Her reaction was a very perplexed look.

Before arriving, I made a stop at another thrift store, this time in Michigan City, where I loaded up a basket with socks, bras, panties, men's underwear, and some rope to use as a clothesline. I decided to wait until I left Illinois, hoping nobody would recognize me. This time at checkout, there were two guys standing behind the counter who were dying to know what I was up to. They loved the idea.

Our house and the one next door shared a double driveway. Pulling in, I saw two twenty-something girls sitting on their front porch. After getting out of my van, I said hello, then started unloading my stuff. It didn't take long before they walked over because, just like the guys at the thrift store, they had to know what I was up to, and just like the guys at the thrift store, they loved the idea.

So after I had known them for just a couple of minutes, one of the girls got on the hood of her car and helped me run a rope across the driveway from my house to their house. With that done, they helped me hang all the classy-looking clothes.

The decorations were pretty basic. It was kids' cartoon bed sheets and some aluminum foil as drapes, a few religious candles, and yes, the famous bathroom sink. The menu was also pretty basic. It was Spam, pork and beans, luncheon loaf, Cheez Whiz, vienna sausage, moon pies, and Spam. Ring a bell? And don't forget the undies hanging in the driveway.

The next night, our two houses got together for a party in our double driveway. At some point, the conversation turned to nudity, so I immediately mentioned being naked on a couple of beaches while traveling in the Greek islands and, of course, on most of the houseboat trips.

Not surprisingly, the next question was would I get naked there. They didn't know me, but my friends/coworkers Bob and Amy did. Hearing that, they started to run toward me like a scene from a movie run in slow motion. Nooooooo! Too late. I calmly got undressed, sat back down, and finished my drink.

The next afternoon, a few of us were relaxing (that meant drinking) on the front porch. The beach would have been a great idea, but it was a whole block away. While sitting there, a couple in a pickup truck stopped in front of the house. We knew why.

The guy got out, then walked over and asked how much we wanted for the bathroom sink. It was tough, but we had to tell him it wasn't for sale. After they drove away, I thanked everyone for not laughing until the truck turned the corner. In hindsight, I should have sold it and used the money to buy more moon pies.

We are all so precious.

2009 COPENHAGEN

In February, I was hanging out at BJ McMahon's. The reason was Hurricane Gumbo, a band who gets busy in the months leading up to Fat Tuesday. It wasn't actually Fat Tuesday; it was a "holiday" called Chubby Thursday, invented by Roger.

Kenny, who worked at the bar, also played in the band. That night, I hung out with his wife and a couple of her friends. One of the girls was from Belgium, so we started trading stories about our travels in Europe.

When I mentioned my plan to go somewhere in Scandinavia in the fall, she lit up, because she worked for SAS (Scandinavian Airlines). My friend Mike and I hadn't decided where, but SAS had some great airfares coming out of Chicago. She gave me her email address and said to contact her when we figured out our schedule.

Our original plan was to make Helsinki, Finland, the first stop because the Blackhawks were playing their first two games of the NHL season there on October 2 and 3. Sounded good, until we learned the only way to see the Hawks was to purchase the whole package, which included hotel and airfare. It was expensive, with the hotel a couple of stars higher than what we needed, plus Mike had been to Finland before, so we took a pass.

With Helsinki off the short list, our next two choices were Stockholm and Copenhagen. After a little research, we learned the Detroit Red Wings and the St. Louis Blues were opening their season against each other in Stockholm on the same two days. We weren't really interested in hanging out with Red Wings or Blues fans, so we decided to start in Copenhagen.

After locking in our air and hotel reservations, we learned the Olympic Festival and 2016 Summer Olympic announcement would be taking place in Copenhagen while we were there. Not that big of a deal for the average

American, but Chicago was one of the final four cities pursuing the Olympic bid. Rio, Tokyo, and Madrid were the other three.

In hindsight, had we known what was going on before making our reservations, we probably would have taken Copenhagen off the list, assuming the city was booked solid. Sometimes, not knowing what you're doing can go a long way.

With our plans set, I sent my SAS friend the flight information, and she was able to move us up to business class. Since we were big shots for the day, the two-hour layover in Stockholm was spent in the first-class lounge. We took full advantage of it.

When we arrived in Copenhagen, the weather was cold, windy, and rainy, and stayed like that for most of our time there. We had a room at the Ansgar Hotel, a short walk to the city's main train station and, coincidentally, a short walk to the city's red-light district. So that's why it was easy to find a place. We took a pass on the local entertainment.

Not counting the hookers, a couple of things stood out. The first one was a 7-Eleven convenience store every couple of blocks. They were small and didn't have the inventory of stuff we're used to seeing in the stores at home, but on a good note, most of them sold alcohol.

The other thing was bicycles. There were more bikes parked by the train station than there were cars. We also noticed there weren't many overweight women in the city. That's because they all rode bikes, some in high heels, and it didn't matter what time it was. We would be walking back to our room from some bar around two in the morning and would see women pedaling home alone, completely safe.

Chicago and Copenhagen have a few similarities. They're both very flat, near a body of water, and bike friendly. The difference is for every bicycle in Chicago, there are probably a thousand bikes in Copenhagen. On day 2, we noticed a good portion of the city's bike paths had left-turn lanes.

While walking home from the bars the first night, we got a lesson on how to cross the street. One never crosses against the light, even when there isn't any traffic. No jaywalking allowed. You only cross at the light and with the light, because you can be ticketed at any hour of the day. What a difference a year makes. I took my life in my own hands trying to cross a busy, wide, one-way street in Cairo, Egypt. There is one good thing about having to wait at a traffic light in Copenhagen. You can cross the street at any time of the day with a drink in your hand, so a red light wasn't that big of a deal.

At the same time the Olympic Festival was going on, Copenhagen was hosting its annual Blues Fest, with a Chicago flair to it. We got to see Eddie "The Chief" Clearwater, a Chicago blues icon, plus a Swedish band called Thorbjorn Risager. The Chief! The Chief!

Friday was Copenhagen's all-day party, which took place in the city's main square, followed by the Olympics announcement in the early evening, followed by more partying. That meant we played tourist early, taking the mandatory water tour and obligatory stop to see the statue of the Mermaid. For some reason, she's the city's most popular tourist attraction.

After that, we hung out in Nyhavn, a neighborhood full of colorful 300- to 400-year-old buildings along a canal that connects the city's harbor to the sea. One side is mainly personal residences and the other mainly shops, cafés, and bars. The food and drink places got the sunnier side, so that's where everyone hangs out.

If you don't want to sit inside, remember, there are 7-Elevens everywhere. What you do is grab a couple of drinks and something to munch on and head back to the canal. Then, you sit your ass down near the water and make yourself at home. It's been called the longest bar in Scandinavia.

We chilled out for a while, then it was time to start our walk to the city square for the Olympic celebration. On the way there, we saw President Obama's motorcade. I gave Michelle a call, but she blew me off. Can you believe that?

Funny thing; while Mike and I were waiting for the motorcade to pass, we struck up a conversation with a local Dane. He freaked us out when he used the words "I reckon." Can't imagine anyone else in Denmark using those words.

Being in the city square that evening was a blast until the announcement telling everyone Chicago was the first city eliminated. Huh? Mike and I looked at each other, not wanting to believe what we heard. I had been waving my City of Chicago flag but quickly folded it up and stuck it in my bag.

It wasn't much fun anymore, so we left the square and headed to the Hotel D'Angleterre to drown our sorrows. I picked it because it's listed in the book *1,000 Places to See Before You Die*. Walking in, I could tell we were in the home hotel of the Madrid Olympic Committee.

At the bar, we struck up a conversation with the people drinking there. It was pretty obvious they were from the committee, so after learning we were from Chicago, they expressed their sympathies and their amazement. Nobody thought we would be eliminated first. The common assumption was Tokyo and Madrid would be the first cities to go, with Rio and Chicago fighting it out for the Olympic bid.

I told the group once Chicago was voted out, Madrid was my next choice, because it would give me a good reason to return there. After some curious looks, I was able to tell them about my semester of school at the University of Madrid in the fall of '72.

One of the men from the committee had this faraway look on his face, trying to remember where he would have been at that time, then it came to him. He was in London for a semester of school. It was like talking to me. He did the same thing I did, at the same age.

With a drink in hand, I walked into the lobby and took a seat at a long banquet table. It had a few boxes of Madrid Olympic stuff, so I grabbed a few brochures and started to browse through them. I also grabbed a commemorative bracelet and a few committee IDs from another box. The bracelet didn't fit, but I hung an ID around my neck, immediately becoming Julio M——.

Soon after that, with my access to the IDs, Mike became "Miguel." Miguel—I mean, Mike kept coming out from the bar to tell me he wasn't going to bail me out of jail. I told him to relax. As long as it looked like I knew what I was doing, nobody would even raise an eyebrow. I was right.

The final straw was rolling up the tablecloth and putting it in my bag. Madrid's Olympic logo was sewn into both ends, so I couldn't pass it up. I took a small piece of the tablecloth home, cut out the logo, and hung it on a wall.

On Saturday, we took a short train ride to Roskilde, which was the capital of Denmark until 1450. The wind and rain continued, only this time it was sideways. Not counting the weather, it was a good trip, with an awesome museum of old Viking ships. I purchased one and brought it home, but don't think it's authentic. It's only four inches long.

The city also has a beautiful cathedral, which was built during the twelfth and thirteenth centuries. We tried to go in, but we were denied because of a wedding going on at the time. Mike tried to explain he was the best man and was running late, but it didn't work.

Sunday was last call. Our first stop was Rosenborg Slot, the Danish Royal Palace, where we took the tour, saw the Danish crown jewels, and got to walk the palace grounds. Then it was time to head to our favorite place in Copenhagen. Yes, that would be Nyhavn.

On our way there, we found Ida Davidson's, a restaurant famous for its smørrebrød sandwich. It's also in the *1,000 Places* book, so we had to check it out. Unfortunately, we picked Sunday, the one day of the week they were closed, which meant it got an asterisk on my *1,000 Places* list.

Near the end of our walk, Mike finally lost it. I think every bike in the city is equipped with a bell so riders can alert the people walking in front of them. Mike was usually walking in a bike path, so he kept hearing "ring, ring, ring" behind him. He finally went on a short rant, got it out of his system, and finally started getting out of the bike paths.

While drinking by the water's edge, we met a couple from Chicago who were kind enough to give us two 2016 Chicago Olympic pins. I'm guessing they had access to a few more because he happened to be the president of the Southland Tourist Bureau, which covers Chicago's south suburbs. One more thing: the sun was out.

On our final walk to the hotel, we stopped at a bar called Sprecher's, had one drink, then calmly waited for another, and waited. It was a male bartender, so I'm guessing the reason was our lack of boobs. Jeff must have relatives in Denmark (inside joke). We actually had to leave and go to a Hard Rock Cafe to end our night.

My final thought was I might come back and sell umbrellas on a street corner. Other than the weather, Copenhagen was great. Next stop, Stockholm.

2009 STOCKHOLM

On Monday, October 5, we arrived in Stockholm and checked into our hotel somewhere around 3:00 p.m. Walking into the room, we immediately noticed the two single beds had been moved together. A little weird, so we quickly moved them apart, way apart.

Our plan was to ride the Hop-On/Hop-Off bus to get a quick feel for the city, but couldn't even hop on. By the time we got out of the room, the buses had stopped running for the day, but there was a backup plan.

It was time to take a walk around the neighborhood and find a bar we could call home. You know the drill. We play tourist during the day, then settle into our new home every night. In Stockholm, it would be Molly Malone's.

On Tuesday, we found Stockholm in a Nutshell. It's similar to the Hop-On/Hop-Off tour, but only half of it is spent on a bus. The other half is on a boat. Stockholm is a city of fourteen islands and around fifty bridges, so the bus/boat combination was the way to go.

When it was over, we walked through an area called Gamla Stan, the old town section of the city. It's where I had my first and, probably, my last Swedish beer. Working our way back to the main part of town, we discovered Drottninggatan (Queen Street). It's pedestrian only, with a lot of shopping choices and a lot of places to eat and drink, similar to Stroget in Copenhagen.

Returning to the room, we sat our asses down, looked at the clock, and started laughing. It was six o'clock. Once we stopped laughing, it was time to rally, hitting an Aussie bar called Boomerang's to wake up, followed by a Greek restaurant for dinner.

Our next stop was the Nordic Sea Hotel and a room just around the corner from its front desk. It was time to go to the Absolut Ice Bar, where everything, from the bar, to the seats and tables, to the glasses, is made of ice. The temperature was posted at -5 degrees Celsius, which translates to about 23 degrees at home. The $35 entrance fee seemed a little steep, but it included our first drink and a parka to keep warm.

It wasn't busy, so after sitting on an ice sofa for a few minutes, we moved to the bar. Our second drink would have cost about $15, so we decided it was one and done, but while talking to the bartender, I mentioned how we were in the same line of work. Hearing that, he bought our next drink, then let me take my parka off and go behind the bar for a cool photo op.

Mike took a great picture of me leaning on the bar, holding a bottle of Absolut Mango. It became one of the pictures I considered putting on the cover of this book. A couple of more stops and it was time to crash. We made it all the way to 11:00 p.m.

On Wednesday, a long walk got us to Djurgarden Island. A bus would have been easier, but we thought the walk would give us a chance to soak up a little of the local atmosphere.

One of the must-see things on the island is the Vasa Museum. In 1628, the Vasa was about to become the most awesome warship in existence, but ran into a problem on its maiden voyage. Long story short: It was top-heavy and a strong wind blew it over. Finally lifted out of the water in the early '60s, it's gone through a slow restoration and is kept in a huge climate-controlled room.

The other highlight is Skansen. It opened in 1891 as the world's first open-air museum, showing how Swedes lived in the late 1800s. There are over one hundred historic buildings, including some windmills. We even saw some real reindeer, plus a great view looking back across the water at the city. Hope that wasn't too boring.

Now it's Thursday, and it was our "get away from your roommate" day. Amazingly, I was up by 7:00 a.m. and out the door thirty minutes later.

An hour boat ride got me to the town of Vaxholm, known as the Gateway to the Archipelago. Believe it or not, the area in and around Stockholm consists of over 30,000 islands, with ferryboats stopping at over 200 of them. Vaxholm, with a population of only five thousand, has sixty-four small islands. Its main tourist site is a fort built in 1549, but was closed that day. Luckily, the city itself was worth the trip.

Back in Stockholm, I took a walk around Sodermalm, one of the city's largest islands, then Fjallgatan, an interesting street located on a bluff looking down at the city center. After seeing the old cemetery in Vaxholm, these houses were pretty new. They were from the early 1700s.

It was time for a few drinks, so I barhopped back into Gamla Stan. Nothing out of the ordinary, except for a bartender I met who was from Montenegro. He was a little surprised I heard of his country and even more surprised I knew where it was. And that would be the end of my "get away from your roommate" day.

We started Friday with a two-hour tour called Under the Bridges on a boat that seated around one hundred people, going from the Baltic Sea through a set of locks to Lake Malaren. The majority of the seats were inside, with maybe twenty outside at the back of the boat. We sat outside.

The tour went by the Parliament Building, City Hall, and the building where the Nobel Prize Dinner takes place every year. It also passed a cute little sandy beach, which the locals think is a gift from God. It's a little bigger than a postage stamp.

We also met Kyle and Nicole, a couple from Detroit who were there to see their Red Wings open the NHL season. We had scheduled Stockholm after Copenhagen so we wouldn't be around any Detroit or St. Louis fans, but got lucky and continued partying with them.

During our stop at a TGI Friday's, the bartender heard us talking about them being big hockey fans from Detroit, so he introduced himself. His name was Frederick and he was the best friend of Johan Franzen, who played for the Red Wings, so of course, we were instructed to say hello to Johan if/when we met him.

One more thing about the boat tour: Over the years, I've gotten used to getting out of the way of some stupid American being stupid. This time, it was a stupid Ugandan. One guy stood at the back of the boat and, while loudly talking on his cell phone, began narrating what he was seeing. His friend never said a word, but when the boat docked, they had to be the first ones off, pushing aside Kyle, Nicole, and a few other people. I actually felt bad for a couple of Red Wings fans.

After that, it was a good walk to Molly Malone's, with one small detour. Mike's a biker, so he was thrilled when we found a Harley-Davidson Store and spent over $100 on T-shirts. In an emotional show of gratitude, the store owner gave him a handful of store pens.

Even though it was our last night in Stockholm, we left our home bar to check out a few other places in the area. A few minutes later, we asked a doorman if he could give us a little insight as to what was around.

In both cities, we had gotten into a habit of asking people where they were from because we kept meeting people from so many different countries. The doorman didn't look Swedish, so I asked. He said he was Greek, so my response was "Haga misu, malaka." The look on his face was priceless, and he needed to know where I learned Greek, especially the words I spoke to him.

I explained when you work in the bar/restaurant business in the Chicago area, you can't help but pick up a little bit of the Greek language. He said I just made his day, because nobody ever spoke Greek to him in Stockholm. Mike was quietly standing there, dying to know what was going on. He got his wish when the doorman said it meant "Fuck you, jagoff." Now the priceless look came from Mike.

Once the laughing stopped, we thanked him for the information and started to walk away, but it wasn't over. I thought a little *apo piso* might be fun later that night. After another priceless look, while laughing, he ordered me never to speak to him again.

Now it's déjà vu for Mike as he waited for the translation. I explained it was slang for "the Greek way," which means "up the butt." Sorry. Mike shook his head, the doorman kept laughing, and we moved on.

We stopped at Boomerang's again, followed by TGI Friday's, where Fred, the bartender, had an extra beer for Mike. He must have felt guilty because shortly after that, I got one too. A few minutes later, it was two free Long Islands. And a few minutes later it was a giant mojito. That's right, just one, and it wasn't for me.

That might have been last call for drinks in Scandinavia, but the night wasn't over. On our walk to the room, we joined a handful of people who got to listen to a guy singing opera from his balcony. Turning the corner, I had to take one more picture. It was a 7-Eleven store, which would remind me of all of them I saw in Stockholm and Copenhagen. Oh, and Fred went home alone.

We're at the airport the next morning, and after flying business class to Copenhagen, my SAS friend told me to ask at the desk if there was a chance to get bumped up for our flight home. The employee told me the flight was full, but to ask again during boarding to see if everyone showed up. Unfortunately, everyone did, because my gut feeling was, we would have gotten the upgrade.

Anyway, home safe.

On this trip, Mike and I talked to people from all over the world. Here's our list:

1. England
2. Ireland
3. Norway
4. Sweden
5. Denmark
6. Brazil
7. South Africa
8. Austria
9. Thailand
10. Spain
11. Japan
12. Venezuela
13. Iraq
14. Kurdistan
15. Montenegro
16. Mexico
17. Greece
18. Iceland
19. Australia

Oh yeah, almost forgot Indiana and Wisconsin.

And here's our list of the different ethnic foods we sampled: Danish, Italian, English, Spanish, Greek, German, Mexican, Swedish, and Indian.

2009 Bears in Cincy

The Bears were in Cincinnati on Sunday, October 25, to play the Bengals. I got a group together and rented an RV, arriving Saturday afternoon. We stayed at the Travelodge in Newport, Kentucky, not in the RV and, as usual, ended the night at Kelly's Keg, now called Bart's.

Instead of walking a half mile across the river to the stadium, I drove the van so we could tailgate. For $90, I got to park about a half mile from the stadium. As it turned out, we picked a good spot, because one of the guys in the motor home next to us was a great cook who loved sharing his stuff. The fact that we were Bears fans didn't matter. We all dined together on steak, shrimp, scallops wrapped in bacon, and homemade chocolate chip cookies for dessert. That's when my friend, Brenda, asked their chef to marry her. Didn't happen.

The game was over in a hurry. Ten minutes in, and we were already down 14-0. By halftime, it was 31-3. The final score was 45-10.

There was one highlight. Two weeks earlier, at a bar in Stockholm, Sweden, I was talking to another American, who happened to be from Cincinnati and, of course, had tickets to the same game. We met up at halftime for a drink and a few laughs.

Most of the group was back at the RV before the game even ended. As soon as we had a full crew, it was time to get outta town.

Home safe.

10's

2010 SHAWNA

While I worked at the bar one night in February, a beautiful blonde walked in. She was a friend of a couple of waiters from Fox's, so when there was a lull in the action, I came over and had the guys introduce me. I discovered she was a big Blackhawks fan, so about a month later, on Thursday, March 25, we drove to Columbus, Ohio, because the Blackhawks were there to play the Blue Jackets.

We stayed at the Drury Inn, about a half-mile walk to the arena, and like the one in St. Louis, it offered free appetizers and a couple of drinks for their customers in the hotel lobby from 5:00 p.m. to 7:00 p.m. While checking in a little after five, we got more than a few stares, probably because Shawna was about thirty years younger than me. Once up in the room, she threw on a Hawks jersey and we headed back down. The majority of the customers seemed to be middle-aged women, and most of them seemed to be looking our way, which was an ego boost for me. Shawna's take on it was that we had walked into a menopause convention. A couple of snacks and a couple of drinks and it was time for some hockey.

Columbus scored in the first minute of the first period, scored four more times in the second period, and went on to win 8-3. During each intermission, we would go down to one of the bars in the concourse, where I got to watch guys line up to buy her a drink. She always let them know if they were going to buy her one, they had to buy me one. She was awesome.

After the game, the routine continued at a couple of bars near the arena. Then it was a slow walk to our hotel. And what did we do after getting back to the room? Made a couple of drinks, turned on the TV, and curled up on the couch. Minutes later, Shawna was in the bathroom, kneeling in front of the porcelain. Not long after that, we crawled into bed and passed out. I woke up the next morning and found her asleep on the couch. She had puked again and figured it was closer to the bathroom and a lot safer for me. What a thoughtful woman.

On the way home, we stopped to hydrate, gas up, and stuff down some hangover food, somewhere in Indiana. She went to the Burger King while I got the gas and the Gatorade. Back at the van, both of us were laughing. It was like we were reading each other's mind, thinking everyone we saw looked like they were related to each other.

Home hydrated, but still hungover.

We had a great time together, but I knew I wasn't young enough to pursue her. Soon after that, she moved to Las Vegas, we think in search of a husband. In late 2013, I learned Shawna had died in a car accident earlier that year.

I miss her.

2010 Fraternity Reunions

In March 2010, a dozen fraternity brothers got together at Tailgator's. We sat around for hours trying, usually unsuccessfully, to remember things from college, but did agree on one thing: this would happen again.

After that, John V. took charge. One year later, around eighty fraternity brothers showed up at the bar on a Sunday afternoon, some from over forty years ago. Included in the group were two of the founding fathers who had graduated in the late '60s. Absolutely amazing!

The most-used line of the night? "Oh yeah." Three guys would be standing together and would spot another fraternity brother walking into the bar. Two of them wouldn't be able to place him, but the third guy would say, "That's Dickie Groth."

"Oh yeah!"

But easily, the best line of the night came from Radar, an old roommate of mine: "If we did today what we did then, we would either be dead or in jail." Nobody argued.

The reunions continued, and on July 18, 2017, we met at Lewis University to celebrate the fiftieth anniversary of the founding of the fraternity. About fifty brothers showed up that day, with around fifteen of them staying overnight in Sheil Hall.

The university gave us some tours on golf carts to refresh our memories and an area to play some Bags and Horseshoes where they set up a mini-bar that served beer and wine. That's right, no rum.

Dinner was next on our schedule, again with an open bar. Learning it also was beer and wine only, two of us made the ten-minute drive to a liquor store for some rum.

The biggest surprise was nobody made the short drive into town (Lockport) for a few drinks at the bar we lived in during school. OMG, did we mature?

2010 Cubs in Cincy

The Cubs were in Cincinnati in early May for a weekend series with the Reds. I got a group together and rented an RV. We had tickets for the Friday and Saturday night games.

The drive there is usually a no-brainer, but this time I had to battle a strong crosswind on the way south through Indiana on Route 65. It was so bad, I had to pull over because we were about to lose the RV's side awning. That's when Jaime stepped up and donated her cute pink belt. We used it to secure the awning, and it stayed there for the rest of the trip.

For Friday, I got a group of cheap seats down the right field line in the upper deck. It was a memorable night because of Cub shortstop, Starlin Castro. At his first at-bat in his first game as a major leaguer, he hit a home run and finished the night with six RBIs. The Cubs won 14-7.

After the game, we went directly to Bart's, the old Kelly's Keg, because we were staying across the street at the Travelodge Motel. Sound familiar?

The ten of us settled in, but after a couple of hours, our group was a little disappointed. We made up a good portion of their crowd, spent a lot of money, and never got a free drink. As a bartender, I usually side with the bar because you never go into a place expecting a free one. I think this time was a little different. It now seemed like a good idea to get some beer to go and finish the night in the RV. A couple of guys on the trip talked me out of buying the beer, but agreed it was a good idea to go. Minutes later, the rest of us learned why. While the barback was bringing cases of beer up to stock the bar, one of the guys from our group saw them unguarded for a minute and grabbed a couple.

On Saturday afternoon, Jaime needed some alone time and hung out in the motorhome for a while. It was quiet until a few teenage boys walking through the parking lot stopped and asked if she could buy them some beer. She said no, lifted up her shirt to give them a quick look at her boobs, then told them to move on. They did as they were told.

That night, the seats were on the first base side again, but a little better than the night before. Yeah, we were in the upper deck, but this time in the Club Level with an all-you-can-eat buffet. Needless to say, the infamous water bottle with rum made an appearance and I needed it. The Cubs lost 14-2.

After the game, it was back to Bart's. No free drinks and no free cases of beer, but we closed the place anyway. Location was its selling point.

Home Sunday night.

2010 Michigan City

We're back in late August, and the theme for the house was Wild West Saloon, not that it mattered. I thought the decorations looked great, but I was one of only a few who made it to the house that week. It was so bad that two people, with no connection to each other, called before leaving home to make sure I would be there when they arrived. I'm still waiting for them.

On one of my free nights during the middle of the week, while walking through Washington Park on the way to a couple of bars, I spotted a wallet in the grass. It belonged to a young guy from Pennsylvania. My first stop was the Shoreline Brewery, but before getting there, I had to walk past the Michigan City Police Station, so I stopped to turn in the wallet. It took a little longer than I thought because there was a woman in front of me trying to find out what jail her son was in. Was it La Porte or Michigan City? Unfortunately for her, it was La Porte, about thirty minutes away.

Then it was my turn, so I stepped up and handed the wallet to the officer. He thanked me, then asked for my name, phone number, and social security number. My SSN? That seemed a little strange. Anyway, I did my good deed so it was time to drink.

When the bartender at Shoreline had a minute, I told her my story about the wallet. She stared at me for a second with a funny look on her face, then asked if it belonged to a young guy from Pennsylvania. Now it was my turn to give her "the look."

If I had gone straight to the bar without stopping at the police station, I could have handed the wallet to its owner. Hindsight is amazing. Hope he got it back.

Oh and the Wild West Saloon wasn't very wild.

2010 STL

In June, the Blackhawks won the Stanley Cup, so I was looking forward to our trip to St. Louis. It was time to rub it in, but the schedule-makers weren't much help. There were no Saturday night games, so I ran a trip for a game on Friday, October 22.

The Saturday games are a no-brainer. We take the train there on Saturday morning, with the return ride getting us home by nine o'clock on Sunday night. The average person can do it without taking time off from work.

Just as I thought, Friday was a tough sell. What made it worse was my inability to book the Drury Inn-Union Station, our place to stay in St. Louis. They directed me to the Pear Tree Inn, also a Drury Hotel, just a few blocks further from the arena but a step down in class. It wasn't the end of the world, but it wasn't the same.

At the Drury Inn, we would scarf down some great appetizers and drink some hard liquor before the game. The Pear Tree only served chips or pretzels and beer or wine, which meant my "water" bottle made an appearance before the game. The good thing was we could still do everything on foot.

In celebration of the 2010 Stanley Cup champions, Anheuser-Busch had produced aluminum Bud Light bottles with the Blackhawk and Stanley Cup logos on them, I'm guessing just in northern Illinois. While talking with my Blues group sales rep, I told her about the bottles and that I would be bringing one for her desk. Her reply: "You wouldn't dare!"

Our train pulled in at 3:00 p.m. I checked my group into the hotel, then immediately headed to the Scottrade Center and the Blues office. When I walked in, the receptionist asked how she could help me. That's when I whipped out one of the Bud Light bottles. She responded with a wave of the finger, telling me: "You can't bring that in here."

A couple of minutes later, I met my rep and got to thank her for the service she provided over the last few years. Then, I presented her with the Blackhawk's Bud Light bottle. She wasn't thrilled, but we stayed friends until she left the organization in 2013. I'll miss her.

The Blues beat us 4-2.

2011 PENSACOLA BEACH

Done working my shift on Easter Sunday night, April 24, I got in the van around 2:30 a.m. and started driving south. Just like in 2000, I was heading to Pensacola Beach, Florida, but after four hours of high winds and heavy rain, it was time to find a rest area.

I got about three hours sleep, then hit the road again. The strong winds started up again as if they waited until my nap was over and would continue for most of the trip. The rainstorms were kinder, letting up around noon.

Before leaving home, I went online to check out the hotel situation, but I didn't make a reservation for the first night. If I was running late, it would be no problem sleeping in the van again.

Arriving early Monday evening, my first thought was if I was in the right place. I didn't think it could change that much in eleven years, then learned about Hurricane Ivan, which hit the area in 2006. A couple of big hotel chains had just reopened in the last few months. I went with the Cabana Motel.

After settling in, a short walk got me to a bar/grill called Sidelines. I met Ashley, a bartender, who assured me the Blackhawks playoff game would be on a couple of the TVs the next night.

It wasn't busy, so we talked about the hurricane and the damage it inflicted. Then it finally hit me. I'd been here before. I thought the place looked familiar. The logo on the employee T-shirts should have tipped me off because I have a Sidelines shirt hanging in my closet.

In 2000, after getting in my van and heading south in search of some warm weather, I ended up in Pensacola Beach and, at some point, ended up at Sidelines. It was also the trip where I was able to get my hockey fix. On 2/11, I saw the Pensacola Ice Pilots beat the Mobile Mysticks in a minor-league game. The next night, on the drive home, I saw the Blackhawks beat the Thrashers 4-3 in Atlanta.

One of the things I liked about the area was the choice of bike trails. Unfortunately, the high winds that kept me company on the way down on Monday were still blowing on Tuesday, so I didn't even attempt a ride. The hotel pool was my backup plan.

I met a few people at poolside. One of them was a woman named Jamie, who had dated a guy named Jamie and had a friend named Jamie. I had to call my friend Jaime (different spelling, same pronunciation), just to tell her.

I also called my daughter after hearing them talking about some tornados hitting the St. Louis area over the weekend. Steph told me how she and her dog had curled up in the bathtub under a blanket while the sirens were going off. A tornado did touch down a couple of miles away, but she was safe.

Now off the phone, I heard the rest of their story. It turned out they were also from suburban St. Louis and had left for Florida the day before the storms hit. The man's brother had called to tell them about their home. It was good news/bad news. Bad news: the house had been severely damaged. Good news: they weren't in it when the storm hit.

It's Tuesday night and time to go to Sidelines to watch the Hawks game. I got a seat at the bar with the hockey game in front of me and the Chicago Bulls game just to my left. The Cardinals game was to my right, with the Cubs next in line, and I quickly found out most of the people around me were from St. Louis.

All the Blackhawk fans were around the corner at another TV, but I survived the night. It was actually a lot of fun talking to a bunch of people from St. Louis. The Hawks didn't have as much fun. They were eliminated by Vancouver.

I also met a couple from Vancouver, and we had a good laugh when they told me Chicago was the next stop on their vacation. They were nice and didn't rub it in too much, probably hoping to get some safe recommendations from me.

On Wednesday, I changed hotels, moving to the Paradise Inn, a few blocks away. My room was pretty basic, plus it left me a long, grueling walk to the pool. It was about ten feet, but I toughed it out. It also had an outdoor bar and an outdoor stage for live entertainment.

It was, by far, the windiest day, so riding the bike was impossible.

There were times when it was difficult to walk. That sand stings. It was also the day the state of Alabama was hammered by around sixty tornados, causing 250 deaths across the state. The storms were so widespread there was even a tornado warning for the Pensacola area. Based on the reaction of some of the locals, it's a rare event.

That evening, I walked across the street to a Holiday Inn and settled in at their bar. It had been open for one month. I met a woman from Wisconsin who was a big Packer fan, a woman from Michigan who was a big Wolverine fan, and a female bartender who was a big Buckeye fan. She was my favorite. OH . . . IO. After that, it was Sidelines again, finishing up at my hotel bar.

The next morning, I took a drive looking for the Flora-Bama Roadhouse, a bar/grill on the Florida-Alabama border. The story I was told was when you get up from the bar to go to the bathroom, you cross the state line. The other story is the Alabama county is dry on Sundays. Don't know how that works, but it didn't matter because I never found it.

That afternoon, the wind died down, so I was finally able to hit the bike trails. I did about twelve miles and got to sweat out a lot of Wednesday.

Later, I made the rounds again, adding Landsharks to my bar crawl. It's owned by Jimmy Buffett and has a great outdoor bar. It's where I ran into the same couple from Vancouver. They were leaving for Chicago in the morning.

It's Friday, and I was back on the bike, trying to work off the damage I inflicted the night before. See a trend? During the ten-mile ride, I ran into Ashley (not literally), the bartender from Sidelines. Things seemed to be going pretty good, that is until her two young kids caught up to her.

I had a great dinner at a restaurant called Hemingway's, made the rounds again, then got back to my hotel's outdoor bar in time for last call. Two guys sitting there were from the band that had just finished playing and I heard them talking about Chicago, so I slid over and introduced myself.

They were blues musicians from the city, so I asked if they knew, or had ever played with Chicago blues legend Buddy Guy. I had gotten to know Buddy's keyboard player, so when they said yes, I asked if they knew Marty. They looked surprised and wanted to know more, so I told them about Marty playing at Tailgator's and at Vino Tinto, a bar just a few blocks from my condo.

With that, one of the guys handed me his business card and told me to say hello the next time I saw him. The name on the card: Biscuit Miller. I later found out he's one of the best blues bass players ever to come out of Chicago.

My drive home on Saturday started around 9:00 a.m. The plan was to get back in time for a drink or two at Vino Tinto. It was the bar's last night, and Marty was their closing act.

Luckily, the people in Alabama and Tennessee drive fast. My drive north on Route 65 was a blast. The posted speed limit was 70 mph, but to blend in with traffic, I set my cruise control near 90 mph, hitting 100mph a few times. I love my van.

The drive through Alabama was also a little sobering. I saw a lot of buildings that had been damaged or destroyed by the tornados, plus a lot of downed trees and towers. The state really took a hit, and that's just what I saw from the interstate.

Approaching Louisville, I talked to my friend Mike. He checked his GPS, predicting I would be home around 1:00 a.m. I got to Vino Tinto's just after midnight. Driving time was about thirteen hours, which averaged out to about 70 mph, including stops. It was worth it, especially seeing Marty's face when he heard I was hanging out with Biscuit in Pensacola Beach the night before.

Home quick and safe.

2011 Old Route 66

In May 2011, I took a drive on Old Route 66 south from Joliet, Illinois. I thought it would be fun to hit some different eateries along that stretch of road. The Old Mother Road still exists, with some drivable stretches on a frontage road running alongside Interstate 55. While on one of those stretches, I noticed a police car behind me. He stayed close for a couple of miles.

I had recently replaced my old van with a not-so-old one, but there was something wrong with my registration. Things weren't adding up, so he pulled me over. After a short wait, the officer walked up to my window and told me everything was in order, but he was curious and asked what brought me down to the area.

I told him my plan, then pulled out my list and rattled off the names of a few places I hoped to hit. That's when he really got interested and took the paper from my hand. Seconds later, he was recommending some of his favorite stops, wondering why they weren't on the list. With that done, we were both free to go.

I ate at, and took food home from

Polka Dot '50s Drive-In, Braidwood
Launching Pad (Giant Spaceman), Wilmington
Wishing Well, Odell
Filling Station, Lexington.

There would be more over the next few years, but I only got as far as Ted Drewes in St. Louis.

2011 AMISH/ROCK
AND ROLL

The Rock and Roll Hall of Fame in Cleveland, Ohio, is listed in the book *1,000 Places to See Before You Die*. My plan was to make it number five on my list of different Halls of Fame. So far, I've been to Cooperstown for Major League Baseball, Canton for pro football, Toronto for pro hockey, and Nashville for country music.

I went online to research it and learned Wednesday was the only day the hall had late hours, staying open until 9:00 p.m. I then discovered the Cleveland Indians were home that afternoon against the California Angels. Perfect, baseball in the afternoon followed by rock and roll at night.

Wednesdays and Thursdays are days off, so I was hoping to hit the road by 3:00 a.m. on July 27, after finishing my Tuesday night shift at the bar. On Monday, while paying bills, I decided money was a little tight and put my trip on hold. I was being mature, but I came to regret it.

I had mentioned the plan to a few of my regulars, so they were pumped up when they saw me on Friday. Why? Because I had witnessed a no-hitter. Huh? That's right, on Wednesday afternoon, July 27, Ervin Santana pitched a no-hitter for the Angels at Progressive Field—so much for being mature.

Two months later, I decided to try it again. The days of the week were the same, but my first stop was gonna be different. The Indians weren't home, so shortly after passing Elkhart, IN, on Interstate 80/90, I exited and found a truck stop to grab some sleep. An hour into my nap and it was time to drag out the sleeping bag. It wasn't July anymore.

Up at 9:00 a.m., I headed about fifteen miles southeast to the town of Shipshewana, located in a predominantly Amish area. It has a flea market with over 1,000 booths, and it is open on Tuesdays and Wednesdays from May through October, and an auction on Wednesdays that is listed in the *1,000 Places to See* book.

I spent about four hours there, buying a couple of things and eating a couple of things. While I walked to my van, an Amish man driving his horse and buggy was headed toward me, so I pointed to my camera asking if it was OK to take a picture. He smiled and gave me a thumbs-up.

On the drive to the interstate, another good photo op appeared. It was a woman in full Amish attire, bonnet included, pushing an extra wide gas-powered lawnmower in front of her farmhouse. I took a pass, thinking it would be rude. Next stop, Cleveland.

The hall was definitely worth the trip. Admission was $20. Not bad, with the only drawback being no pictures. I spent four hours taking in as much as possible, but ran out of time. The music, memorabilia, and classic film footage were awesome, especially for someone my age.

When it closed, my plan was to drive for a while and nap for a while, hopefully not at the same time. Five hours of driving and a couple hours of sleep would have gotten me home around 3:00 a.m., but my nap only lasted thirty minutes. I made last call.

Michigan City 2011

This year, our rental became a '50s diner for seven nights, starting on Monday, August 22.

That morning, I picked up Bob and Carol—sorry, no Ted and Alice. Bob was a coworker, and Carol was a waitress at the restaurant next to the bar. We moved in around 3:00 p.m., and within minutes, the two of them were off, on foot, to the casino about a mile from the house. They staggered back around 10:00 p.m., about the time I was going out for a few drinks.

Tuesday, they were out the door at 7:00 a.m., staggering back around noon. I had gone out to get a few things for the house just before they returned and was greeted by the television with its volume as high as it could go when I came back. It really didn't matter because both were passed out on their respective couches.

Amy (another coworker) and her friend Ashley arrived that afternoon and, instead of going to the casino, went to work, putting up decorations. We also met our neighbors. This year, the group at the house next door was from St. Bernadette's Parish, located in Evergreen Park, my suburban neighbor.

You can probably guess where Bob and Carol went that evening. Amy, Ashley, and I headed to Shoreline Brewery. It was open-mic night, and one of the performers was a next-door neighbor who would eventually make an appearance at open-mic night at Tailgator's.

The girls left on Wednesday and were replaced by Big Don and Slink (John), old friends from grammar school and high school, and part of the group that went to Montreal in 1976 for the Summer Olympics. It turned out to be a beautiful day, so what did we do? Stayed inside, sipped some drinks, and talked for about eight hours.

Bob and Carol stayed the course, hitting the casino on or about 6:00 a.m. to 11:00 a.m. and on or about 6:00 p.m. to 11:00 p.m. Their stay in Michigan City was amazingly consistent. Bob gambled, smoked, drank, and passed out. Carol did pretty much the same thing but also cooked a couple of delicious meals for the house. Finally, after staggering back on Wednesday night, Carol's ex-husband picked them up and drove them home.

Most of Thursday was alone time, so I hit the bike trails near Union Pier, Michigan, maybe twenty minutes from the house. I did about fifteen miles, but after a long day of drinking on Wednesday, combined with the hilly terrain, I thought I was gonna die. My day ended with a slow walk to Shoreline for a couple of drinks and a quick stop at Matey's.

People finally started showing up on Friday, with a few stragglers coming on Saturday morning, so the "diner" was pretty busy.

Even though I had the house until Monday morning, everybody cleared out by Sunday afternoon. After making sure it was in good shape, I made a quick stop at Shoreline, then drove home early like everybody else.

And here's the best Notable Quotable:

What, you're going back to your room and die?

No, I'm going back to my rum and diet.

We are all so precious.

2011 STL

The Blackhawks were in St. Louis on December 3, to play the Blues, so I bought forty tickets for the game, with eight of them set aside for Steph. Of the remaining thirty-two, only twenty-four made the 10:00 a.m. train Saturday morning. Its first stop is Joliet, Illinois, about thirty minutes southwest of Summit, our point of departure and about an hour southwest of downtown Chicago.

As people boarded, a couple grabbed the two open seats in front of me. After taking a quick look around, they took a second look at me because I looked familiar. They recognized me from McMahon's, where they used to drink maybe nine or ten years earlier. Travel as usual.

On the way down, I sent my daughter a text, telling her about the eight extra tickets. She got back to me, saying she would go online and try to sell them. She was successful but, unfortunately, too successful. She sold nine instead of eight, so I ended up paying a scalper to get into the game.

The Saturday train trips are always rough on me. I work at the bar on Friday nights, get a few hours' sleep, then board the train late Saturday morning. And soon after that, I have to start drinking.

It's a five-hour ride and we were on schedule, so there was plenty of time to check into the Drury Inn before the free appetizers/drinks started. And as usual, the front desk gave me a few extra drink tickets for my daughter and her little group, and for me.

After the game, which we won 5-2, some of us did a little bar crawl, finishing up at a place called Maggie O's. Returning to our hotel, a few of us went down to its basement bar, hoping for a late last call. We got one.

Demma's, a bar about two miles from Tailgator's, also had a group come down for the game also staying at the Drury Inn. We were on different trains on different days on the way down, but we had tickets on the same train home Sunday afternoon.

Saturday night must have taken its toll because it wasn't one, but two very boring groups on the ride home. I called our car a library, Sue (Demma's) called it a morgue. The only highlight was a drunk woman dancing through the train, wearing the conductor's hat. Oh wait, that was Sue.

MICHIGAN CITY 2012

Medieval Times was the theme this summer, but that's about all I got.

When renting the house, I always hoped for a day or two alone during the middle of the week. My wish came true, so I drove to Fish Lake, just south of La Porte, Indiana.

From the mid-'50s into the early '60s, my family would get away for a few weekends during the summer at my grandparents' cottage at . . . Fish Lake. My grandmother died in late '63, so within a year or so, my grandfather sold the place because it wasn't the same without her. Before it happened, my dad, who was an accountant, had started doing the taxes for a couple of the families that had cottages in our cul-de-sac.

In 1987, I returned with Vic and Steph, who had just turned two. It was my first time back in almost twenty-five years, and I couldn't believe how close together everything was. As a kid, I remember telling my mom I was heading down to K——'s house because there were other kids to play with and an awesome tree to climb. Looking at it in '87, it was maybe a twenty- to thirty-second walk to the tree.

Now, it's another twenty-five years, and my drive into the area brought back a lot more memories. I parked in the same cul-de-sac and walked down to the lake. A right turn and a short stroll past three more cottages got me to the pier where most of us went swimming. After a few of minutes of nostalgia, I turned around and walked past our cottage, trying to match the names of the families I remembered to the houses they lived in.

Over the years, some of the cottages had become year-round homes. As I got to my van, I heard this coming from one of the porches: "Excuse me, are you Jim [my younger brother] or Dick?" It was a woman from one of the old families who actually recognized me. She even called her husband to see if he could leave work early. He couldn't, so the two of us talked for a while, then I had to head back to Michigan City because I was expecting people at the rental.

I'll probably drive out there again.

On November 11, 2015, I did, this time with my brother, who went through some of the same emotions I did three years earlier. This time, nobody recognized me.

2012 STL

This year, the Saturday game was on December 15th. The day the schedule came out, my awesome group sales rep called to see if I was interested. I was, and so was Sue from Demma's. This year, our groups would be on the same train on Saturday and Sunday.

The great thing about the hockey trips to St. Louis is once you're there, everything can be done on foot. You know the drill. It's a short walk from the train station to the Drury Inn Hotel, followed by a short walk to the arena for the game, and finally, a short walk to a few local bars after the game.

If you want to go to Soulard or to a casino, or get real adventurous and go across the river to a strip joint, you need a taxi.

And just like last year, Maggie O's was our last stop. The bars in St. Louis close at 1:00 a.m., so of course, we stayed for last call. The walk to the hotel wasn't bad, except for the torrential rain, and even though it was closing time and we were soaking wet, we headed to the basement bar. Drying off was not an option. And just like last year, we got what we wished for, then were treated to a couple more drinks. It reminded me of London in '97 when Mo, Tracy, and I got locked in with the regulars for last call, twice. We must have been in the basement a long time, because the next day I was informed about finishing the night with a beer in my hand, not a rum and Diet Coke. Didn't believe it either.

The train ride home was pretty funny. On Saturday, the ride to St. Louis was one big party, with people walking around the whole time. Not on Sunday. Even though it included the group from Demma's, it didn't matter. Half of us were in the "library" and the other half in the "morgue." And nobody danced down the aisle wearing a conductor's hat.

Home sober.

2013 STL #1

The Blackhawks were in St. Louis on Thursday, February 28, so with a ticket purchased online, I hit the road around 11:00 a.m. Traffic was light and moving fast, so I moved a little faster, doing the three-hundred-mile trip in just over four hours.

My first stop was a travel agency in South County, about twenty minutes southwest of downtown. Steph was getting married in August in the Riviera Maya, Mexico, so I went to see Kelly, who was handling the arrangements. I introduced myself, paid for my trip, then paid for a good portion of my daughter's trip because her birthday was a week later.

Steph was super busy at the time, between law school and a job at a law firm. For my birthday and for Christmas, she sent me a text. Now it was my turn. I sent a text telling her about a minor problem with the trip and that she needed to talk to her contact at the agency. That's when Kelly would lead Steph on before telling her about her birthday present. It worked, but it took a while because Kelly was sick for a couple of days. Then after my daughter called the agency, she actually called me.

With my work done in South County, I drove downtown and parked at Union Station. It was a short walk to the hockey arena to pick up my ticket, then a short walk back to the Drury Inn. I asked one of the girls at the desk about availability on April 27. The Hawks were in town that night and I already knew the hotel was booked, but it was time to suck up.

I was hoping to grab some food and maybe a drink or two. What clinched it was mentioning my rep from the Blues group sales office who had recently left the organization. The girls at the desk missed her too, then handed me a couple of drink tickets.

Now it's game time. Hockey or baseball, Chicago and St. Louis have a great rivalry. The place was rocking as the game began but got real quiet, real fast when the Hawks scored twelve seconds later. Have you ever been at a game where a fan sitting in your section constantly yelled about everything that happened?

"Hey, that was offside! How could you miss that?"

"Hey, they got too many men on the ice! Can't you count?" etc., etc.

I really paid for my mistake because that guy was sitting next to me.

During the second intermission, Louie, the Blues mascot, was making the rounds when two young women flagged down this ugly blue polar bear for a photo op. Yes, they were sitting in front of me. While dealing with the girls, he noticed the Blackhawk fan sitting behind them and waggled his finger as if disciplining a child. After pointing to my hat and then to the scoreboard, he quickly stopped.

With the clock winding down and the Blackhawks up 3-0, Blues fans started heading to the exits. When the final horn sounded, the only people in the arena were Hawk fans, so we got to celebrate safely. Because of the amount of Chicago fans and construction on I-55, getting across the Mississippi River into Illinois was going to be slow. Knowing that, I was forced to kill some time at the Drury Inn's bar. After that, it was an easy drive home, making it back a little before my regular bedtime.

What surprised me was not running into anyone I knew.

2013 Cubs in Cincy

After finishing my shift Monday night, April 23, I got in my van around 3:00 a.m. and headed to Cincinnati for a couple of Cub games and a couple of days by myself. It's an easy drive, this time including a four-hour nap in a truck stop near Indianapolis.

I went straight to the Travelodge in Newport, Kentucky, our hotel of choice over the years. It's just across the Ohio River from the ballpark and just across the street from Kelly's Keg (now called Bart's), our bar of choice over the years.

Walking in, I asked for a Jacuzzi suite. My AARP card helped me get it for $115. It was on the third floor, and the view from the balcony looked across the river, directly at Great American Ballpark. Settled in, I took a quick walk around the neighborhood to a dollar store for some cheap snacks and a liquor store for some Bacardi rum. Then it was game time. And yes, a water bottle with my buddy Bacardi accompanied me.

My seat was in section 102, deep in the left-center-field bleachers. During the game, as I started to feel comfortable with the people around me, it was time to tell them my all-time favorite baseball story. I was pretty confident it would get a good reaction because it involved Frank Robinson, a Cincinnati icon. Remember? It's the Phx '84 story where I ended up standing next to the third base line with him. The older Reds fans within earshot loved it.

Wednesday's game started at noon, and the weather sucked. As it got a little better, I went across the river but walked past the ballpark. My destination was a Cincinnati neighborhood called Over-the-Rhine, which was put on the National Register of Historic Places in 1983.

It's an area of around 1,000 historic buildings not far from downtown that were built in the 1800s, mainly for German immigrants, hence the name Over-the-Rhine. The neighborhood eventually became mainly African American, but it was neglected over time. There are hundreds of vacant buildings, many of which are deteriorating, and in 2009, it was called the most dangerous area in the city. The clock is ticking.

I estimated my walk that afternoon at around six miles. Back at the room, after relaxing in my Jacuzzi for a while, it was time to regroup. A short walk got me to a couple of bars along the levee, with a Hooters restaurant being the last stop.

My plan was to have a couple of drinks after ordering some wings to go, but there was a minor problem. The special that night was all-you-can-eat wings and they were cheap, but had to be eaten in the restaurant.

As I waited for my waitress, a manager came over to help because the girl assigned to my table was tied up with another customer. I told her what I had hoped to do, so she took care of me. I could take ten wings home if I had ten wings in the restaurant. OK.

My drive home Thursday afternoon had a slight detour, this time going straight west into Illinois so I could pick up I-55. After stops at a few Old Route 66 eateries for lunch and for some to-go food for dinner that night, I headed home.

One more thing: While finishing this book, I read an article about the OTR neighborhood. The clock stopped ticking. It has gone through an amazing renovation with new residents and new investments. After being listed in Frommer's *500 Places to See Before They Disappear*, it's back from the dead.

2013 STEPH

My daughter got married on Saturday, August 16, at the El Dorado Resort on the Riviera Maya. That's right, Mexico in the middle of August. Heat is one thing, but humidity is another. The weather was horrible, with the dew point nudging over 80.

The story starts a few months earlier while thanking my daughter for having the wedding on the beach. For me, it meant I didn't have to dress up. Remember, I live and work in shorts and a T-shirt for a good portion of the year, but she had bad news. Since I was the father of the bride, I was expected to dress appropriately. That meant khakis and a long-sleeved white shirt, with a collar.

A couple of weeks later, while hanging out with Danielle, a bartender friend of mine who's a couple of years older than my daughter, I told her the story I just told you. And guess what? She reacted the same way Steph did, explaining almost word for word that I had to wear real clothes since it was my daughter who was getting married. Hearing it from another woman confirmed it.

A couple of drinks later, she actually volunteered to take me shopping. We met a couple of nights later and went to a local mall, where she picked out clothes she thought I should wear. Then she stood outside the dressing room door, waiting while I tried on her choices. I'd walk out, she would give me a quick once-over then tell me what else to try on.

At one point, she handed me a white shirt, but I hesitated because it was still folded and the pins were still in it. She grabbed it, yanked the pins out, shook it, and handed it back. It was a keeper.

When we got done, it was time to thank her, which meant it was time for a few drinks on me, but she had to take a pass. When I protested, she explained it wasn't going to happen that night because she had plans, but I would definitely be buying her some drinks in the near future.

I called Steph the next day to give her a wardrobe update, making it clear if my clothes weren't right, it wasn't my fault.

Now, the wedding.

On Friday the 15th, I landed in Cancun around 1:00 p.m. The first thing I noticed was water. It was everywhere because of a tropical depression. It had poured the previous two days and continued on and off through most of Friday. Then on Saturday, for Steph's wedding, the clouds magically disappeared.

Only twelve people were able to attend the festivities, all arriving on Friday. When I walked into the hotel, my daughter was at the front desk. She was in good spirits, considering she had been waiting almost an hour to check in. I think the close proximity to the lobby bar is what kept her sane.

The plan for Friday evening was to meet for dinner, so I settled into my Jacuzzi suite for a while. With that done, a ten-second walk got me to one of the pool bars. After dinner, we went in search of another pool bar, but remember, we were there in August. It was off-season, which meant most of them were closed by 8:00 p.m., with some of bars and restaurants never opening.

Steph and I got lucky and found one open past eight. It's where we met the Others. They were two girls her age who were doing Cancun on their own, so we adopted them for the weekend.

Not surprisingly, my Saturday started out at a pool, and yes, it had a bar. Then at 5:00 p.m., we were scheduled to meet on the second floor of a bar/restaurant called Bellini's, leaving us about a one-minute walk to the beach where the ceremony would take place.

Andy, my ex's boyfriend, and I were the first ones to arrive, literally. There was not one other person in the place, and not just customers, there were no employees either. As the rest of our group started to show up to this empty, hot restaurant, we tried to turn on the A/C but needed a passcode.

Seconds later, someone spotted a house phone and called the front desk to find out what was going on. We were told the bar wasn't scheduled to open and there weren't any employees scheduled to work, even though we were scheduled to meet there before and after the wedding.

That meant it was time for me to go to work. I found an ice machine, so even though the room was hot, my drinks were cold. It wasn't like we were stealing; we were scheduled to be there, plus we were at an all-inclusive resort. After ten minutes behind the bar, I was ready for another shower. Oh no! My special outfit was all sweaty. Sorry, Danielle.

Things quickly got better. My daughter was beautiful, so was the ceremony, and so was the cool breeze off the water. Then the resort found us a spot at another restaurant for dinner.

After that, it was time to get rid of the nice clothes and get to one of the 11:00 p.m. bars we heard about. This is where the Others stepped up and told us about the one bar in the resort that stayed open until 2:00 a.m. I knew we adopted them for a reason.

Sunday was pretty low-key, with most of the group leaving that afternoon. It was also the start of Steph's honeymoon, so I had Sunday night to myself.

Back home on Monday, I sent Danielle a text saying, "Good choice, my daughter thanks you." Her response: "Phewwwwww!"

2013 E-L-C

I flew out of Midway Airport around 6:00 p.m. on Wednesday, October 23. The plan was to spend a few days in Edinburgh, Scotland, then take the overnight train to Cardiff, Wales, where I would spend a few more days before flying home. After a second look at the map, I realized Liverpool, England, was about halfway between the two cities and on the same train route. Yes, it was time for my Beatles pilgrimage.

My reservation with KLM had its good and bad points. The good things were the airport and the price. I was flying out of Midway, just four miles from home, plus the price seemed cheap. My theory was confirmed after calling the airline to see what an upgrade would cost. I considered spoiling myself but when the rep on the phone saw what I paid, she warned me it would be expensive. She was right, so I took a pass.

The downer was my flight plan. It went from Chicago to Detroit, east to Amsterdam, then back to Edinburgh. The flight home from Cardiff again went east to Amsterdam, then west to Minneapolis before landing at Midway. Is that why it was cheap?

There were two things that stood out on this trip. One was my health; the other was the weather. A couple of days before leaving, I started having some weird stomach problems. That's all I'll say. The weather was amazing. It only rained a couple of times, each day.

The flight from Detroit left late, so after landing in Amsterdam, I had about ten minutes to catch my flight to Edinburgh. I ran through the airport to the assigned gate, but it was empty. Either the time was wrong or the gate number was wrong, but it didn't matter. I missed my flight.

Because of that, the airline gave me a ten-euro coupon to be used in the airport. It got me a bottle of water, a small sandwich, and a banana.

I thanked them by leaving some of my stomach problems in an airport bathroom.

I checked into the Royal British Hotel, but it was too late to grab a Hop-On/Hop-Off bus. You know what that means. The hotel was across the street from Waverly Station, the city's main train stop, and everything around it was pretty commercial, so it took a little longer than I planned before finding my home away from home.

My first drink in Edinburgh was a Bacardi and Diet Coke, and I had it in the basement, or should I say at the Basement, a pub maybe three or four blocks from my hotel. I also had my first dinner there, which was a little more traditional than my first drink. It was a steak pie with a puff pastry lid. Look it up.

One of the first things I noticed was the lack of seats at the bar. Sitting there and not in a booth is important because it gives me the opportunity to talk to the bartender and trade stories about the business we work in. Luckily, I was able to grab one of the four seats. It wasn't just in the Basement; it was something I would see throughout my trip.

At some point, I got up and walked around to the other side of the bar to check out the selection of Scotch whiskeys. I was looking for Laphroig, so the bartender grabbed the bottle and got ready to pour me a drink. I stopped him just in time because I had no intention of drinking it. We carried it at Tailgator's for a while, but most people, including me, couldn't even get past the smell. The bartender was stunned because he loved it.

While closing my tab that night, the woman behind the bar informed me of the 20 percent industry discount she was able to give me. Thank you so much, considering I don't even live in the country. And that's one reason I sit at the bar.

After a quick stop at my room to regroup, I found Mitre's, a bar in the Old Town area about a half-mile walk in the opposite direction. It was another pub with a good feel, so I finished my night there.

The next morning got me on the Hop-On/Hop-Off bus I missed the day before. Back at my room, I went online and found a ten-hour bus tour that would take me to Rosslyn Chapel, Hadrian's Wall, and a couple of other stops. Cost: about $55.

Then it was time for my hike up to the castle. Edinburgh is another city with seven hills like Rome and Amman, and its castle sits on some volcanic rock with an amazing view of the city. I wasn't ready for the walk, so this time, I hopped on the bus and actually hopped off.

During my time there, I got someone to take a picture of me standing next to a cannon. That's right, next to a cannon. When I travel with my friend Maria, the photo op would have been her straddling a cannon—no straddling for me.

With the castle tour over, I took the long walk down Edinburgh's famous Royal Mile. The area is full of shops, pubs, restaurants, and a lot of steep streets. Mitre's was one of the pubs, so I made a quick stop there and learned about a bar with live blues music on Saturday nights just one street over. The name of the bar? Whistle Binkies. Couldn't make that up.

I stopped there for a drink to confirm the schedule, and yes, a blues band was playing at 7:00 p.m. on Saturday, right around the time the bus tour would be getting back. And yes, I only had one drink.

After an unplanned nap, I went back out around 9:00 p.m. and walked the neighborhood, looking for a different bar, ending up at the Basement. Besides the comfort zone I felt, one other thing stood out. It was the employee uniforms. They all wore Hawaiian shirts, which was a little strange because there was nothing else Hawaiian about the place. I told them about my annual New Year's Day party and its Hawaiian theme and promised to send them a couple of shirts. I did in early December.

Last call was at a pub called Conan Doyle's, and two drinks later, I was given a loyalty card for 20 percent off all future purchases. Another seat at the bar and another industry discount. Amazingly, I never made it back. My stomach problems returned overnight, so I canceled my day trip. Ten hours on a bus without a bathroom? Don't think so. Instead, I went to the Tourist Information Center across the street from my hotel and was directed to Boots drugstore, a five-minute walk down the street. The pharmacist on duty was awesome. She listened to my problem, and a few minutes later had me on the phone with a doctor.

I was hoping he would suggest something available over the counter, but thought I should come to his office to get checked out. It was across town and my stop would have cost about $150, so I took a pass and decided to ride out the storm.

One other thing about the pharmacist: She used the words "okey dokey" more than a few times. It reminded me of a local guy I talked to in Copenhagen in 2009 who used the words "I reckon." Never expected to hear either phrase while traveling in Europe.

After a thrilling start to the day, a short walk got me to Scotland's National Gallery. A couple of hours later, I took a walk down Princes

Street, through the old town, and up to Calton Hill and a tower built in honor of Admiral Nelson.

Around 150 steps gave me a great view of the area. I could look back and see the Castle and Princes Street, then turn and see Holyrood Palace. One more turn got me a view of the Firth of Forth, an inlet of the North Sea and the royal yacht *Britannia*. It's where Queen Elizabeth of England has spent some of her vacation time over the years.

Now it was time for some blues, getting to Whistle Binkies around 8:00 p.m. The band was good, but they were more rock than they were blues. Maybe my expectations were too high, but I thought they needed to add some soul. And of course, I left in time for a stop at the Basement.

I walked my ass off on Sunday, starting at Holyrood Palace. One highlight was an exhibit of some of Leonardo Da Vinci's works. It was good, but nothing like the Da Vinci Museum in Milan, Italy, which I toured about twenty years earlier. I also saw the bedroom the queen uses when she's in Edinburgh. And, Mo, I'm sorry, Queenie didn't ask about you.

After that, it was a tough hike up to Arthur's Seat, another rocky volcanic crag located across the city from Edinburgh Castle. It wasn't a steep walk, but it was a long one. At a little over 800 feet, it almost qualifies as a mountain.

The sun was finally out and it wasn't raining, so I gave it a shot, joining a group of other hikers. The wind was in the 30–40 mph range, so about halfway up, we voted unanimously to stop our walk and not get blown off the mountain.

The rest of the night was uneventful because the rain had returned and the walk had kicked my ass. It wasn't my first choice, but I stayed in and had a few drinks at the hotel bar, skipping the Basement on my last night in Edinburgh. With a 7:00 a.m. train the next morning, being close to home was probably a good thing. Liverpool was next.

After checking into the Aachen Hotel, about a ten-minute walk from the main train station, I went out and found the city's Hop-On/Hop-Off bus and got a quick, one-hour orientation.

With some new information from the bus ride, it was time to plan the next day. I already knew my schedule that night. It was the Cavern Club, where the Beatles got their start, located in the Cavern Quarter, a neighborhood less than a mile from my hotel.

My first stop was the Glass Onion where I discovered pint drink prices for liquor. Add one British pound to the price of your drink and you get a double. One more stop and it was time to enter the Cavern Club. I was drinking in the most famous part of Liverpool and in one of the most famous bars in the world, and the price of a double was cheaper than a single in the bars I went to in Edinburgh. I'm gonna like this place.

None of my friends will believe this, but I got up Tuesday, worked online, had the breakfast that came with my room, and was out the door by 9:00 a.m.

A mile walk got me to the Albert Dock, where I took a quick tour of Liverpool's Maritime Museum. The Beatles Museum was next and just like the Rock and Roll Hall of Fame in Cleveland, there wasn't enough time. I was only in Liverpool for a day and a half and was scheduled to take the ferry across the Mersey that afternoon. Need I say more?

The rainy weather on this trip started to remind me of London with Mo and Tracey in 1997, but it didn't deter me because I was ferrying across the Mersey River. The commentary on the boat's sound system was provided by Gerry Marsden, the lead singer of Gerry and the Pacemakers. They're the ones who made the song "Ferry Cross the Mersey" a hit in the mid-'60s. Didn't make you look that one up.

When the boat tour ended, I headed back to the Cavern Quarter to get some pictures while it was still light out. On my walk through the neighborhood, I saw Eleanor Rigby sitting on a bench. It was a statue.

I returned to the Glass Onion, but it was full so a few seconds later, I walked into a pub called the Grapes. It doesn't take long to find a place to drink in the quarter.

I actually took a seat in a booth, then walked up to the bar after learning there wasn't a waitress on duty. A local patron sitting at one of three seats struck up a conversation with me. He was an older white-haired man with a cane leaning against the bar, who wondered if I was going to order some food. If I was, he suggested the chicken curry, homemade by Julie, the bartender that night—good enough for me.

He also figured I was a Beatles fan, so after I'd known this guy for a whole minute, he offered to show me something the average Beatles tourist never saw. I jumped at the chance, but felt a little bad when he got up and, with the help of his cane, had me follow him as he limped out the door.

We took a short walk down a cobblestone lane to a very unassuming doorway and walked in. It was a tiny atrium with entrances to a couple of small shops—oh, and life-sized statues of John, Paul, George, and Pete. This was pre-Ringo.

Back at the pub, while waiting for my food, my new friend hobbled over to ask if I noticed the picture on the wall behind me. I had, but since there were pictures of the Beatles everywhere, I only gave it a quick glance.

What I didn't see the first time was a small plaque explaining the photo was taken here, in my booth. He told me I was sitting in the same booth "the boys" were sitting in when they were photographed in 1962. He never said it, but I had this gut feeling he knew at least one of them.

The Grapes was one of the shorter stops of any pub during my trip, but the people, the food and "the boys," made it the most memorable one. Last call was at a place called McCartney's.

Wednesday morning was a 9:00 a.m. train to the central station in Cardiff, Wales, arriving around 1:00 p.m. and, just like the first two cities, a short walk to my hotel.

Before leaving home, I did some research on city walking tours, hoping to find something to do by myself for free and not with an organized tour group. I found one, hit Print, and twenty pages later, had a three-mile walk.

Cardiff's city center is similar to Edinburgh's, just more compact and, thankfully, much flatter. A couple of the highlights from the first ten pages were the Old Arcade Pub, which opened in 1835 and Spiller Records, the oldest record store in the world, which opened its doors in 1894.

Dinner and drinks that night were at O'Neill's, a pub down the street from my hotel and, yes, the pubs in Cardiff did the doubles for the extra pound. I made one more stop, at a place called the Queen's Vault, where I overheard three men talking about entertainer Tom Jones as a friend of theirs and what a nice guy he was.

I had to get into the conversation. Remember, in early '77 working at Condesa del Mar as an assistant manager, I met him while checking on a problem with the thermostat in his dressing room.

I told them how patient he was with everything going on around him and how his ego never seemed to get in the way. All three men nodded in agreement. Being able to tell that story in Wales to guys who knew him was pretty cool. Having them agree with me was also pretty cool. One more drink and it was time to crash.

Thursday was Halloween, waking up to cold, rain, and wind again. Up earlier than normal, I had a traditional English breakfast at my hotel. It consisted of toast, eggs, bacon, mushrooms, tomatoes, sausage, and beans. Did you get all that?

I took a walk down to Cardiff Bay, spending the rest of the morning there, then toured Cardiff Castle in the afternoon. After that, it was back to the bay, but having my fill of castles and museums, I went to a hockey game, joining about a thousand other people. It was the Cardiff Devils hosting the Hull Stingrays. This was minor-league hockey and I'm in Wales, so I was able to go down to ice level, stand behind the goal, and snap a couple of pictures. Cardiff won, 6-5.

After the game, I returned to O'Neill's and closed the place. Remember it was Halloween, so I was curious to see how it was celebrated in the UK. The pedestrian area that ran from the bar to my hotel was basically made up of costumed women and drunken men. Yes, the end of the night was loud.

The goal for Friday was to finish the rest of the walking tour. Some of the second half highlights were the City Hall building, the National War Museum, and old St. Luke's Church. I stopped at the church because the sign by its front entrance caught my eye. It had a list of upcoming events and the next movie scheduled to be shown there, just days after I left, was *The Blues Brothers*.

After finishing the twenty pages, it was time for a quick break at my room before the long walk to a place called the Jazz Bar/Restaurant. Friday was the last day of my vacation and a blues band was scheduled to play there, so after walking out my front door and taking a right turn, three strides got me to the bar's front door.

Earlier in the day, I stopped in and was able reserve a small table for 9:00 p.m. It turned out to be a good move because the place filled up.

During my late dinner and the band's break, I went over and put in a request for "Sweet Home, Chicago." An older guy, whom I soon learned was the band's promoter, came over to apologize because the song wasn't on their playlist.

We ended up trading a few stories with me dropping the names of Buddy Guy and Marty Sammon, Buddy's keyboard player. His story was better. When he was young, he lived in Los Angeles for ten years and actually played the saxophone for six months with Jimi Hendrix's band.

Now it's Saturday morning and time to catch my 10:30 flight home, but there's one more story before leaving Cardiff. The bus to the airport cost five pounds, but when I handed the driver a ten-pound note, he had to scramble for change, eventually giving me all coins.

At the airport, I had just enough money to buy a sandwich and a bottle of water, but the clerk didn't recognize a couple of the coins I handed him. Huh? I never got an explanation and was only able to buy the bottle of water. Not a clue.

The rest of the way home was uneventful—long, but uneventful.

2013 STL #2

For a few years, my Blues group sales rep had spoiled me. She would call me the day the hockey schedule came out, but had left the organization during the off-season. That meant I had to call them because the Hawks were there on Saturday, December 28. My new sales rep informed me the only way to get tickets to a Chicago game was to buy the same amount for another non-Chicago game.

It happened to me twice in just a few weeks in the same city. The Bears were playing there on November 24, so I tried to get a group of tickets for that game but got the same answer from the St. Louis Rams office.

It had been happening to a lot of Chicago fans because we travel well. The home teams get worried because they want more home fans in their arenas than people from the visiting team. I heard the new motto in St. Louis was "Keep the Red out."

The same thing occurred in Nashville on November 4, 2012, but my guess is the local liquor establishments wouldn't have a problem with the amount of tickets sold to Chicago fans. That's because the lead story on the news that night was how we drank most of the downtown bars out of beer after the Bears destroyed the Titans 51-20.

Then, in mid-November, the Blues group sales office called, asking if I still wanted tickets for the 28th. Really? I bought thirty tickets, with six more for Steph, but there was a problem. The Drury Inn was booked, which meant it was time for us and my "water" bottle to return to the Pear Tree Inn.

I reserved a room for Steph and her husband for the night, so she brought a few friends and a beer-pong table so they could entertain before and after the game.

The hotel bar was where my Chicago group hooked up with Steph's St. Louis group. For the people from Chicago who had never met my daughter, the response was the usual: "Oh my God, you look just like your dad." She's so lucky, although her reaction never really shows it.

It's finally time for some hockey. The walk to the arena took us past the Drury Inn, so a few of us stopped in, hoping to grab a drink or two and something besides chips and beer. They're always good to me, so it wasn't a problem.

After the game, which we lost in overtime, we walked back through the neighborhood, stopping at a couple of bars. Maggie O's was the last one I remember. When it closed, Dave K. became my chaperone and got me safely back to the hotel.

And here's the icing on the cake. In April, when the season ended, I got a call from the Blues group sales office. We were matched up against St. Louis in the first round of the playoffs, and they wanted to know if I was interested in tickets to a couple of their home games. Evidently, nobody in the office noticed my (708) area code.

Again, it was on short notice, so I bought six tickets for Steph.

2014 Nashville
Pensacola Memphis

It started in January with a voicemail from Ted, my best and oldest friend, and it sounded a little ominous, with him telling me to call back as soon as possible. At our age, my first thought was somebody died.

He had recently retired and had two words for me when I called him back: road trip. With the itch to go somewhere, he rang up four old friends with the hope of replicating our trip to Florida during spring break '73. I was the only one who could go. All of us together again? Holy shit! This time, our stop in Florida would be Pensacola Beach, not Fort Lauderdale.

After working my shift at the bar on Tuesday, April 22, I hit the road around 3:00 a.m., stopping in Lockport to pick up Ted. He got about three hours sleep before I picked him up, and I got about three hours sleep on the way south when he took the wheel. Nashville was first, checking in to our hotel around noon on Wednesday.

Our first stop was the Country Music Hall of Fame. I was there in 2006, but this trip had a bonus. The tickets we bought included a short bus ride and admission to historic RCA Studio B, Nashville's oldest surviving record studio. It opened in 1958, with the Everly Brothers one of the first to record there. They were followed, in no particular order, by Elvis Presley, Roy Orbison, Dolly Parton, Chet Atkins, Charlie Pride, Waylon Jennings, and a lot more.

Then it was time to find the Market Street Ale House, my home bar during the trips to Nashville in 2006. After all the dead brain cells, I did remember one thing: there isn't a Market Street in the city. We quizzed employees in a couple of bars about the Ale House's location, but always got the same answer.

"Sorry, I haven't been in the city that long."

My backup plan was I would recognize the place when I saw it, and that's what happened. Its new name was McFadden's. I kept looking around, hoping to find the same girls that took care of us in 2006, but no luck.

The Blackhawks were playing the Blues in game four of their playoff series that night. A couple of local citizens overheard us talking about it and suggested a place called Bailey's on Lower Broadway. A few minutes later, we were sitting at the bar, watching the game on a large TV directly in front of us.

Sometime during the game, a guy from St. Louis sat down next to us. A few minutes later, after the Blues scored two goals to tie the game, we made him change seats. Our stay ended on a good note when the Hawks won 4-3 in overtime.

I made it till 2:00 a.m., Ted not so late. Remember, he's retired and eats dinner around four in the afternoon. I was amazed he made it as long as he did.

The most important thing to do on Thursday was find a drugstore. We both needed earplugs after trying to get some sleep Wednesday night. Once that was taken care of, it was a short walk to the Ryman Auditorium.

The Ryman is a national historical landmark, originally built as a church in the 1890s and turned into a theater about ten years later. Our entrance fee included a backstage tour and a few steps onto the stage of the Grand Ole Opry, which called the Ryman home from 1943 until 1974.

Next was about a ten-minute walk to a large building called Music City Center. Nashville? Music? We're going in. We quickly learned it was a convention center that was hosting an expo for the Rock Marathon, a footrace that takes place in a handful of cities around the world and was coming to Nashville. We knew we were out of shape and definitely out of place, but did enjoy checking out the women who belonged there.

Dinner was at a Mexican restaurant's outdoor patio where we got to watch a guy crash his car into the patio fence about twenty feet from our table. A few seconds later, we got to watch him calmly drive away. Another short walk got us to the Market Street Ale House—sorry, I mean McFadden's. We liked their prices, and I liked coming back to the bar I called home in 2006, so we closed it.

It's Friday morning and time to drive to Pensacola, Florida, arriving at the Paradise Inn around 2:00 p.m. As I pulled into the parking lot, one thing jumped out at me. It was the hotel sign. You'll never guess who was playing at their outdoor venue. It was Biscuit Miller, whom I met during my stay in 2011.

We walked into our room, and after one whole minute, Ted walked out and went to the hotel's outdoor bar. A few minutes later, I caught up and found him talking to a woman who had lived in the area for a few years but was originally from New Orleans.

My first question was if she was familiar with the Tropical Isle, a bar in the city's French Quarter. Here's the rest: "Pam's place?"

"Yes, you know Pam?"

"Yes, do you know Pam?"

I told her I was from the southwest suburbs of Chicago and knew a family from the area who invaded New Orleans almost every year. Then, out of her mouth: "Sure, I know the F———s." Travel as usual.

After some quality time at the hotel bar, it was time to walk over to Sidelines. It's the bar I found on my previous trip where I was able to watch the Cubs, Blackhawks, and Bulls at pretty much the same time. Nothing had changed; the Bulls and Blackhawks were both on.

And it didn't take long to find another travel connection. A guy I was talking to mentioned he was from the far southeast side of Chicago, so I mentioned the name of a local funeral home. Of course, he knew Jim. I did too. He was a fraternity brother of mine from college. We met a few other people from the Chicago area, but that was the only weird connection. And both Chicago teams won.

On Saturday, it was time for me to hit the bike trails, but I had a setback when I opened the back door of my van. My bike had a flat tire. I got lucky when the hotel clerk directed me to a bike shop two blocks down the street.

After starting my ride about a half hour later, I discovered another problem. The odometer/trip meter wasn't working. Returning to the shop, they quickly figured out what was wrong. The new guy who repaired it put the wheel on backward. Had I gone in reverse, it probably would have worked.

By this time, my ambition had slumped. I only did about six miles; at least that's what the odometer said. During my short ride, I saw Landshark's, another hangout from 2011, but it wasn't open. It wasn't officially shut down; it just had some weird hours. It was actually closed on Saturdays. I didn't believe it either, but took a picture of the sign that listed its schedule.

Back in the hotel parking lot, I heard a couple of guys talking and heard the word "Marist," the name of the high school I attended on the far southwest side of Chicago. It was a guy and his son who were both Marist grads and another guy from Joliet, Illinois, who had graduated from Lewis University, which, of course, is my alma mater. They might have graduated years before me but, again, travel as usual.

The Paradise Inn is located in a great spot because we could do almost everything on foot. When we left the room Saturday night, traffic was backed up big-time on the road in front of the hotel. It wasn't critical because we were walking, but the bar/restaurant area a few blocks down was full of young, loud partiers. Our guess was they were leftovers from spring break.

One other thing stood out. Based on the way some of the younger people were dressed, we figured out it was prom night, so we kept walking and found a place called Shaggy's. It was reasonably priced and wasn't inhabited by any crazies or prom kids, so we settled in and finished the night there.

Sunday's schedule was simple: bike, Blackhawks, and Biscuit. The Hawks played at 3:00 p.m., so I did my bike ride before the game, somehow doing fourteen miles. We were at Sidelines for the game, which the Hawks won 5-1, eventually walking over to Landshark's because I remembered it was open. Trouble was I didn't remember its hours. The place closed at 7:00 p.m.

Now it was time to head back to our room to regroup so we could hear Biscuit Miller and his Blues Band at the hotel's outdoor venue. That's when we learned they had played from 4:00 p.m. to 7:00 p.m., not the later shift.

He was sitting at the bar, just like in 2011 when I overheard his conversation and slid over and met him. I reintroduced myself, telling him how we met three years earlier. The story sounded vaguely familiar, but he wasn't sure so I let him slide. Their group was heading to another bar down the street and he invited us to join them, but we were out of gas. One more drink at the outdoor bar and Sunday came to a close.

Monday, the 28th, and it was last call for Pensacola. After a non-alcoholic lunch at Sidelines, I got on my bike and did twelve miles. Back at the hotel, it was time to finish the half-gallon of Bacardi rum Ted brought as a backup. Once it was gone, another bottle magically appeared. That would be the backup bottle I had waiting in my van.

We got lucky because Biscuit had talked his band into playing for a couple of hours, even though they were only scheduled to play Sunday and Tuesday. That meant we got to finish our stay in Pensacola listening to some great Chicago blues at Paradise's outdoor bar.

We were leaving for Memphis in the morning, but not before waking up a few times because of some severe storms that came through the area. Somehow, we were on the road by 9:00 a.m., and we got out of town in the nick of time because another line of severe storms was heading our way. Had we been booked for one more day, we might have been stuck there for a couple more.

Our drive took us through Mobile, Alabama, arriving in Memphis around 4:00 p.m. That's when we learned Pensacola got twenty-six inches of rain in a forty-eight-hour span, including Tuesday evening's 5.7-inch deluge that came down in one hour. Luckily for us, it wasn't Tuesday morning. *USA Today* said the one-hour storm was 200–500 year event. We also missed the rain in Mobile. They only got about ten inches.

In 2011, it was the tornados that ripped through Alabama two days after I drove down to Pensacola. This time, it was the rain/flooding the day after we left Pensacola. Don't think I'll be going back.

Our hotel was the Hampton Inn on Peabody Street, recommended by a friend from the bar who had stayed there a couple of weeks before Ted and I left on our trip. He raved about its location and insisted we make it our home. He was right. It was just around the corner from Beale Street.

Our first meal in the city was at Rendezvous, a place known for its BBQ and another place recommended by people from the bar. On the walk there, we made a stop at the Blues City Cafe, but only for drinks.

When we arrived at Rendezvous, the long line almost scared us away. We stayed, which was a good move, because they turned over tables faster than any place I've ever seen. We were seated just a few minutes later, and that's when I received some devastating news. They didn't carry Bacardi rum. Actually, they didn't carry any hard liquor, just beer and wine, so I treated myself to a delicious diet pop, sorry, diet cola. The food was good, the prices were good, and we left there stuffed.

After that, we walked off a little bit of the meal, ending up at a Hard Rock Cafe. Ted was one and done and headed back to the hotel. One drink later, the handful of people left in the place got to put in their requests for videos that would play on the bar's TV screens. I got to watch "Mustang Sally" and "Try a Little Tenderness" from the movie *The Commitments*, then it was my turn to head to our room.

Now it's Wednesday morning. After a quick stop for some Gatorade, we took a nice, slow one-mile walk to Sun Records. It was opened by Sam Phillips in 1952 as an independent record label with its own recording studio, and it became famous after he discovered Johnny Cash, Carl Perkins, Jerry Lee Lewis, Roy Orbison, and Elvis.

Next was Stax Records, another famous recording studio that opened shortly after Sun Records and became the place for black and soul music. Some of its early artists included Booker T and the MGs, Isaac Hayes, Sam & Dave, and Otis Redding.

It was about two miles for this part of our walking tour, but the further we went, the worse the neighborhood got. Ted finally talked some sense into me, and we headed downtown.

Two more miles got us to the Rock and Soul Museum, which covers about sixty years of Memphis music history. Then two minutes got us to the Gibson Guitar Factory/Museum. It's where we were reprimanded by a woman behind the counter. Her quote, which included a wave of the index finger, was "You don't ever walk to Stax Records."

As I was leaving there, it was time for last call at the Rum Boogie Cafe. It wasn't for the whole day, just our afternoon shift, but we did break down and make one more stop at our hotel bar. We had no choice; it was blocking our path to the elevators. A little R&R and it was time to start our evening shift.

Game 7 of the Minnesota/Colorado series was that night and the winner would play the Blackhawks, so we were interested. I left the room first, went on a scouting mission, and minutes later, found a local bar and grill on Main Street, coincidentally called Local. When I updated Ted, he was thrilled it was only five minutes away because the Florida sun and the walk earlier in the day had taken their toll on his feet. There weren't any seats at the bar, so the hostess took me downstairs to a banquet room they used for the overflow on busy nights. She then sat me down in front of a very large TV screen and turned up the volume. I was the only one in the room.

I thanked her, then asked if she could be on the lookout for a redheaded senior who might be limping and might look a little lost. A few minutes later, she escorted Ted down to his special seat. Now there were two. A few more people eventually made it down to my room, topping out at eight.

Minnesota won in overtime, which meant the game ran late, which meant Ted had to stay up way past his bedtime. He actually made it to midnight. I stayed until 2:00 a.m.

We checked out the next morning, hitting the road around 10:00 a.m. for what was a long and uneventful ride home. Thankfully uneventful, because my "service engine" light had been on since Pensacola.

MICHIGAN CITY 2014

We skipped 2013, and part of me said, "Don't do it," but I rented the house in Michigan City for a week, starting on Thursday afternoon, August 21. "Oktoberfest" was the theme.

The previous renter exited the house on Tuesday, and the cleaning was done by Wednesday afternoon. Knowing this, I got an early start. Instead of arriving on Thursday morning, I was there and already unpacked by 8:00 p.m., Wednesday night. Perfect, because it gave me plenty of time to spend on the top deck of Matey's Bar and Grill.

With the head start, I was done with the shopping and most of the decorating by noon Thursday, finishing just before some severe storms moved into the area. No bike ride, but later, when it cleared up, I made the leisurely walk to Shoreline Brewery, ending the night at Matey's.

Friday was the beginning of the Oktoberfest weekend and again, no bike ride because it rained all day. My evening was spent keeping track of the cancelations and no-shows, again finishing my night at Matey's. Finally, on Saturday afternoon, people started showing up. It was Brenda, JD, and Carolyn with Martin, her eight-year-old son. Nobody was remotely interested in my German menu, probably because it included beets and sauerkraut. OK, I can understand that, but not one brat was thrown on the grill. So what did we do for dinner? We ordered a pizza. Ach du Lieber!

There were still a few people I hadn't heard from, but when the house phone rang a couple of times, it surprised us. Nobody knew the house number, and when someone picked up the phone, there was never anybody on the line. Brenda figured it out: "I bet it's your mom." (Mom called, 2008.)

On Sunday, the weather cleared up, and I was able to do thirteen miles on the bike. It would be the last time because the rain returned for the next three days. Amazingly, the nights were clear so you can guess where I ended up.

The list of no-shows made it an easy decision. This would be the last house.

2014 STL

The Hawks were in St. Louis on Saturday, October 25, so it was time to call my contact in group sales. His response was similar to what I heard the previous year. The decision wasn't final, but the organization was leaning toward making people buy tickets to a second game if they wanted tickets to a Chicago game.

When a group of thirty tickets opened up, I somehow qualified. It was twenty-six for me and four for Steph. My group sales rep was also nice enough to warn me the tickets were at the end where the Blues shot twice. Bring it on.

Because of the late notice, the Drury Inn Union Station was already booked, which meant our group was heading back to the Pear Tree Inn.

After getting the OK for the hockey tickets and finding a hotel, I needed twenty-six train tickets. Amtrak needed a passenger list in seven days, but I couldn't do it. That meant everyone was on their own. I drove down alone, getting there in just over four hours.

While checking in, I pleaded my case, explaining how we usually stayed at the Drury Inn, where the snacks were better, they served mixed drinks, and the hotel was closer to the arena. Learning I was the group leader, they upgraded me to a Jacuzzi suite.

Remember, it's the Pear Tree, so my "water" bottle made another appearance. Then, just like the last time we stayed at the Pear Tree, it was a quick stop at the Drury Inn, where a few of us were able to grab a couple of free drinks before the game. Déjà vu?

After the game, I ran into Sue (Demma's) at Maggie O's. I was jealous because she was able to book her group at the Drury Inn—that is, until she told me how they had been banned from the hotel bar. Evidently, one of the guys from their trip had caused some problems, so nobody from their group was allowed to eat or drink there.

On Sunday, I decided to get rid of my hangover in Illinois at the Cahokia Mounds, walking four to five miles and spending time in its awesome museum. It's the largest prehistoric Indian site north of Mexico, with as many as 20,000 people living there from 800 AD to around 1300 AD. Check it out.

The Hawks lost 3-2.

2014 Madrid

Remember how I turned twenty-one in Madrid in 1972? The plan was to turn sixty-three there, so after landing at Barajas Airport on the morning of November 20, about seven dollars got me a bus to Madrid's Atocha Train Station. From there, it was about a five-minute walk up Atocha Street to my room.

One thing immediately stood out; it was the trees. I'm pretty sure there weren't any in '72, but that's when it hit me. I'm old. There had been plenty of time for them to grow.

Before leaving home, I went online and found a hostel in the same area I lived forty-two years earlier. The toilet and shower were in my room, not down the hall, and it only cost about $40/night. Not only was it in the same area, it was on the same street.

After checking in, I took a walk around the neighborhood to see if anything had changed or was the same. It had and it was.

The "fun" began at an ATM when my MC and AMX cards were both denied because of wrong PIN numbers. Strange, because my AMX card worked fine in the UK the previous year and I hadn't changed the number on my MC card.

After failed attempts at a couple more ATMs, it was back to my room. Online, I found an American Express office walking distance from my place. It wasn't there.

With not much cash, it was gonna be tough to make it all five days. Heading home early was a distinct possibility. I didn't do much eating or drinking that night, so after a couple of tapas (appetizers) and one large glass of sidra (cider), it was back to my room.

I had a wake-up call on Friday morning, but it wasn't a phone call. My room was at the top of the stairs, there was no carpeting, and the walls were paper thin. That meant it was loud, which meant I was up early.

The drapes in my room had stayed shut on day one, so when I pulled them open, it was time for a flashback. What I saw was a small open-air atrium that included all four floors. It also included laundry hanging out on the top two floors.

During my semester in Madrid, the women who ran our hostel did our laundry and hung it out to dry outside their windows in a small open-air atrium. That means, for the moment, I was in the same place I called home in '72.

Later that morning on the way up the street to the subway stop, I remembered the walk and like in '97, remembered my building. I might not have been staying there, but the memories were the same. After that, I hooked up, by accident, with a free walking tour while making my way through the Puerta del Sol, done in English by an energetic young woman from Latvia. That's right—Latvia. Its starting point was the statue of the Bear and the Strawberry Tree, the symbol of Madrid, but before leaving the plaza, we got to step on a plaque that symbolizes the center of the city and, amazingly, the center of the country. Like throwing a coin into the Trevi Fountain in Rome, stepping on it guarantees you will return.

The rest of the tour consisted of a couple more plazas, then the Royal Palace, but only from the outside. Remember, it's a free tour. Next to the palace is the Museo de Catedral, and next to it is the Suicide Bridge. It was described to us as an old stone overpass built in the 1500s, then a viaduct built in the 1870s and rebuilt in the 1930s and 1970s. Anyway, nobody jumped; we just took pictures.

After my three-hour tour, it was back to the room for a couple of things. One was a nap, and the other was to go online again to try and get my credit cards to work. No luck online.

I went out for dinner around 8:00 p.m., which is early if you live in Madrid. I found a restaurant whose sign said they accepted American Express, so I went in and asked if they could run my card to see if it would work. It did, so it was time to eat, oh yeah, and drink.

After that, I joined the Paseo, a Madrid tradition of walking, snacking, and drinking, done by most people before their late dinners. Yeah, I did it backward, but my credit card worked, so I continued. Last call was at a bar/restaurant called El Diario. I liked the place and wanted to buy a bar T-shirt to add to my collection, but they didn't sell them. I then asked if it was possible to buy one off the back of one of the bartenders. Still no luck, but I'll be back.

On Saturday, it was a short walk up the street to the Plaza Mayor, where I had lunch at the Meson del Champignon, another old haunt from '72. Then it was another walk past the Royal Palace, this time to the Temple of Debod.

In 1960, everything on the island of Philae, located on the Nile River, had to be moved when the Aswan Dam was built. If it wasn't, it would have ended up underwater, so the temple was donated to the city of Madrid, finally opening in 1972. Somehow, I missed it during my semester that fall.

Saturday night's Paseo was the busiest, and this time, I did the tapas crawl before my late dinner, ending the night at El Diario.

On Sunday morning, my destination was Avila, an old medieval town about two hours away, but I overslept and missed the morning bus. The next bus wouldn't have left me much daylight, so I took a pass and walked across the street to a travel office, hoping to book a hot-air balloon ride that floated over Madrid. The plan was to do it on Monday morning because I was leaving on Tuesday. The office was closed, so I missed that too.

My backup plan was to explore the Prado, one of the top art museums in the world. I didn't see much of it in '72, this time spending around four hours. Then it was siesta time.

Sunday's tapas crawl took me back to the area around the Plaza Mayor, where I hoped to end my walk with dinner at Botin's. It's listed in the *Guinness Book of World Records* as the oldest continuously active restaurant in the world, supposedly opening in 1725.

While waiting for a table, I got a quick look at the menu and the prices. Dinner and a couple of drinks would have cost me about $150. Think I'll sit outside in the plaza.

This is where I learned drinks are poured in front of you no matter where you're sitting. It seemed a little strange when my first drink on my first night in Madrid was poured in front of me, but I was sitting inside at a bar. I didn't expect it to happen outside.

My night ended at El Diario again, where I learned a couple of interesting things, at least interesting to me.

One: A couple of bartenders, even though they didn't speak English, would say, "Oh my God."

Two: A couple of bartenders knew of the phrase "Ay de mi," which I remembered from my time in Madrid in '72. It didn't translate with

Hispanics at home, but with the older Madrid citizens, it translated as "poor me."

After midnight, the bar bought me a drink for my sixty-third birthday.

On Monday, I went to the Museo de Americas, which holds a lot of interesting stuff from North America. Because of a problem connecting to the hostel's free Wi-Fi, I wasn't able to check the museum's hours until I got there. That's right, closed on Mondays.

My next stop was Estadio Bernabeau, home to Real Madrid, one of Europe's top soccer teams over the years, where my luck improved. I took the stadium tour and had a "free" picture taken of me with one of their large championship cups. Actually, the picture was only free until I wanted to get it developed, then my 5×7 photo cost about $14, not too bad.

Another nap, another tapas crawl, and another late dinner and it was time for last call at El Diario on my last night in Madrid. As promised, they found a T-shirt, but warned me about its size. It might have fit when I was ten. Adios.

Home Tuesday.

One more thing. Food on the trip: patatas bravas, jamon, gambas, jamon, chorizo, calamari, paella, jamon, anchovies, gazpacho, jamon, champignons, swordfish, moussaka (that's right, moussaka), Pringles, and jamon. And no, I never made it to the Museo de Jamon.

2015 St. Joseph, Michigan

Buddy Guy was playing at a BBQ/blues festival in Centennial Park on Saturday, May 16. I had never seen him live, so it was time for a little road trip.

St. Joe's is only a two-hour drive from home, and Buddy wasn't playing until around 6:00–6:30 p.m., so it fit nicely into my schedule after working Friday night.

I got a parking spot in the neighborhood and walked the couple of blocks to the park, just a stone's throw from Lake Michigan. It was the first really warm day that month, so after finding the ticket booth and getting a feel for the area, I headed to the beach for a while. Bad move.

Returning to the park about an hour before the show, I got to read the sign at the ticket booth informing everyone it was sold out. My solution was to take a slow walk outside the fence and find a spot to sit my ass down, pretty sure I would still be able to hear the concert. That's when I heard, "Dickie!" Yes, somebody knew me.

It was Mo, a local bartender/friend whom I've known for about twenty years. She's now a schoolteacher and happened to be there with a group of teachers for a little weekend getaway, not knowing what was going on when they made their reservations.

After catching up for a few minutes, she noticed I didn't have a wristband. Standing on the other side of the fence didn't help, so she gave me her ticket, then told me the plan.

She pointed to the hotel they were staying at, then instructed me to tell the person at the gate about my stomach problems. My lack of confidence in the park's porta potties sent me back to the safety of my room. I still had "my" ticket, so he waved me in and gave me a replacement wristband.

Since Tailgator's opened, I got to know Marty S., Buddy Guy's keyboard player. He played at our bar a few times and at Vino Tinto, a small bar in downtown Oak Lawn, walking distance from my condo. Now with a wristband, I left the park and walked around to the back of the stage, hoping to track him down.

My plan was to get Marty's attention and talk for a few minutes, hoping he could maybe get me backstage or into the VIP section. When he finally spotted me, the band was heading to the stage to start their set, so it was a quick conversation.

I reentered the park using my new wristband and found Mo so I could thank her for the great advice and return her ticket. She was involved with her friends, so I found my own spot on the lawn, inside the fence, and got to see Buddy Guy live—definitely worth the trip.

2016 Lisbon

First of all, I was in Portugal for nine days and nobody recognized me.

Before I left, people had been asking if had a plan on how or when to end my book. The answer is at the end of this trip, after landing at O'Hare Airport.

My flight to Lisbon was on Air Canada with a stop in Toronto. While on their website, I saw an opportunity for a reasonably priced mini-upgrade. It wasn't first class, it was something called Preferred Seating. My seat was in the first row on the aisle, with only six seats across the plane. Not only was there more legroom, there was almost a foot between me and the window seat.

Before dinner, the drink cart appeared with a choice of water, juice, or wine. I jokingly replied, "Bacardi and Diet Coke," and I was surprised when the flight attendant reached down for one of those little bottles and poured me a drink. She surprised me again when I learned it was free, at least in my section.

Here's something Mo, a good friend and travel partner, will appreciate. During one of my standing breaks, I got to tell three flight attendants the story of me and the "smoking lady" on our flight home from Greece through London in '98. They loved it.

I arrived in Lisbon on Monday morning, September 5, and my first impression wasn't good. It was hot, with the temperature topping out at 100 degrees. My second impression was better after walking into the studio apartment I reserved. It had a toilet/shower, Wi-Fi, fridge, microwave oven, and even a small washing machine and all for about $60/night. Almost forgot, it had air conditioning too.

It cooled off enough that evening so dinner outside was comfortable, but my "local bar" search didn't work because the area was too touristy. There were plenty of restaurants with outdoor seating, but no bars. After a few stops and a climb up the hilly city to the Bairro Alto neighborhood, I ended up at Lisbon's Hard Rock Cafe.

The place was crowded, with no seats at the bar. Back outside, I asked a couple of guys standing near the front door if they knew a local bar where I could go and just chill out. They looked at each other, and after a quick laugh, one of them told me to follow him. I happened to be talking to one of the restaurant managers.

He ushered me back in and up to the second-floor service bar. After sliding over a few racks of glasses, then sliding over a bar stool, a spot magically opened up. In the next few minutes, I met the bartender and a couple of waitresses and quickly made friends. Now with my own special spot, I decided to make it my home away from home.

After missing the Hop-On/Hop-Off bus on Monday, I listened to Rick Steves, the PBS travel guru and started Tuesday at St. Jorge's Castle, which overlooks the city. I also listened to myself and found a city bus that got me there in a couple of minutes for a couple of euros. Don't walk up. Walk down.

A few hours in and around the castle and it was time to head down to the Alfama neighborhood. After a quick walk through Lisbon's cathedral, the Fado Museum was next. It holds about 200 years of fado music history, which has been described as Portuguese blues, but I missed it after getting a little lost in the area's maze of streets.

Dinner and drinks were outside again, this time in Rossio Park, just a short walk from my place. I read somewhere that most of the outdoor tables sat four people, and if you're alone at a busy restaurant, there's a good a chance other people might be seated with you or vice versa.

It only happened once, when a couple from Salzburg, Austria, was seated at my table. We had a good time trading stories about our travels in Europe, but what impressed them most was my stop in their city. They loved the fact I did the hike up to a fortress that overlooks the area. After that, it was time for a few last calls at the Hard Rock.

I walked in and headed up to the second-floor service bar, where I slid over a few racks of glasses then slid over a bar stool so my spot would magically open up. It was a different bartender, so I got a strange look after rearranging the furniture. I told her how the manager gave me this spot the night before, and luckily, one of the same waitresses was working. The first words out of her mouth were "You're back. I guess you like your spot."

On Wednesday, the temperature dropped down to the low eighties, right where it should have been. My day started with a leisurely mile walk to the Tagus River. After taking a right turn and heading west, I immediately noticed the 4/25 Bridge in the distance and its similarity to San Francisco's Golden Gate Bridge.

There was another similarity. On a hill across the river is a 330-foot statue of Christ. If you watched the 2016 Summer Olympics, it's a copy of the statue in Rio de Janeiro, done by Lisbon's Catholic cardinal after a trip to Brazil.

It was a good walk just getting to the bridge, but I kept going. The huge Discovery Monument was next but was covered in scaffolding. Again, I kept going, making it to the Belem Tower and up to the top of the 100-foot structure. It's where I got to enjoy a great view and a great breeze. Back at ground level, it was time to treat myself and grab a taxi. Online, I learned my walk was about six miles.

After a late dinner, a quiet end of the night was on the agenda. It didn't happen. Heading back to my place through Rossio Square, I stopped to watch a bunch of Aussies walk by with drinks in hand. When one of them noticed my sad (jealous) face, I was quickly invited to join their bar crawl.

The first stop with my new friends was a cool rooftop bar. At the next stop, I realized we were starting to duplicate my afternoon walk along the river. Elise, the only non-Aussie, and I agreed we had gone far enough, called it a night and shared a cab back to Rossio Square.

In those few minutes, I learned she was a Detroit Red Wing fan, a little strange since she was from Toronto, Canada. We exchanged email addresses with the possibility of meeting in Detroit for a Blackhawk/Red Wing game. That's all.

Thursday, when I finally started moving, it was back to the river, this time heading east. Lisbon had hosted the '98 World's Fair and I wanted to check out Nation's Park, where it was held. After I toured the park on foot, the mile-long ride across the area in a small cable car was the highlight.

And after missing my home bar because of Wednesday night's bar crawl, I was back at the Hard Rock, but not before another outdoor dinner.

On Friday, day 5, I took the subway to the city's main bus station. From there it was a thirty-minute ride to the town of Mafra, spending the early part of the day walking around the city and its national game reserve.

I finished up with a tour of the city's National Palace, which is also home to its monastery, basilica, school of sculpture, and library. The library is where I learned about the bats. For the last 300 years, a colony of bats has lived there to protect the ancient books from insect damage. True story, they can eat their weight in bugs every day.

Dinner was outside again, but it was time to change the menu. When in Portugal, plan on eating a lot of cod. Whenever I've been in Milan, Italy to see my relatives, one of my aunts would always cook rabbit. Now it was time to try it somewhere else. It wasn't good, so after a low-key complaint, the chef actually came out, apologized, then offered to send me out more rabbit. Uh, no.

He had only worked there for a couple of months and wanted to make some changes to the menu. I'm hoping my opinion helped. After a couple of drinks on the house, it was time to leave and end the night at the Hard Rock.

After a long day on Friday, Saturday became a mini-vacation day while on vacation. I slept in, then walked down to the river and took a 1 1/2-hour boat tour. Dinner was outside again, and the Hard Rock was my last stop again.

After a few drinks or maybe a few nights in the average bar, you'll usually get a free one. The Hard Rock is corporate, so it doesn't happen there. The handful of employees I met were awesome, and I would like to thank them for the "mistakes" I got during my stay.

Sunday the 11th and it was back to Belem to check out what I missed the first time, this time taking the trolley. The Coaches Museum was first, where I saw the evolution of coaches and carriages, starting in the 1600s, followed by the Maritime Museum that showed the history of Portugal's Age of Discovery. I finished up at the Archeology Museum, where I saw a lot of old stuff.

There was one more stop to make in Belem. It's a small bakery called Pasteis de Belem, which opened in 1837. When you're in Lisbon, make sure to stop there and try its famous custard tart called the pastel de nata. OMG.

On Monday morning, eight of us left in a small van from Rossio Square for an eight-hour tour. There were couples from San Francisco, New York, and London, a woman from Vancouver, Canada, and me. Our first stop was Sintra, a UNESCO World Heritage site. I picked Monday because a lot of things in Lisbon were closed, and everything in Sintra was open. It's actually home to ten national monuments. We didn't see all of them, but did see the Pena Palace, which has an amazing mix of Gothic towers, Renaissance domes, and Moorish minarets. After that, it was the National Palace, followed by a couple more castles. Sorry, yawn.

While walking through a city park, we learned about the prominence of cork trees in the area. It didn't take long before the guy from New York and I looked at each other and started laughing. If you haven't seen the SNL skit about cork soakers, look it up.

The next stop was Cabo da Roca, the westernmost point of Portugal and the westernmost point of mainland Europe. I got some great pictures, including one looking down a 500-foot cliff at the Atlantic Ocean. Back in the van, our driver told us how lucky we were because the area is usually cloudy, misty, and windy. We had picked the nicest day in almost two months.

Tuesday the 13th was my last day in Lisbon, and it was pretty low-key. The highlight was another walk through the Alfana neighborhood, this time making it to the Fado Museum. It was followed by another outdoor dinner, which meant I was nine for nine, and yes, last call was at the Hard Rock.

On Wednesday the 14th, I left for home. There's more.

2016 Lisbon Flight Home

My flight was on Lufthansa Air, which meant it went east to Frankfurt, Germany, before heading west to Chicago. It left late, so I missed my connecting flight.

At the customer service desk in Frankfurt, the clerk informed me the next flight to Chicago wasn't until the next afternoon. He said not to worry because he would get me a hotel room and transportation to and from the airport at no cost, then made a phone call to confirm everything. Seconds later, I knew something wasn't right.

He apologized, explaining there were no rooms available because of a huge expo going on in the city. His solution was a forty-five-minute flight to Munich's International Airport, located about twenty miles outside the city. Here's the next problem.

Munich had hosted a European soccer tournament game on Tuesday night, and the 2016 Oktoberfest was starting on Friday. That meant there were no rooms in the city center. The best they could do was a hotel in an industrial area about halfway between the city and the airport.

As the cab pulled up to the Dolce Hotel, my first impression was a good one. Walking in, the woman at the front desk welcomed me and asked how she could help. I started to explain the problem with my connecting flight, but she quickly stopped me. Her quote: "Oh, you must be the Lufthansa guy." When I answered yes, she told me about the free room and free dinner waiting for me. And yes, it was a Jacuzzi suite. Surprised?

I had been to Munich before, so the ten-mile cab ride to and from the city made it an easy decision. I got a table at the hotel's outdoor patio and had my free dinner. Drinks were extra.

The icing on the cake came the next day when a short walk down the hall got me to the hotel's spa room. With time to kill before my departure, I was able to take a sauna, so basically, I got a free spa day in Germany for missing my flight home.

"You know those things only happen to you." That's the response I got from a few friends after hearing my story.

Now, here's my answer on when to end this book. On November 2, seven weeks after landing in Chicago, the Cubs won the World Series. That's a wrap.

APPENDIX

Countries

1. Canada

2. Mexico

3. France

4. Spain

5. Germany

6. Italy

7. Vatican City

8. Monaco

9. Austria

10. England

11. Switzerland

12. Belgium

13. Netherlands

14. Luxembourg

15. Lichtenstein

16. Greece

17. Czech Republic

18. Hungary

19. Denmark

20. Sweden

21. Scotland

22. Wales

23. Portugal

24. Jordan

25. Egypt

26. Iceland—airport only

27. Ireland—airport only

Canadian Provinces

1. Alberta

2. British Columbia

3. Manitoba

4. Ontario

5. Quebec

6. Saskatchewan

US States—46
Missed:

1. Alaska

2. Hawaii

3. Oregon

4. Washington

Minor-League Baseball

1. Crestwood Cheetahs, Illinois 2002

2. Akron Aeros, Ohio 2001

3. Jamestown Expos, New York '91

4. Huntington Cubs, West Virginia '91

5. Winston Salem Spirits, North Carolina '91

6. Charlotte Knights, North Carolina '91

7. Peoria Chiefs, Illinois '91

8. Des Moines Cubs, Iowa '91

9. Cedar Rapids Kernels, Iowa '92

10. Clinton Giants, Iowa '92

11. Davenport River Bandits, Iowa '01

12. Burlington Bees, Iowa '01

13. Harrisburg Senators, Pennsylvania '02

14. Edmonton Trappers, Alberta Canada '81

15. Columbus Clippers, Ohio '90

16. NWL (Northwoods League) All-Star Game in Rochester, Minnesota '97

Hockey

1. Chicago Old Stadium. Blackhawks

2. Chicago United Center. Blackhawks

3. St. Louis Checkerdome. Blues

4. St. Louis Kiel Center/Savvis Center. Blues

5. Detroit. Joe Louis Arena. Hawks/Red Wings '85

6. Boston Garden. Hawks/Bruins '87

7. Pittsburgh. Civic (Mellon) Arena. Hawks/Penguins '91

8. Hartford. Civic Center. Hawks/Whalers '91

9. Minneapolis. Met Center. Hawks/North Stars '90 '92

10. Toronto. Maple Leaf Garden. Hawks/Maple Leafs '90 '97

11. Washington DC. US Air Arena. Hawks/Capitals '94 '95

12. Montreal Forum. Hawks' last game there/Canadiens '95

13. Miami Arena. Hawks/Panthers '96

14. Tampa Bay. Ice Palace. Hawks/Lightning '96

15. Atlanta. Phillips Arena. Hawks/Thrashers 2000

16. Columbus. Nationwide Arena. Hawks/Bluejackets 2001

17. Nashville. Gaylord Center. Hawks/Predators 02/2006 12/2006

18. Pensacola Ice Pilots. Florida 2000

19. Sparta Prague. Czech Republic '94

20. Cardiff Devils. Wales 2013

Basketball

Professional
Bulls at the old Chicago Stadium and the United Center
New Orleans Superdome—Utah Jazz/Golden State Warriors '75
Phoenix Veterans Memorial Center—Suns/Utah Jazz '83
Milwaukee Bradley Center—Bulls/Bucks playoff game '90
Indianapolis Market Square Arena—Bulls/Pacers '91
New Orleans Superdome—Bulls/Denver Nuggets '91

College
Depaul and Loyola at the Rosemont Horizon
NCAA Semifinals and Final at the St. Louis Checkerdome '78
Ohio State at Wisconsin '81
Wichita State at Illinois State U
Notre Dame/Virginia at the Rosemont Horizon '81
NCAA Midwest Regionals at the United Center '98
Quincy at Lewis U 2012

Soccer
Chicago Sting—indoor and outdoor. Chicago Stadium, Wrigley Field, and Soldier Field
NASL All-Stars vs. Santos, Brazil (Pele) Soldier Field '71
Santander vs. Cadiz in Cadiz, Spain '72
Burgos vs. Real Madrid at Estadio Bernabeau in Madrid, Spain '72

Major League Baseball Parks

1. Wrigley Field, Chicago 8/8/88. '84 NLCS Game 1. MLB All-Star Game 7/10/90. Others

2. Comiskey Park, Chicago MLB All-Star Game 7/6/83. Others

3. Cellular Field, Chicago ALCS Game 1 10/5/93

4. Tiger Stadium, Detroit 9/99

5. Riverfront Stadium, Cincinnati '82, '91, '93, '94

6. Great American Ballpark, Cincinnati 2003, 2007, 2010, 2013

7. Veteran's Stadium, Philadelphia '92 home opener vs the Cubs

8. Three Rivers Stadium, Pittsburgh 6/87

9. PNC Park, Pittsburgh 5/08

10. Fulton County Stadium, Atlanta 8/86

11. Fenway Park, Boston 4/02

12. Old Yankee Stadium (its last year), New York 5/2008

13. Camden Yards (first game), Baltimore 4/6/92, also 7/93

14. Jack Murphy Stadium, San Diego 5/85

15. Royals Stadium, Kansas City '78 playoffs Game 2 and '80 World Series Game 3

16. Busch Stadium, St. Louis '82 World Series Games 6

17. Busch Stadium (same name/new park), St. Louis

18. Mile High Stadium, Denver 4/94

19. Astrodome, Houston 5/96

20. The Ballpark, Arlington, TX 5/96

21. County Stadium, Milwaukee '82 Al-CS Game 3 and '82 World Series Game 3

22. Miller Park, Milwaukee 8/2002-Matt 9/2003 7/2005

23. Jarry Park (Expos) during '76 Olympics, Montreal 7/76

24. RFK Stadium, Washington DC 5/2005

All-Star Games

7/6/83 MLB All-Star Game @Comiskey Park

2/8/84 NASL Indoor Soccer All-Star Game Sting vs. All-Stars @Chicago Stadium

2/18/86 MISL Indoor Soccer All-Star Game @Chicago Stadium

2/6/88 NBA Slam Dunk Contest @Chicago Stadium

2/7/88 NBA All-Star Game @Chicago Stadium

7/9/90 MLB Home Run Derby and Old-Timers Game @Wrigley Field

7/10/90 MLB All-Star Game @Wrigley Field

1/19/91 NHL All-Star Game @Chicago Stadium

7/19/97 NWL All-Star Game @Mayo Field, Rochester Minnesota (Matt)

World Series Games

10/17/80	Kansas City	KC beats Phi 4-3
10/15/82	Milwaukee	STL beats Mil 6-2
10/19/82	St. Louis	STL beats Mil 13-1

Movie Extra '90s

TV:
Early Edition
Untouchables—called, but couldn't work.

Movies:
Hero
Rudy
Gladiator
Rookie of the Year
Mercury Rising
Natural Born Killers

Commercials:
Advocate Health Care

Music

Rock and Roll Hall of Fame—Cleveland, OH

Ryman Theater Grand Ole Opry—Nashville, TN

RCA Studio B—Nashville, TN

Country Music Hall of Fame—Nashville, TN

Sun Records—Memphis, TN

Rock 'n' Soul Museum—Memphis, TN

Gibson Guitar Factory/Museum—Memphis, TN

Art

Art Institute—Chicago, IL

Louvre—Paris, France

Prado—Madrid, Spain

Reina Sofia—Madrid, Spain

Uffizi Gallery—Florence, Italy

Alte Pinakothek—Munich, Germany

Swimming

Atlantic Ocean: Fort Lauderdale, Florida, and Cadiz, Spain

Pacific Ocean: Ixtapa, Mexico

Gulf of Mexico: Florida and Cancun, Mexico

Dead Sea: Jordan. Didn't swim, floated.

Mediterranean Sea: Ostia, Italy

Aegean Sea: Naxos and Santorini, Greece

Lake Michigan: Illinois, Indiana, and Michigan

Fish Lake: LaPorte, Indiana

Football

Professional
1. Wrigley Field. Bears/Lions '63
2. Soldier Field Bears
3. Astrodome. Houston Oilers/Bears '77
4. Municipal Stadium. Cleveland Browns/Bears '80
5. Memorial Stadium. Baltimore Colts/Bears '83
6. Busch Memorial Stadium. St. Louis/Bears '84
7. Silverdome. Detroit Lions/Bears '85
8. Lambeau Field. Green Bay Packers/Bears '88
9. Superdome. New Orleans/Bears '91
10. Sun Devil Stadium. Arizona Cardinals/Bears '90 and '94
11. Paul Brown Stadium. Cincinnati Bengals/Bears 2009

College
1. Tennessee @ Notre Dame '78
2. Michigan Stadium (Slippery Rock vs. Shippensburg State) '79
3. Northern Illinois @ Kent State '83
4. Northwestern @ Minnesota '90
5. Texas Tech @ Ohio State '90
6. Purdue @ Ohio State 2001
7. Kent State @ Ohio State 2007

Olympics

Montreal 1976
7/18 Men's Basketball
7/19 Boxing
7/21 Soccer
7/21 Boxing
7/23 Track and Field

7/24 Track and Field

Lake Placid 1980
2/16 Men's and Women's Luge
2/17 Women's Downhill
2/18 Men's and Women's Ski-jumping
2/19 1000 meter Men's Speed-Skating
2/19 Men's Figure Skating
2/20 Women's Speed Skating
2/20 Hockey—USSR beats Canada 6-4
2/20 Hockey—US beats West Germany 4-2
2/21 Women's Figure Skating
2/22 Men's Slalom Skiing
2/22 Hockey—The Game, US beats USSR 4-3
2/23 4-Man Bobsled

Atlanta 1996
7/31 Women's Basketball
8/1 Baseball
8/1 Boxing Quarterfinals
8/2 Track and Field

Halls of Fame

Baseball—Cooperstown, NY
Football—Canton, OH
Hockey—Toronto, ONT
Country Music—Nashville, TN
Rock & Roll—Cleveland, OH

Autographs

Matt Cepicky
Muhammad Ali
Lou Boudreau
Frank Robinson

Lee Smith
Tommy John
Cliff Lee
Brandon Phillips

National Parks

1. Grand Canyon, AZ
2. Rocky Mountain, CO
3. Everglades, FL
4. Mammoth Caves, KY
5. Gateway Arch, MO
6. Glacier, MT
7. Badlands, SD
8. Grand Teton, WY
9. Yellowstone, WY
10. Gettysburg, PA
11. The Alamo, TX

National Preserves, Lakeshore, Seashore, and Recreational Areas

1. Indiana and Michigan Dunes
2. Padre Island, TX
3. Lake Mead, NV/AZ
4. Ozarks, MO
5. Big Cypress–Tamiami Trail, FL

National Monuments, Memorials

1. Craters of the Moon, ID
2. Devil's Tower, MT
3. Little Bighorn Battlefield, MT
4. Mount Rushmore, SD
5. Pullman (Chicago), IL
6. Washington Monument, Washington DC

7. Lincoln Memorial, Washington DC
8. Jefferson Memorial, Washington DC
9. Vietnam Veterans Memorial, Washington DC
10. WWII Memorial, Washington DC

UNESCO World Heritage Sites

1. Salzburg, Austria
2. Vienna, Austria
3. Schonbrunn Palace—Vienna, Austria
4. La Grande Place—Brussels, Belgium
5. Bruges, Belgium
6. Rocky Mountain National Parks (Banff and Jasper) Alberta, Canada
7. Waterton-Glacier International Peace Park—Montana and Alberta, Canada
8. Prague, Czech Republic
9. Roskilde Cathedral, Denmark
10. Vatican City, Italy
11. Cairo, Egypt
12. Great Pyramids of Giza, Egypt
13. Philae-Nubian Temple Complex on Agilika Island, Egypt
14. Grande Ile-Strasbourg, France
15. Banks of the Seine River—Paris, France
16. Cathedral of Notre Dame—Paris, France
17. Roman ruins—Trier, Germany
18. Cologne Cathedral, Germany
19. Upper Middle Rhine Valley, Germany
20. Acropolis—Athens, Greece
21. City of Rodos on the Island of Rhodes, Greece
22. Delos Island, Greece
23. Budapest, Hungary
24. Luxembourg City, Luxembourg
25. Historic Center of Rome, Italy
26. Last Supper at Santa Maria della Grazie Church—Milan, Italy
27. Florence, Italy
28. San Gimignano, Italy
29. Piazza del Duomo and Tower—Pisa, Italy

30. Venice, Italy
31. Naples, Italy
32. Siena, Italy
33. Mount Etna—Sicily, Italy
34. Petra, Jordan
35. Wadi Rum, Jordan
36. Edinburgh, Scotland
37. The Alhambra—Granada, Spain
38. Segovia, Spain, and its aqueduct
39. Toledo, Spain
40. Cuenca, Spain
41. Sevilla, Spain
42. Berne old city, Switzerland
43. Tower of London, England
44. Westminster Abbey—London, England
45. Canterbury Cathedral, England
46. Liverpool Waterfront, England
47. Yellowstone National Park, Wyoming
48. Everglades National Park, Florida
49. Grand Canyon National Park, Arizona
50. Mammoth Cave National Park, Kentucky
51. Cahokia Mounds, Illinois
52. Tower of Belem-Lisbon, Portugal
53. Monastery of the Hieronymites—Lisbon, Portugal
54. Cultural landscape of Sintra, Portugal

500 Places to See Before They Disappear (2009)

1. Everglades, FL
2. Grand Canyon—south rim, AZ
3. Columbia Icefield—Alberta, Canada
4. Dead Sea—Jordan (I floated)
5. Adirondack Mountains, NY
6. Lake Mead, NV/AZ
7. Glacier National Park, MT
8. Miami Beach, FL
9. Biscayne Bay Shores, FL

10. Cahokia Mounds, IL
11. Over-the-Rhine, Cincinnati, OH
12. Yellowstone National Park, WY
13. Rocky Mountain National Park, CO
14. Badlands National Park, SD
15. Banff National Park—Alberta, Canada
16. Giza Pyramids, Egypt
17. Valley of the Kings—Luxor, Egypt
18. Petra—Jordan
19. Acropolis—Athens, Greece
20. Colosseum—Rome, Italy
21. New Orleans, LA
22. Venice, Italy
23. Florence, Italy
24. Salzburg, Austria
25. Prague, Czech Republic
26. Tower of London, England
27. Alhambra—Granada, Spain
28. La Sagrada Familia Cathedral—Barcelona, Spain
29. Gettysburg, PA
30. Cook County Hospital—Chicago, IL
31. Leaning Tower—Pisa, Italy
32. TWA Terminal @ JFK Airport, New York, NY
33. Double-decker bus in London, England
34. Da Vinci's "Last Supper"—Milan, Italy
35. Fenway Park—Boston, MA
36. Wrigley Field—Chicago, IL
37. Houston Astrodome, TX
38. Seven Dwarfs Sign—Wheaton, IL
39. Superdawg Drive-in sign—Chicago, IL
40. Cressmoor Prairie—Hobart, IN

1,000 Places to See (2011)

England
1. Windsor Castle
2. Canterbury Cathedral

3. London Buckingham Palace
4. London Hyde Park/Kensington Gardens
5. London St. Paul's Cathedral
6. Tower of London
7. London Westminster Abbey
8. London Camden Market and Locks

Scotland
9. Edinburgh Castle

Austria
10. Kitzbuhel
11. Salzburg
12. Wachau Valley/Melk Abbey
13. Vienna Hofburg Palace
14. Vienna Schonbrunn Palace
15. Vienna St. Stephen's Cathedral

Belgium
16. Antwerp
17. Bruges
18. Brussels La Grande Place
19. Beer in Belgium
20. Belgian chocolate, waffles, frites, and mussels

France
21. City of Strasbourg/Cathedral
22. Paris Eiffel Tower
23. Paris Louvre—Mona Lisa
24. Paris Notre Dame
25. Paris Arc de Triomphe

Germany
26. Romantic Road (Rothenburg, Dinkelsbuhl, and Nordlingen)
27. Alte Pinakothek Munich Art Museum
28. German beer culture ('72 Oktoberfest in Munich)
29. Rhine Valley Mosel and Rhine Rivers (Lorelei)

Greece
30. Mykonos and Delos
31. Naxos
32. Santorini/Akrotiri
33. Rhodes
34. Athens, Acropolis
35. Athens, National Archeological Museum

36. Monaco

37. Luxembourg City, Luxembourg

Italy
38. Pisa Leaning Tower
39. San Gimignano Towers
40. Siena Piazza del Campo
41. Lucca walled city
42. Naples
43. Lake Maggiore
44. Rome Colosseum
45. Rome Pantheon
46. Rome Piazza Campidoglio
47. Rome Forum
48. Rome Spanish Steps
49. Rome Trevi Fountain
50. Rome Piazza Navona
51. Vatican City/Sistine Chapel
52. Ostia Antica
53. Milan Da Vinci's "Last Supper"
54. Milan Piazza del Duomo
55. Milan La Scala Opera House
56. Catania Sicily Mt. Etna
57. Florence "David" Galleria del Accademia
58. Florence Duomo-Baptistery
59. Florence Basilica of Santa Croce
60. Florence Medici Chapels
61. Florence Pitti Palace
62. Florence Ponte Vecchio Bridge

63. Florence Uffizi Galleries
64. Florence Piazza della Signoria
65. Florence Piazzale Michelangelo
66. Venice Grand Canal
67. Venice Doges Palace
68. Venice Gallerie dell'Accademia
69. Venice San Marco Piazza and Basilica
70. Venice Carnevale

Spain
71. Barcelona La Sagrada Familia Church
72. Cuenca
73. Granada, the Alhambra
74. San Sebastian
75. Segovia—Roman aqueduct
76. Sevilla—three weeks in college
77. Toledo
78. Madrid Reina Sofia Museum
79. Madrid Prado Museum
80. Madrid Royal Palace
81. Madrid Plaza Mayor
82. Madrid El Rastro (churros y chocolate)
83. Madrid Retiro Park
84. Madrid tapas crawl

Portugal
85. Lisbon Barrio Alfama
86. Sintra Pena National Palace

Switzerland
87. Lucerne
88. Lugano
89. Zermatt-Matterhorn

Czech Republic
90. Prague Castle District
91. Prague Old Town Square—State Opera House (*La Traviata*)
92. Prague

93. Czech beer

Hungary
94. Budapest Castle Hill
95. Budapest Hotel Gellert Spa/Bath

Denmark
96. Copenhagen Hotel D'Angleterre (bar only)
97. Roskilde Viking Ship Museum and Cathedral

Sweden
98. Stockholm Archipelago—Vaxholm
99. Stockholm smorgasbord
100. Stockholm Vasa Museum and Skansen Outdoor Museum
101. Stockholm Gamla Stan neighborhood

Egypt
102. Giza and Saqqara Pyramids
103. Nile River Cruise
104. Aswan and Lake Nasser
105. Luxor—Valley of the Kings (hot-air balloon)
106. Cairo Museum of Egyptian Antiquities

Jordan
107. Petra (Siq, Treasury, El Deir Monastery)
108. Taybet Zaman
109. Dead Sea (I floated)
110. Jarash
111. Wadi Rum
112. King's Highway—Mt. Nebo, Madaba, Kerak Castle, and camels

Mexico
113. Zihuatanejo

Canada
114. Banff National Park, Alberta
115. Jasper National Park, Alberta
116. Calgary Stampede, Alberta

117. Montreal Old Town, Quebec

United States
118. Grand Canyon, AZ
119. Rocky Mountain National Park, CO
120. Everglades National Park, FL
121. Florida Keys, FL
122. Miami South Beach, FL
123. Walt Disney World, FL
124. Chicago, IL Art Institute
125. Chicago Blues scene
126. Chicago Museum Campus
127. Chicago Museum of Science and Industry
128. Chicago Wrigley Field
129. Chicago Magnificent Mile
130. Chicago Millennium Park and Grant Park
131. Chicago Taste of Chicago
132. Chicago Ravinia Festival
133. Chicago food scene (pizza, hot dogs, and Italian beef)
134. Old Route 66 IL and MO
135. Shipshewana, IN
136. Kentucky Derby Louisville, KY
137. New Orleans French Quarter, LA
138. Boston, MA Freedom Trail
139. Boston Fenway Park
140. Boston North End
141. Glacier National Park, MT Going-to-the-Sun Road
142. Las Vegas Strip, NV
143. Adirondack Mountains Lake Placid, NY 1980 Olympics
144. Cooperstown and the Baseball Hall of Fame/Museum, NY
145. Old Yankee Stadium, New York, NY
146. Rock and Roll Hall of Fame Cleveland, OH
147. Gettysburg, PA
148. Badlands National Park, SD
149. Black Hills, SD
150. Mount Rushmore, SD
151. Memphis BBQ (Rendezvous), TN
152. Memphis music scene (Sun Studio, Rock and Soul Museum), TN

153. Nashville music scene—Ryman Theater/Grand Old Opry, TN
154. River Walk, San Antonio, TX
155. Grand Teton National Park, WY
156. Jackson Hole, WY
157. Yellowstone National Park, WY (Old Faithful)

Washington DC
158. National Mall
159. Smithsonian Museum
160. Arlington National Cemetery
161. *White House (missed the tour I set up)